LOCO MOTION

THE WORLD'S OLDEST STEAM LOCOMOTIVES

LOCO MOTION

THE WORLD'S OLDEST STEAM LOCOMOTIVES

MICHAEL R. BAILEY

First published 2014

The History Press
The Mill, Brimscombe Port
Stroud, Gloucestershire, GL5 2QG
www.thehistorypress.co.uk

British Library Cataloguing in Publication Data.
A catalogue record for this book is available from the British Library.

ISBN 978 0 7524 9101 1

Typesetting and origination by The History Press
Printed in India

CONTENTS

Foreword by Sir Neil Cossons   6

Introduction   8

Acknowledgements   12

Glossary   13

1   The Progenitors – Trevithick's Locomotives, 1803–08   17

2   The First Industrial Locomotives, 1812–15   23

3   The George Stephenson Types, 1820s   31

4   John Rastrick's Locomotives, 1828–29   39

5   The Locomotive Comes of Age – Robert Stephenson's Designs, 1828–30   47

6   *ROCKET*'s Rivals, 1828–30   57

7   The *Planet* Suite, early 1830s   67

8   The American Progenitors, 1825–31   77

9   The Grasshopper Type, 1830s   89

10 The Patentee Type, mid-1830s to early 1840s   95

11 The Bury Type, mid-1830s and 1840s   129

12 The Norris Type, late 1830s to 1850   141

13 The Long-Boiler Type, 1840s   152

14 The Crewe Type, 1840s   157

15 Other Single Driver Locomotives, 1840s   165

16 The American 4-4-0 Type, 1840s   178

17 Mineral Locomotives, 1838–50   183

18 Locomotive Plates, 1830s to 1850   200

19 Conclusion   204

Appendix – Museums Displaying Pre-1850 Locomotives, Components
                and Replicas   206

Bibliography   210

FOREWORD

by Sir Neil Cossons

Of all the extraordinary new technologies of the nineteenth century it was the railway, beyond all others, that captured the imagination of the public. But in order to flourish, the railway, which had existed in various forms for over 200 years, needed motive power other than man, horse or gravity. Enter the steam locomotive. The arrival of steam power, specifically, of a locomotive engine moving with the load – as opposed to a stationary engine pulling trains by cables – was to effect the crucial transformation that gave birth to the railway as we know it today. The steam railway was to define the nineteenth century.

From primitive origins shortly before Trafalgar it had reached sturdy adolescence by the time of Waterloo. Just 15 years later, on 15 September 1830, the victor of Waterloo, the Duke of Wellington – by then Prime Minister – opened the world's first public passenger carrying railway, between Liverpool and Manchester. The railway revolution had begun. Throughout Europe and North America, and ultimately across the world, the railway was to have a profound effect on the building of societies and the shaping of nations. Central to all this was the steam locomotive engine.

Much has been written in contemporary accounts, and since, about early steam locomotives. They were an immediate source of wonder and enchantment. But it is difficult to match the lyricism of the actress Fanny Kemble, then aged 20, after travelling with George Stephenson on the footplate of ROCKET shortly before the Liverpool and Manchester opening:

We were introduced to the little engine which was to drag us along the rails. She (for they make these curious little fire horses all mares) consisted of a boiler, a stove, a platform, a bench, and behind the bench a barrel containing enough water to prevent her being thirsty for fifteen miles […] She goes upon two wheels, which are her feet, and are moved by bright steel legs called pistons; these are propelled by steam, and in proportion as more steam is applied to the

upper extremities (the hip-joints, I suppose) of these pistons, the faster they move the wheels […] The coals, which are its oats, were under the bench, and there was a small glass tube affixed to the boiler, with water in it, which indicates by its fullness or emptiness when the creature wants water […] This snorting little animal, which I felt rather inclined to pat, was then harnessed to our carriage, and Mr Stephenson having taken me on the bench of the engine with him, we started […] the motion is as smooth as possible, too. I could either have read or written; and as it was, I stood up, and with my bonnet off 'drank the air before me.' […] When I closed my eyes this sensation of flying was quite delightful, and strange beyond description; yet […] I had a perfect sense of security, and not the slightest fear […].

Now for a word or two about the master of all these marvels, with whom I am most horribly in love. He is a man from fifty to fifty-five years of age; his face is fine, though careworn, and bears an expression of deep thoughtfulness; his mode of explaining his ideas is peculiar and very original, striking, and forcible; and although his accent indicates strongly his north country birth, his language has not the slightest touch of vulgarity or coarseness. He has certainly turned my head.

Here, in a few romantic words, we have a picture of the world's most celebrated locomotive and the most renowned man connected with the birth of the early railway. But until recently, of the first generations of locomotives themselves – including ROCKET – we knew surprisingly little, of their design, construction or performance. This book sets out, for the first time, to identify all those in the world that still survive, and to describe and analyse them.

From the outset the faith placed in the powers of the steam locomotive, and in its future prospects, was astonishing for, despite its still indeterminate form, investors and the wider public saw immediately the opportunity presented by the steam railway. But, it was not until well into the 1840s – when Britain was overwhelmed by a hysterical infatuation with railway investment – that the essential morphology of the locomotive began to crystallise, broadly into the form that it was to retain until the end of steam over a century later. The path towards maturity was one of trial, error and experiment, of operational experience, incremental improvement and the application of science.

Today, in an age where we are once again turning to the railway to fulfil our demand for high-speed intercity travel, understanding the part played by these remarkable precursors of the modern world is all the more enlightening. From a worldwide total of rather less than 5,000 locomotives from this dawning of the railway age, there are just a few dozen salutary survivors from the period to 1850. Here, Michael Bailey analyses the evidence they present. He is especially well qualified to do so, not only as the leading historian in this field but as one who has built and operated working replicas in order to analyse forensically their performance and test the claims of those who built and operated these first locomotives more than a century and a half ago. As a result, we now know more about *ROCKET* than ever before, despite the fact that the original has been in the collections of the Science Museum, and its predecessor in the Patent Museum, since 1862.

It has been these illuminating experiments that have, in part, inspired the writing of this book. But it has also been an appreciation of the richness and veracity of the material evidence that the early locomotives offer. In this invaluable new study this evidence is brought together for the first time, from the remaining locomotives themselves – mainly in Europe and North America – some important surviving components, and the operable replicas.

Sir Neil Cossons
Former Director of the Science Museum, London
Past President of the Newcomen Society for the History of
Engineering and Technology
March 2013

INTRODUCTION

The world's museums of science, industry and transport possess major collections of machinery, both on display and in store. These have been collected over many years, in some cases since the mid-nineteenth century. Together they form a major resource providing us with the opportunity to learn much about the history of mechanical progress through design, materials and manufacturing methods.

However, museums have not always pursued comprehensive archaeological and archival research of their artefacts, and in many respects we remain ignorant of these important details. To examine artefacts closely requires time and money, as well as historical and archaeological skill. Sadly, curators have been largely under-resourced, with little or no time or funding to carry out the requisite investigations. Notwithstanding the interest and enthusiasm on the part of some curatorial staff over the years, artefacts have most often been collected, cleaned and placed on display without follow-up investigations that would have provided us with extended knowledge.

All such machines are displayed in the form in which they ended their working life. It is, however, a characteristic of machines that the longer they were in use the more they were subject to modification, or even rebuilding. Improvements, not only in design, materials and manufacturing practices, but also with operating and maintenance procedures, are therefore reflected in the surviving machines. It is possible, however, through close examination, to reveal evidence of their earlier forms, giving us a deeper insight into mechanical progress.

EARLY LOCOMOTIVES

Railway locomotives form a particular example of machinery for which surviving artefacts provide us with a major resource towards a better understanding of their design and manufacture. Enormous strides were made in design practice and adopted materials, together with manufacturing and casting techniques. To overcome the very particular dynamic and efficiency problems of locomotives, their operating and maintenance procedures also evolved quickly, leading to many modifications and improvements during the life of the machines.

This volume looks at the development of locomotives during the first half of the nineteenth century. At first, the notion of moving loads and passengers by steam power along a rail track was pursued by the Cornish engineer, Richard Trevithick. His first trial locomotives were not taken up, however, but in 1812 the world's first commercial use of locomotive power, in Leeds, opened a remarkable era in railway and economic development. Such was the rapid progress made in succeeding years that, by 1850, locomotive technology had reached extraordinarily confident designs that allowed passenger trains to exceed a mile a minute (100kph), and mineral train loads to approach 1,000 tons.

Many museums in Europe and America have in their collections a largely untapped resource of early locomotives that provide us with the opportunity to study their design and mechanical progress. In addition, there are several examples of surviving components, either separately displayed or incorporated into replicas. Each component has a story to tell and each forms a small part of the jigsaw of locomotive development.

This study has been made possible through the examination of many of these artefacts by the author and his colleagues, backed up by archival and secondary research to provide context to the archaeological work. The author and Dr John Glithero, aided by our colleague Peter Davidson, have undertaken a number of archaeological investigations on early locomotives in museum collections. In some cases, studies have been undertaken by other distinguished engineering historians. The findings from these investigations have been published in most cases, and some, notably those derived from work carried out on Robert Stephenson's *ROCKET* (Chapter 5), have significantly altered our understanding of their design features and subsequent modifications.

REPLICATION

There are, inevitably, many gaps in the representation of locomotive types in museum collections. In quite a number of cases these gaps have been filled with full-size operable replicas. The correct terminology for such machines should be 'reproductions', but it is clear from common usage that 'replicas' is the term now most often used and understood. Such machines ought to adopt the same materials, tolerances, and manufacturing practices as their forebears. However, the lack of appropriate materials, such as wrought-iron plate, and the inevitable adoption of the locomotives for public demonstration, has dictated the use of later materials and safety features. The minimisation of such compromises is the goal of every replica project leader.

Replicas benefit from a considerable amount of research that has been required by the project teams to provide accuracy. They allow discerning students the opportunity to understand design and component progress, and to learn about operating and maintenance practices. Furthermore it is possible to translate information gained from replicas into useful data about the originals. Nevertheless, some readers will disagree with the elevation of replicas to the same level as original artefacts, on the grounds that the compromises are unacceptable. But to avoid replication altogether on the grounds of compromise is a sterile argument.

There is a long history to the practice of recreating locomotives from previous eras, the first such example being the 'Hetton' locomotive which purports to date from 1822, but the replica actually dates from the 1850s (Chapter 3). The author and his colleagues from the Museum of Science and Industry in Manchester have undertaken the design and erection of the *PLANET* replica (Chapter 7), the first main-line locomotive design. All the many findings, in relation to performance and maintenance, as well as design, from this project have been fully written up. With the research that is required in order to undertake and successfully complete a replication project, it is highly desirable for project leaders to ensure that everything learnt from their projects is written up for the benefit of future generations.

In addition, other full-size replicas made of wood are displayed in several locations around the world. Some, such as *L'ÉLÉPHANT* and *LE BELGE* in De Mijlpaal (the Milestone) museum in Mechelen, Belgium, are very well executed – others are not. Although it is interesting to see them, they are actually 'sculptures' which offer visitors only an impression of early design. We learn little about materials or operating and maintenance characteristics, and they have therefore been excluded from this volume.

Much could be learned about early locomotives from the examination of contemporary scale models, but these have not been considered in this volume. There is indeed scope for a further volume about all that can be learned from them. Two exceptions have been made, however, and these are the half and quarter-scale models of the 'Cherapanov' locomotive and *PROVORNY (AGILE)* which are on display in the railway museum in St Petersburg, Russia (respectively Chapters 7 and 10). Made by technical students at the St Petersburg University in the few years after the delivery of the original locomotives, they offer important evidence about these long lost full-size examples.

MECHANICAL PROGRESS

With so many surviving and replicated locomotives in the first half-century, the opportunity has been taken to describe them, and the design characteristics they represent, in clusters, brought together by their common evolutionary design 'schools'. Thus, the seven examples of the Stephenson 'Patentee' type locomotives (Chapter 10), or the five examples of the 'Norris' type (Chapter 12) are grouped together to allow comparison between them and to demonstrate the evolution of the type over time.

Other groups, such as locomotives used in the various mineral industries of the 1840s, have been brought together into one chapter. This allows for comparison of the several ways that engineers interpreted the needs of those industries and their associated railway systems, or the main-line railways that served those industries. This arrangement of chapters inevitably leads to overlaps within the timeline of locomotive innovation, but provides a more meaningful explanation of design progress. Nevertheless, the chapters proceed in a general chronological order from the earliest locomotive experimentation at the beginning of the century through to the giant *MEMNON* mineral locomotive of 1848 (Chapter 17), and the standard 4-4-0 American locomotive in the form of *Rochester* from 1850 (Chapter 16).

Throughout the volume are the recurring themes of mechanical progress. The steam locomotive is a complex machine of interdependent components. Its advancement in load-hauling capability, speed and economy has been made possible through design innovation, improvements to machining and casting methods, and material developments, as well as a better understanding of dynamics. The investigations carried out on a number of the locomotives have served to highlight component progress over time, both with new designs and retrofitting on older examples to extend their useful lives.

Many readers of this volume will be familiar with locomotive components and other terms associated with locomotive design and driving. The author is, however, aware that other readers, with a strong interest in locomotive history, may not be familiar with all the terms adopted in the book. A glossary of these terms has therefore been included to assist with the fullest understanding of locomotive descriptions.

Boilers were a principal consideration for locomotive engineers. Designs to achieve improving levels of thermal efficiency and cost-effectiveness presented major challenges to designers and builders, some of whom were notably more successful than others. Undoubtedly, the breakthrough was the boiler adopted for *ROCKET* in 1829 (Chapter 5). Not only did it provide increased heating surface through the use of multiple fire tubes, the increase in speed of the flue gases ensured a better heat transfer. Local availability of different forms of fuel played an important part in the types of boilers selected. The initial use of coal gave way to expensive coke in the early main lines in Britain, whilst in North America wood and, eventually, anthracite fuel were more readily available and were a lot less expensive than European fuels.

Following the earliest years of main-line operation, when component reliability was the primary issue, efficient use of steam became a preoccupation of locomotive engineers. In the 1830s and 1840s the development of valve gears to increase efficiency and minimise wastage became a particular characteristic of each design. The many mechanical and geometrical variations are described in these pages to allow the reader to comprehend the variety of solutions to the efficiency challenge. From the earliest forms of manual valve gear allowing only for directional change, came the search for a variable steam cut-off to the cylinders to reduce steam usage and fuel costs. A number of separate cut-off slide valve designs, such as that on the *Pays de Waes* (Chapter 15), were adopted before the variable cut-off link motion was introduced in 1842. The earliest example of the link motion may be seen on *L'AIGLE* (Chapter 13).

The variety of frame designs, and the introduction and development of suspension systems are integral parts of the locomotive story. Some early designs, such as *Samson* (Chapter 17) adopted frameless layouts, whilst the built-up 'sandwich' frame on *John Bull* (Chapter 7), and the bar frame 'Bury' type on Braithwaite's *ROCKET* (Chapter 11) became competing standard designs. The former led on to the standard plate frame designs in Europe such as *L'AIGLE* (Chapter 13), whilst the bar frame became the standard form in North America, as seen on *Pioneer* (Chapter 15).

The progress made with the many other components is reflected in the descriptions that follow throughout the volume. Lubrication, safety valves, boiler feed pumps, regulator valves, try-cocks and sight glasses all evolved during this first half-century.

However, it is material development in order to meet the special requirements of locomotive components in this pre-steel era that is the recurring theme. New material supply industries, such as for copperplate in Britain, grew to meet the increasing demands of the locomotive industry, but availability and cost constraints dictated different materials elsewhere. The iron fireboxes of early American locomotive builders may not have been as durable as the copper fireboxes of British-built locomotives, but lower first costs of manufacture, even allowing for mid-life replacement, made them attractive against the high costs of copperplate.

Serious failures of some components, notably wheels and axles, forced manufacturers to develop more robust materials and more reliable manufacturing methods. What we see in museums today, therefore, are the successful replacements. To better understand the original arrangements is a further justification for operable replicas, albeit with the need to adopt materials that are now acceptable for everyday use. This was well illustrated with the failure of the axles on the *PLANET* replica (Chapter 7).

A summary of the life history and dimensions of each locomotive is tabled alongside the text to serve as a reference addendum allowing readers to seek further detail. Certain dimensions have been provided by museums from their technical papers that have perhaps been archived for many decades. Some of the dimensions may therefore be more accurate than others, but time and lack of opportunity have prevented the detailed checks that would be necessary to confirm every measurement.

LOCOMOTIVE NAMING

The names by which each artefact and replica are known vary widely. The origins of their names reflect many influences, each of which is explained herein so far as is known. Some names are geographic or named after people associated with the region or the railway itself. To assist the reader in readily distinguishing locomotive names in the text, they are shown throughout in italics.

Some locomotives carry cast nameplates, usually, but not always, fitted to their boiler sides. It is noteworthy that all such names are in upper case lettering, and are shown here accordingly, for example *LAFAYETTE* (Chapter 12). Some locomotives have well-known names to which they are regularly referred, but which actually carry no nameplates. These are shown in lower case, for example *John Bull* (Chapter 7).

A third category is for locomotives that have no name at all, and are usually referred to by their geographical association. A case in point is the 'Hetton' locomotive (Chapter 3) which is shown throughout in this form.

DESCRIPTION

The book will appeal to a wide readership of locomotive and other railway historians; engineers and scientists; model-making practitioners; museum curatorial professionals with an interest or involvement in the archaeology of machinery; and lovers of steam locomotives. Although the artefacts are largely in the keeping of museums of transport, science and industry in the United Kingdom, Continental Europe and in the Americas, its appeal will be well beyond these boundaries.

The challenge, therefore, has been to find a form of presentation to satisfy such wide interests. We live in a world of change, with our everyday dimensions evolving from 'imperial' to 'metric' units. There is strong advocacy for one or other according to custom and practice. The resolution has been to adopt the units of the 'home' country with appropriate conversions for the benefit of all readers. Thus a French-built locomotive, such as *SÉZANNE* (Chapter 13) is shown with metric dimensions and imperial conversions.

The locomotive wheel arrangements have similar affiliations between different parts of the world. The 'Whyte' notation, traditionally employed in the Americas and in the United Kingdom, shows leading wheel, driving wheel and carrying wheel numbers in that sequence. The similar 'French' notation, but adopting axles rather than wheels, has been traditionally adopted in its particular market areas. The 'German' system, which has also been strongly followed in its sphere of influence, adopts leading axle numbers, driving axle letters and carrying axle numbers. To simplify presentation however, the use of three different notations has been avoided in favour of the Whyte system.

MUSEUMS

The book provides nearly a hundred entries from almost fifty sites in Great Britain, Continental Europe and in North and South America. With minor exceptions, all the locomotives can be seen by museum visitors at some time during the year. A list of museums and their contact details are provided in the appendix, allowing readers to plan visits according to the sometimes restrictive opening hours. Certain museums now move some artefacts to other sites to broaden the opportunity of seeing them, and it is therefore essential to check regarding their current locations. The internet plays an important part in keeping everyone informed of the current position. Museum websites are shown for readers' guidance, but it is a shame that the excellent web pages offered by some are not matched by all.

ACKNOWLEDGEMENTS

There have been many distractions during the course of preparing this work, which began nearly two decades ago. Finding out and researching details about all the locomotives and components has involved a large amount of research amongst the publications of other distinguished locomotive historians, and the author is particularly pleased to acknowledge their works, which are listed in the bibliography. It has also required an extensive series of communications with, and visits to, museums and other locations on both sides of the Atlantic. In almost every case museum curators have been most helpful in providing access to their artefacts and background archival material.

The interest shown by curators in the novel approach taken by the author and colleagues to understand the history of their locomotives has been rewarding. In three cases this resulted in moving film being taken of the processes involved. Over the years some curatorial staff have been promoted elsewhere or have retired, whilst others continue to provide valuable advice about their historic charges. To them all, the author offers sincere thanks for the assistance that has been provided.

Over the last two decades there have been a number of changes affecting the artefacts, and it has been difficult to ensure that this volume represents correctly the current position at the time of publication. The author is conscious that changes, both in the location of exhibits and of knowledge about them arising from further research, will bring about the need for an update of this volume at some stage. Readers who have more advanced information about any of the entries, and who are willing to share this, will be warmly acknowledged should further editions be feasible.

The author is very pleased to acknowledge the considerable work of his colleague, Dr John Glithero. Our several detailed joint studies, both with the examination of original locomotives and on the design of replicas, has been a particularly rewarding experience for us. We are both, in our turn, very pleased to acknowledge the work of our colleague, Peter Davidson, who has accompanied us on museum visits, and played a major part in building the *PLANET* replica locomotive at the Museum of Science and Industry in Manchester (Chapter 7). Particular thanks must also be accorded to Peter for his reading of the draft text of this volume. Each of his criticisms and suggestions has been responded to, but of course responsibility for any errors rests with the author.

Lastly, I would like to thank my wife for all her assistance and good humour during the preparation of this volume. Without her forbearance and encouragement the book would not have been possible.

Michael R. Bailey
March 2013

GLOSSARY

Whilst many readers will be familiar with the terms used for pre-1850 locomotives in this volume, the following glossary is included to assist with the fullest understanding of the locomotive descriptions.

Traction

Adhesion	Movement along edge rail or plate rail track achieved through friction between locomotive driving wheels and rails. Dependent upon both piston power and locomotive weight.
Rack & pinion	Movement along a toothed track achieved through a driven pinion wheel. Adopted when track was otherwise too fragile to carry an adhesion locomotive, or gradient was too steep for friction to suffice.
Tractive effort	Nominal assessment of locomotive starting effort in pounds (kilos), determined by cylinder bore, stroke and driving wheel diameter, together with a proportion of boiler pressure. Often limited by the adhesive weight on adhesion locomotives.

Frame

Sandwich frame	Formed of timber (usually oak or ash in Europe, and coniferous wood in North America) with wrought-iron plates bolted on both sides.
Bar frame	Formed of rectangular, round or channel-section wrought-iron bar.
Plate frame	Formed of full-length deep wrought-iron plates, usually placed inboard of the wheels.
Stretcher	Transverse wrought-iron bar or plate bolted between the main frames and providing shape and stiffness to them.

Spectacle frame	Stretcher adopted for some inside cylinder designs in a 'spectacle' form to give clearance for the connecting rods and providing attachment points for slide bars.
Equalising beam	Suspension lever linking adjacent driving axle spring sets to ensure that the sprung wheels continue to share the locomotive weight over undulating track.
Drawbar	Coupling bar between locomotive and train, with an eye at each end, for coupling to fixed brackets using vertical pins. The locomotive bracket on early designs was attached to the back plate of the firebox, and on later designs to a frame stretcher or buffer beam.
Motion plate	Vertical bracket, fitted outside the main frame, to support driving motion components.
Flexible beam truck	Adopted by the Baldwin locomotive works in the 1840s for long wheelbased designs allowing the front driving wheelsets to slide laterally on curves whilst remaining coupled to the other wheelsets.
Axle box	Axle bearing, usually capable of limited vertical movement within slides, as determined by suspension springs.

Boiler

Long-plate boiler barrel	Formed of wrought-iron plates laid longitudinally and rolled across their width, to be riveted to adjacent plates to form the barrel.
Concentric-ring boiler barrel	Formed of wrought-iron plates rolled circumferentially to form rings, to be riveted together to form the barrel.
Flue	Single tube passing through the boiler on earlier locomotives, to carry hot flue gases from the fire grate

	at one end to the chimney at the other. Its external surface area, in contact with the water, forms the heating surface.
Return flue	Flue incorporating a 'U'-bend with its chimney end adjacent to the fire grate.
Tubes	Multiple tubes introduced into locomotive boilers from 1829 to carry hot flue gases from the fire to the chimney, transferring heat to the water on the way.
Siphon tubes	Water tubes inserted across a flue to increase heating surface, and to stimulate water circulation within the boiler.
Combustion chamber	Length of flue beyond the fire grate (and preceding a tube plate) which extends combustion space and time, thereby increasing fuel efficiency.
Tube plates	End plates at both ends of the boiler barrel with multiple drilled holes to receive tubes and forming the pressure envelope. The length of the barrel is the external dimension over the plates.
High pressure	Greater than atmospheric pressure (14.7lbf/in^2 or 1bar).
Regulator valve	Controls the rate of steam flow from the boiler to the steam chests.
Plug valve regulator	Cone-shaped regulator valve, seated in cone-shaped housing with apertures, so that rotation provides regulated steam flow to the steam chests.
Grid-iron slide valve regulator	A slide valve with a perforated square plate moving over a face with an equal number of holes. A small movement of the regulator handle provides a large area of opening.
Clack valve	Boiler feed water non-return valve.
Perforated steam pipe	Steam pipe with perforations uppermost, allowing collection of dry steam from above the boiler water level, for direction via the regulator valve to the steam chests.
Spring balance safety valve	Safety valve restrained from lifting by the force of a lever fitted with a calibrated spring balance. Its conical seat allowed a progressive increase in discharge area.
Pop safety valve	Safety valve restrained from lifting by the force of a helical spring. Once it had started to open, the geometry quickly made it open fully, discharging steam until the pressure fell below the specified level.

Water tube boiler	Small barrel with multiple tubes filled with water and exposed to hot gases and radiant heat from the fire.
Porcupine boiler	Small vertical boiler with multiple small flue tubes protruding sideways through the water space to an outside jacket to increase heating surface.

Firebox

Wrapper plates	External firebox plates enclosing water and steam surrounding the inner firebox.
Gothic firebox	A vaulted upper casing above the inner firebox crown plate, the side and end plates forming a pyramidal shape, its large steam space allowing dry steam to be collected.
Haystack firebox	A hemispherical upper casing also providing steam space for the collection of dry steam.
Grate area	Area of fire grate within the inner firebox walls.
Foundation ring	Peripheral (usually rectangular) iron ring riveted to the inner firebox and wrapper plates to maintain a secure pressure boundary at the base of the firebox.
Crown stays	Robust beams fitted to firebox crown plates to add stiffness against pressure distortion.
Side stays	Threaded round bars that connected inner fireboxes to the wrapper plates to maintain a uniform separation resisting the boiler pressure.
Brick arch	Adopted from the 1850s. Erected in front of the firebox tube plate beneath the tubes and sloping upwards. Products of combustion were swept backwards allowing them to mix with secondary air to ensure that combustion was completed before passage through the tubes.

Driving Motion

Flywheel	Heavy rotating wheel, used on the earliest single-cylinder locomotives, driven by the piston and developing kinetic energy for release between subsequent strokes to maintain continuous traction.
Piston rod	Round bar fitted to the piston and connected to a crosshead, providing linear movement as the first driving action.

Crosshead	Link converting linear piston rod movement to rotary driving motion. Transverse bar guided by vertical slides on early locomotives, with pivoted connecting rods to fly cranks on gears or wheels providing rotary drive motion. Reduced in size on later designs to a small casting guided by horizontal slide bars, with a central connecting rod pivot.
Slide bars	Parallel guides within which a crosshead maintained a linear reciprocating action.
Connecting rod	Wrought-iron bar connecting crosshead to gear shaft or driving wheel crankpin, fly-crank or crank axle.
Crankpin	External driving wheel pin, fitted to a spoke or boss, driven by a connecting rod to convert linear motion to rotary motion on outside cylinder locomotives.
Fly-crank	Drive arm fitted to an axle end and driven by a connecting rod giving rotary motion for gear shaft or driving wheel, and providing a 90-degree separation from opposing crankpin drive.
Crank axle	Driving axles for inside cylindered locomotives, with crank webs and crankpins converting linear piston thrust to rotary motion.
Fremantle 'grasshopper' parallel motion	Drive motion developed by William Fremantle in 1803 for stationary engines and later adapted for early locomotive use. On early designs motion beams ('walking beams' in North America) were used. They were pivoted at one end and driven by a piston rod at the other, between which a connecting rod was lowered to a gear shaft or driving axle. On later designs crossheads were used which drove connecting rods directly. To maintain a vertical straight line movement of the piston rod, the parallel motion employed a swing link to support the far end of the beam, with a further link from this support to a fixed point on the path of the crosshead.
Watt parallel motion	Developed by James Watt in 1784 and later adapted for early locomotive use. It employed a 'motion beam' pivoting about its mid-point, driven by a piston rod at one end and with a connecting rod at the other dropped down to a cranked gear shaft or driving axle. The vertical piston alignment was assured by use of a parallelogram linkage, with a fixed point on the path of the crosshead forming a pantograph.
Jack shaft	Powered axle, without wheels, coupled to a driving axle to provide traction whilst allowing the use of springs on the driving axle.

Valve Gear

Eccentric	Driving axle fitting which rotated eccentrically to provide reciprocating movement to the valves through straps, rods and links. Later adopted for boiler feed pumps.
Slip-eccentric	Eccentric free to rotate on the axle until it engaged the selected forward or reverse driving dogs. After engagement the eccentric rotated with the axle. Engagement with the dogs was by circumferential contact on early locomotives and by sideways displacement on later designs.
Driving dog	Axle-fitted slip-eccentric restraint which provided forward or reverse valve movement after engagement.
Fixed-eccentric	Eccentric fixed to the axle providing reciprocating movement to pre-selected forward or reverse eccentric rods.
Eccentric rod	Iron rod bolted to a strap fitted around an eccentric which communicated reciprocating movement to a valve through links.
Gab (British)/ 'drop-hook' (North America)	Notch at the valve-end of an eccentric rod allowing it to be engaged or disengaged with a rocker shaft drive pin providing reciprocating movement to a valve rod as required. Its early 'D'-form notch, when disengaged, required manual valve repositioning. Its later 'V'-form, with a 'spreading jaw', engaged the drive pin, wherever located, to reposition the valve in the same action.
Bell crank	A combination lever that provided a generally 90-degree change of movement.
Carmichael's valve gear	Arranged for ferry boat operation by Charles Carmichael of Dundee in 1818. Adopted a fixed-eccentric driving an eccentric rod fitted with upper and lower 'V'-form gabs allowing alternative

	engagement of forward or reverse rocking shaft drive pins. It was only viable with 100 per cent cut-off.
Cam	Rotating or sliding piece with an irregular shape used in a mechanical linkage. The irregularity strikes a lever at one or more points on its circular path especially to transform rotary motion into linear motion or vice versa.
Rocker shaft	Rocking linkage, driven by eccentric rod, to valve spindle using alternate drive pins engaged by gabs, for forward or reverse valve movement.
Weigh bar	Shaft fitted with weights, whose rotation lifted or lowered the links supporting the valve gear to change the direction of travel or the cut-off. The weights counterbalanced the weight of these links to ease the rotation of the shaft and reversing lever.
Link motion	Mechanism based on a slotted expansion link providing adjustable valve travel for forward or reverse movement and hence variable steam cut-off to the cylinder.
Steam cut-off	The proportion of the piston stroke during which steam is permitted to enter the cylinder. The cut-off was fixed for the earliest locomotives, but some early American designs introduced separate cut-off valves to reduce steam consumption and save fuel. Later designs, first introduced in Britain, allowed variable cut-off using a link motion.
Stephenson link motion	Convex expansion link adjusted vertically by reversing rod, bell crank and lifting link. The curve of the link was centred on the eccentric centre. The die block, connected directly to the valve rod or via a rocker shaft, responded horizontally to move the valve as

	required. Developed by Robert Stephenson & Co. in 1842.
Gooch link motion	Concave 'stationary' expansion link provided an arc for the adjustable die block. The block connected with the valve spindle through a radius rod. Raising or lowering of the block selected the direction of travel and the cut-off, the link curve being centred on the pivoted end of the radius rod. It was developed in 1848 by (Sir) Daniel Gooch, locomotive superintendent of the Great Western Railway of England.
Radius rod	Rod linking the valve spindle to the die block on Gooch link motion, the lifting or lowering of which moved the die block in an arc within the expansion link.
Valve rod	Rod connected, through a gland in the steam chest, to the valve controlling steam movement into and out of the cylinder.

Railway Track

Edge-rails	Flat- or round-topped iron bars supported on sleepers, either directly or using chairs, requiring flanged wheels, usually with coned treads for guidance.
Plate-rails	'L'-shaped iron rails supported on sleepers, requiring flangeless wheels guided by the rail uprights.
Strap-rails	Wooden edge-rails, with wrought-iron strips fitted on their upper face, adopted for many early routes in North America. They minimised rail wear whilst avoiding the expense of imported iron edge-rails.

THE PROGENITORS – TREVITHICK'S LOCOMOTIVES
1803–08

The work of Richard Trevithick (1771–1833) in pioneering the use of high-pressure steam engines made possible the earliest development of railway steam locomotion. Much has been written about Trevithick's work over the years (Dickinson and Titley, 1934), but recent research by Rees and Guy (2006) shows that the Trevithick 'type' of locomotive played a more influential role in railway development than had previously been supposed.

His 'puffer' engines, originally developed for pumping water from Cornish tin mines, were soon adapted for other industrial uses. From 1798 Trevithick began work on ideas for mounting his engine on wheels to pursue his ambition for self-propelled vehicles. His earliest model has survived in the London Science Museum.

Following his encouraging experiments with the model, Trevithick built a full-size travelling engine which operated successfully on a road in Camborne in Cornwall on Christmas Eve, 1801. Although the exact form of the vehicle is unknown, a full-size operable replica of its assumed form (the so-called *Puffing Devil*) was built by members of the Trevithick Society in 2001, incorporating known characteristics from his 'puffer' engines and later waggonway travelling engines.

Following his high-pressure engine patent in 1802, Trevithick promoted its use amongst industrial companies, advising them on several applications. These included the Coalbrookdale Ironworks, with whom he also discussed installing an engine on a vehicle with the potential for use as a travelling

Right: First experimental steam locomotive model made by Richard Trevithick in 1798. Displayed in the London Science Museum. (Science and Society Picture Library)

Far right: Replica of Trevithick's road locomotive *Puffing Devil*. (Philip Hosken, Trevithick Society)

The 'Llewellyn' drawing of Trevithick's 'Coalbrookdale' 'Tram Engine'. (Science and Society Picture Library)

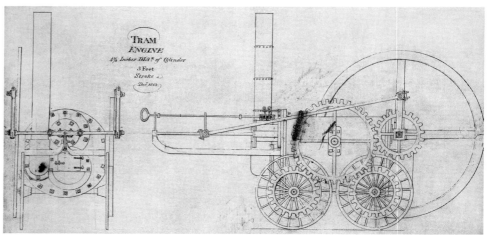

engine on the ironworks' tramroad. In a letter written by Trevithick in August 1802, he indicated that construction work had then begun: 'The Dale Company have begun a carrage [*sic*] at their own cost for the realroads [*sic*] and is forcing it with all expedition.' The proprietor of the ironworks was William Reynolds (1758–1803) who died at about the time the travelling engine would have been completed.

Only fragmentary information is available about this vehicle and it is still not possible to confirm that the engine was actually completed. Reynolds' nephew, W.A. Reynolds, later claimed (Randall, 1880) that the engine had been built and that the cast-iron boiler had survived in use as a water tank, whilst other components remained in the yard at the nearby Madeley Wood works. With the distorting effects of time, however, it cannot be proved whether he was remembering a travelling engine or another engine of the period.

A remarkable drawing of Trevithick's 'Tram Engine', dated December 1803, was acquired in 1862 by the new Patent Office Museum in London. The drawing had come to light in 1855 through research carried out into Trevithick's work by his son, Francis (1812–77). It had been prepared by John Llewellyn, later described as being a mining agent from Merthyr Tydfil in South Wales. It remained in his family's papers until his nephew, William, made it available to Francis Trevithick. For nearly a century the Merthyr connection had given rise to the belief that the drawing was of the later 'Penydarren' travelling engine that operated on the Merthyr Tramroad (p.19). In 1952, however, E.A. Forward noted that the drawing illustrated a 3ft (915mm) track gauge, as used on the tramroad serving the Coalbrookdale Ironworks, rather than the 4ft 2in (1,270mm) gauge of the Merthyr Tramroad.

In the early 1800s, such a drawing would have been prepared to illustrate what had just been built rather than being plans for the machine's construction. Although this adds weight to the likelihood that the engine had been built at Coalbrookdale, it is still insufficient to confirm that. The hypothesis, therefore, is that Trevithick took the drawing with him to Merthyr Tydfil to aid the Penydarren Ironworks' tradesmen with the construction and assembly of the second vehicle.

THE 'COALBROOKDALE' ENGINE
OPERABLE REPLICA

(See p.97 for colour image.) The replica of the 'Coalbrookdale' travelling engine, completed at the Ironbridge Gorge Museum in 1990, is based largely on the Llewellyn drawing. Working drawings for the replica were prepared by Stuart Johnson, a consulting engineer.

With its single horizontal cylinder set into the boiler, the drive from the crosshead, via a connecting rod, crank and gearwheels, is to the wheel-pair on one side of the engine only. The prominent flywheel on the other side follows Trevithick's stationary engine practice. Steam admission is by a quarter-turn plug valve operated by a tappet rod connected to the crosshead. The flangeless tram wheels revolve around fixed axles.

The small boiler, restricted by the 3ft (915mm) track gauge, made it impossible to insert a return flue of the type that Trevithick had adopted for his road vehicle. Two parallel tubes are therefore fitted through the boiler, connected by an extension box at the flywheel end, to achieve the same effect. The configuration of the engine, with the cylinder flange, piston rod and slide bars protruding from the same end as the chimney and the fire grate, does not allow the engine to be fired on the move.

The engine operates periodically on a short stretch of replica tramroad track at the Blists Hill Victorian Town, part of the Ironbridge Gorge Museum, and can be seen at other times at the museum itself.

'Coalbrookdale' Operable Replica

Built

1990	Ironbridge Gorge Museum (with assistance of GKN Sankey, in association with National Vulcan, the Engineering Training Board and apprentices)

Ownership

1990–Present day	Ironbridge Gorge Museum Trust (Accession No. 1999.1078)

Display

1990–Present day	Blists Hill Victorian Town, Ironbridge Gorge Museum

Summary Details

Plateway gauge:	3ft (915mm)
Wheel diameter:	3ft (915mm)
Cylinder diameter:	4¾in (121mm)
Piston stroke:	36in (915mm)
Boiler length:	4ft (1220mm)
Boiler diameter:	3ft (915mm)
Fire tube diameter:	
Fire grate end:	15in (381mm)
Chimney end:	7in (178mm)
Grate area:	2.5ft² (0.25m²)
Working pressure:	60lbf/in² (4.1bar)
Valve gear:	Quarter-turn valve cock operated by tappet rod
Weight in working order:	*c.* 3.5 tons

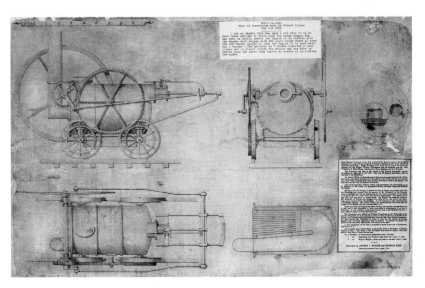

The 'Gateshead' drawing of Trevithick's 'Penydarren' engine. (Science and Society Picture Library)

THE 'PENYDARREN' ENGINE
OPERABLE REPLICA

In the absence of confirmation of the operation of the 'Coalbrookdale' engine, the honour of being the world's first steam-operated railway vehicle has usually been ascribed to Trevithick's travelling engine at the Penydarren Ironworks in South Wales. He clearly discussed the potential for such an engine with the ironworks' proprietor, Samuel Homfray (1761–1822). The latter later agreed a large wager with the owner of the nearby Cyfarthfa Ironworks that an engine would be capable of hauling 10 tons of iron products along the 9½-mile (15km) Merthyr Tramroad. This 4ft 2in (1,270mm) gauge line ran from Penydarren to Abercynon, terminating alongside the Glamorganshire Canal.

The success of the trip by the 'Penydarren' engine, on 21 February 1804, is hailed as the beginning of the steam-operated railway, despite the engine's

weight breaking several of the plate-rails and fixtures, and later reverting to its principal use as a stationary engine powering the ironworks' equipment.

There is no specific drawing of this engine. However, under the same circumstances as the Llewellyn drawing's likely illustration of the 'Coalbrookdale' engine, a drawing attributed to Trevithick's third travelling engine, erected at John Whinfield's works in Gateshead in 1805, is probably representative of the 'Penydarren' arrangement. It portrays an engine that was significantly larger than that attributed to the 'Coalbrookdale' design. The drawing is also preserved in the London Science Museum. It had been taken to Gateshead by John Steel, a millwright from the north-east who had worked with Trevithick in Penydarren when its engine was constructed, and who returned to become Whinfield's foreman. That Steel took the drawing to the north-east is suggested by a later endorsement on the drawing.

This early endeavour at steam haulage was recognised by the building of an operable replica by the National Museum of Wales in 1981. The arrangement of the replica follows the 'Gateshead' drawing, whilst detailed dimensions referred to in correspondence allowed the museum to design the replica locomotive to be 'reasonably representative of the original'.

The museum was obliged by the stringency of regulatory and insurance standards to make modifications to the arrangement. Most notably the

Replica of the 'Penydarren' engine. Now displayed at the National Waterfront Museum in Swansea. (Author)

'Penydarren' Operable Replica

Built

1981	Welsh Industrial and Maritime Museum, Cardiff (with assistance of many engineering firms, colleges of technology, the National Coal Board and apprentices)

Ownership

1981–Present day	National Museum of Wales

Display

1981–98	Welsh Industrial and Maritime Museum, Cardiff
1998–2005	National Railway Museum, York
2005–Present day	National Waterfront Museum, Swansea

Summary Details

	Replica	Original
Track gauge:	4ft 2in (1,270mm)	4ft 2in (1,270mm)
Wheel diameter:	3ft (914mm)	3ft 2in (965mm)
Cylinder diameter:	9in (228mm)	8¼in (210mm)
Piston stroke:	36in (914mm)	54in (1,372mm)
Boiler length:	5ft (1,524mm)	6ft (1,829mm)
Boiler diameter:	4ft (1,220mm)	4ft 3in (1,295mm)
Flue tube diameter:		
Fire grate end:	24in (610mm)	
Chimney end:	12in (305mm)	c. 14in (356mm)
Heating surface:	c. 50ft² (4.65m²)	
Grate area:	6.3ft² (0.6m²)	
Working pressure:	40lbf/in² (2.8bar)	
Valve gear:	Four-way rotary plug valve operated by cams	
Weight in working order:	c. 8 tons	c. 5 tons

cylinder centre line had to be slightly lowered to avoid the conjunction of a number of boiler welds. The knock-on effect led to a redesign, which was undertaken by the South Wales area staff of the National Coal Board.

The single horizontal cylinder was inserted at the opposite end of the boiler from the fire grate and chimney. The original engine could thus have been fired on the move, although it is not known whether the crew stood on an adjacent tram vehicle or walked briskly alongside. The replica is accompanied by a tram vehicle on which the crew can stand.

The crosshead, slide bars, connecting rods, gearwheels and flywheel follow the same arrangement as the 'Coalbrookdale' engine, although the gearing ratios are improved. To avoid the locomotive having to be pinched along until the cranks are at right angles to the connecting rods, a cruciform dog-clutch mechanism, engaging on the primary gearwheel, has been added. This mechanism, a best interpretation from the Gateshead drawing, makes provision for disconnecting the crankshaft from the gearing and its reconnection at the appropriate piston phase.

The exhaust steam is known to have been fed into the chimney, as Trevithick was fully aware of the consequential benefits of helping the fire to

draw. An external exhaust pipe has been fitted to the replica, although none was shown on the 'Gateshead' drawing. As with the 'Coalbrookdale' replica, steam distribution is governed by a four-way rotary plug valve, the design of which was based on a Trevithick drawing in the Science Museum. It is worked by a cam and operating arm from the crosshead.

The replica was given its first trial in Cardiff in June 1981 and for a number of years operated over replica 4ft 2in (1,270mm) gauge plate-rails. On special occasions the engine has visited railway events in other parts of Britain, for which purpose it was fitted with flanged tyres to operate over standard gauge track. Since 2005 it has been displayed at the National Waterfront Museum in Swansea, where it is occasionally steamed.

Right: Detail of the 'Penydarren' engine showing gear drive and cruciform dog-clutch mechanism. (Author)

Far right: Detail of the 'Penydarren' engine showing cylinder-end, valve chest and valve operating-arm. (Author)

Below left: Trevithick's No. 14 stationary engine built *c.* 1803–07 by Hazledine & Co. of Bridgnorth. Displayed at the London Science Museum. (Science and Society Picture Library)

Below right: Ticket issued for the public demonstration of *Catch Me Who Can* in 1808. Retained in the London Science Museum. (Science and Society Picture Library)

CATCH ME WHO CAN

2-2-0 OPERABLE REPLICA

(See p.98 for colour image.) Although Trevithick had played such a major part in these earliest experiments in steam locomotion, his involvement concluded with his *Catch Me Who Can* experimental locomotive. It was manufactured at the Hazledine Foundry in Bridgnorth, under the supervision of John Rastrick (1780–1856), and was the first engine apparently arranged as a locomotive rather than as an industrial engine adapted to self-propulsion. Trevithick demonstrated it publicly in London in 1808. The circular wooden track on which it ran was located close to the New Road (now Euston Road), on a site now occupied by University College (Liffen, 2010). The marshy site made the track unstable and the demonstration was of short duration. It is not known what became of the locomotive thereafter.

To commemorate the bicentenary of this event in 2008, the Trevithick 200 charity was formed to build an operable replica of *Catch Me Who Can*. On behalf of the charity, David Reynolds designed and supervised its construction at the Severn Valley Railway's workshops in Bridgnorth. The design is speculative, and based on a sketch shown on the tickets issued in 1808 for the public demonstration, and on Trevithick's 'No. 14' stationary engine, built at Hazledine's foundry around 1803–07, and displayed in the London Science Museum.

CATCH ME WHO CAN 2-2-0 Operable Replica

Built

| 2008 | Trevithick 200 initiative at Severn Valley Railway's workshops, Bridgnorth |

Ownership

| 2008–Present day | 'Trevithick 200' charity |

Display

| 2008–Present day | Severn Valley Railway's Bridgnorth locomotive depot (not normally on display; occasional public steamings only) |

Summary Details

Track gauge:	4ft 8½in (1435mm)
Wheel diameter:	4ft (1219mm)
Wheelbase:	5ft 2in (1575mm)
Cylinder diameter:	7in (178mm)
Piston stroke:	30in (762mm)
Boiler length:	5ft 8¾in (1746mm)
Boiler diameter:	3ft 11in (1193mm)
Flue tube diameter:	
Fire grate end:	21in (533mm)
Chimney end:	12in (305mm)
Grate area:	4½ft² (0.42m²)
Working pressure:	55lbf/in² (3.8bar)
Valve gear:	four-way rotary plug valve operated by tappets
Weight in working order:	c. 6.75 tons

Detail of *CATCH ME WHO CAN*, showing cylinder and driving motion. (Author)

Detail of *CATCH ME WHO CAN*, showing the valve chest, valve operating rod and tappet. (Author)

Trevithick improved the arrangement over the first two travelling engines by placing the single cylinder vertically in the end of the boiler. The piston rod drove a crosshead and connecting rods directly to cranks on the rear wheels set at 90 degrees to each other. The replica has been designed to demonstrate this arrangement, whilst adopting modern materials and manufacturing standards. The return flue boiler is fired from the leading end, for which purpose a platform has been added. The flue incorporates three siphon tubes to improve steaming capability. The cylinder, cast from the same pattern as the *Puffing Devil* (p.17), is fitted to the boiler end plate rather than fully within the barrel.

As with the other replicas, a four-way rotary plug valve has been fitted to distribute the steam between the cylinder ends, whilst a vertical slotted operating rod, worked by the crosshead, engages the tappet to reverse the plug valve at the end of each stroke.

The replica, based at the Severn Valley Railway's site at Bridgnorth, is steamed occasionally at events in the West Midlands, but was to be fitted with brakes in 2013 for trial operation on the line. It may otherwise only be seen by special arrangement with the charity.

The 1808 locomotive did not come up to Trevithick's expectations and he thereafter turned his attention to other applications of his high-pressure engine. The world was to wait a further 4 years before new projects for locomotion were successfully introduced, in Yorkshire and the north-east of England.

THE FIRST INDUSTRIAL LOCOMOTIVES 1812–15

The difficulties and cost of providing track of sufficient strength for Trevithick's travelling engines offered no immediate financial incentive for coal proprietors to pursue steam locomotion. By 1812, however, Great Britain's economy was badly affected by the Peninsula War with the French Emperor, Napoleon, one consequence of which was the increased cost of horse haulage for coal traffic. John Blenkinsop (1783–1831), the viewer of Middleton Colliery, south of Leeds, reconsidered the use of steam locomotion to reduce the cost of moving coal to the city. He developed the notion of a rack and pinion drive, rather than relying on adhesion as Trevithick had done, to give the required tractive effort. This allowed lighter locomotives to reduce rail breakages.

The successful introduction of the 'Blenkinsop' type of traction gave financial incentive to other mine owners, particularly in the north-east of England, to pursue locomotive power. To avoid the additional costs of casting rack rails and pinion wheels, however, further trials of adhesion haulage were initiated by colliery engineers, namely William Hedley (1779–1843), John Buddle (1773–1843) and William Chapman (1749–1832). This groundbreaking work led to the successful introduction of adhesion locomotives, but only by spreading the locomotive weight over six or eight wheels to avoid problems of rail breakage.

BLENKINSOP/MURRAY LOCOMOTIVE
REPLICA WHEELS

Matthew Murray (1765–1826), the Leeds-based manufacturer of textile and steam machinery, developed a successful design of locomotive to operate the 3½ mile (5.6km) Middleton Colliery railway. Adopting the Blenkinsop rack system, his locomotives made possible the introduction of the world's first commercial operation of railway steam locomotives in 1812.

The boilers of Murray's locomotives were cast in two halves, each incorporating one cylinder set into the top. The halves were bolted together across their central flange, and Davidson (2012) has pointed out that this arrangement was effectively two Trevithick-type engines combined to form the larger twin-cylindered locomotives. The pistons drove the pinion wheel via crossheads, connecting rods and gearing. The gearing set the connecting rods at 90 degrees to each other, ensuring starting from any crank position and a smoother torque.

The edge-rail line, with rack pins cast on one side of the track only, operated with four or five locomotives until the early 1830s. Further examples were built for collieries in Lancashire and the north-east, including Kenton & Coxlodge Colliery. None survived and no operable replica of Murray's

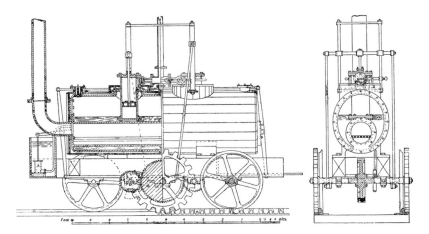

Side-elevation drawing of a Murray locomotive on the Blenkinsop system adopted on the Middleton Colliery railway. (Bulletin de la Société d'Encouragement pour l'Industrie Nationale, *Volume 14e, année 1815*)

Blenkinsop/Murray locomotive Replica wheels

Ownership:

c. 1870–1929	John Spencer & Sons Ltd
1929	T.W. Ward Ltd
1929–47	London & North Eastern Railway
1948–62	British Transport Commission
1962–75	British Railways Board
1975–2012	National Museum of Science and Industry (Accession No. 1975-7143)
2012–Present day	Science Museum Group

Display:

1929–1962	York Railway Museum
1962–1975	Museum of British Transport, Clapham, south London
1975–Present day	National Railway Museum, York

Summary Details:

Track gauge:	5ft 5in (1651mm)
Pinion wheels diameter:	41in (1041mm)
Carrying wheels diameter:	32in (813mm)

Replica Blenkinsop-system locomotive wheels from the Tyne Iron Works site. Displayed at the National Railway Museum, York. (Author)

PUFFING BILLY
STATIC ORIGINAL AND TENDER

(See p.98 for colour image.) Also in 1812, William Hedley, the viewer of Wylam Colliery in Northumberland, sought to confirm the feasibility of traction through adhesion rather than using Blenkinsop's system. A trial was carried out on the 5-mile (8km), 5ft (1524mm) gauge Wylam waggonway between the colliery and Lemington on the banks of the Tyne, which had been relaid with cast-iron plate-rails. To demonstrate that adhesion could be successfully achieved, he constructed a four-wheeled wooden carriage propelled by two men on each side standing on platforms. They turned handles connected through gearing to the axles, and demonstrated that six coal waggons could be drawn along a level track.

Christopher Blackett (1751–1829), the colliery's owner, duly authorised the manufacture of a steam locomotive which, supervised by Hedley, was probably undertaken at Thomas Waters' works in Gateshead, with the assistance of Jonathan Foster (1775–1860), his principal enginewright, and Timothy Hackworth (1786–1850), the foreman smith. The test carriage was used for the vehicle, its gearwheels being modified to suit the piston stroke. The single-cylinder engine began working in early 1813, but was not very successful.

As other engineers in the coalfield began to develop locomotives, Hedley initiated work on two new two-cylinder locomotives which entered service around 1814. They were constructed in accordance with a patent taken out by Hedley (No. 3666) for, *inter alia*, intermediate shafts with toothed wheels. Both these locomotives have survived to take the honour of being the

locomotive type has yet been built, although it is arguable that such a project would provide a much better understanding of its design and operation.

In 1869–70 however, when John Spencer & Sons acquired the former Tyne Iron Works site in Lemington, west of Newcastle, they inherited original patterns of the locomotive pinion and carrying wheels and rack rails. It is thought that the iron works had cast these components for the Kenton & Coxlodge Colliery in 1813.

Examples of the rails and both types of wheels were cast from the patterns in around 1870, and one set, mistakenly having two pinion wheels fitted to the same axle, was transferred to Spencers' main iron and steel works site in Newburn. In 1893 the set was loaned to the South Kensington Museum, but subsequently returned. When the Newburn site was taken over by T.W. Ward Ltd of Sheffield, the company presented the wheelsets and rails to York Railway Museum. They subsequently passed to the National Collection and are now displayed in the National Railway Museum. No attempt has been made to correct the pinion wheel error.

To commemorate the bicentenary of the commencement of steam locomotion, a further replica pinion wheel has recently (2012) been cast on behalf of the Middleton Railway Trust and is displayed in its Engine House Museum.

world's oldest steam locomotives. They are fondly known as *'Puffing Billy'* and *'Wylam Dilly'*, although Guy (2003) indicates that it is possible they were first known as *'Elizabeth'* and *'Jane'*, after Blackett's daughters.

Soon after *Puffing Billy* entered service, the Wylam waggonway suffered broken plate-rails due to its excessive weight. Hedley reformed the engine by spreading the weight over eight wheels, and in this form it ran on the waggonway until approximately 1830. Around that year the Wylam line was relaid with stronger edge-rails which allowed the locomotive to be returned to four wheels, incorporating flanges. The gauge remained at 5ft (1524mm).

The exact provenance of *Puffing Billy* has been discussed in papers and books over a number of years, alternative theories being that it is either the original locomotive or a replacement from the re-wheeling of possibly 1830. However, following detailed examination, Crompton (2003) concludes that the evidence strongly suggests that the boiler, at least, is the original from 1814. The wooden frame, however, shows no sign of an earlier eight-wheel configuration and probably dates from the *c.* 1830 modification.

After operating for just under half a century, *Puffing Billy* was taken out of service in 1862 and loaned by the Wylam Coal Company to the Patent Office Museum in London. An extraordinary and acrimonious negotiation then took place with Edward Blackett, the company's owner, who sought to sell it to the museum for the substantial sum of £1200. In 1865 he accepted payment of £200, and the locomotive has thereafter remained in the collection of the museum and its successors.

Detail of *Puffing Billy*, showing flat boiler end plate, fire hole cover plate and door, and chimney base. (Peter Davidson)

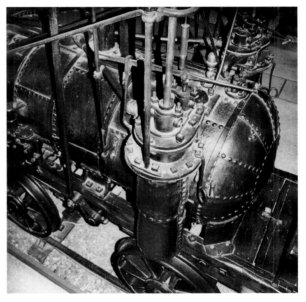

Detail of *Puffing Billy*, showing the boiler's 'egg' end, with cylinder and valve chest. (Author)

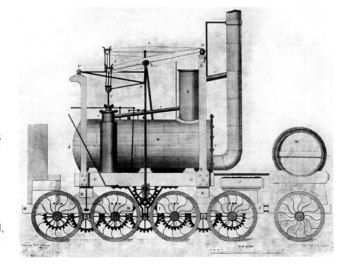

Side-elevation drawing of *Puffing Billy* as an eight-wheel plateway locomotive. (*A Practical Treatise on railroads etc*, Nicholas Wood, London, 1825, Plate VI)

Puffing Billy has provided an excellent opportunity to study the earliest materials and construction methods used in locomotive building. Crompton's survey (2003) has shown that the wrought-iron boiler barrel is built up of five rings, each of twelve wrought-iron plates of about 20½in (520mm) width. Its convex 'egg' end has twelve perimeter plates and a dished centre plate. The other end is flat, the upper segment of which accommodates an inspection/washout hole, its door secured by two bridge stays. The larger segment, accommodating the return fire tube, is badly cracked and patched, as are the firehole cover plate and door, and the chimney. The return fire tube is a later replacement, with 31in (787mm) long plates tapering to an oval at the chimney end.

The boiler is supported on the frame by three brackets on each side. The two vertical cast-iron cylinders are mounted adjacent to the rear barrel ring which is recessed to accommodate them. The external cylinder casings are riveted to the barrel to form part of the pressure envelope, the cylinders thus being encased to aid thermal efficiency.

The driving motion is Freemantle's 'grasshopper' arrangement. This is unlike the 'Watt' type parallel motion illustrated in its eight-wheeled configuration, and probably dates from its rebuild around 1830. Long connecting rods from the motion beams drove the under-frame crankshaft, which set the rods at 90 degrees to each other. The movement of each motion beam was determined by two fixed pivots, provided by a common transverse rod above the cylinder line, and at the base of supporting 'A'-frames at the other end. Each 'A'-frame, the top of which is level with the transverse rod, supported the end of a beam while allowing it to move horizontally, as constrained by links between the beam and the transverse rod.

The valve gear is a simple tappet action adapted from stationary engine practice. Valve handles, pivoted in forks mounted on the cylinder heads, were attached to the valve spindles, the valves being positioned by hand according

Puffing Billy **Static original and tender**	
Built	
1814	? Wylam Colliery workshop
Ownership	
1814–65	Wylam Coal Co.
1865–84	Commissioners of Patents (Accession No. 1862–2)
1884–99	Department of Science and Art
1899–1909	Board of Education
1909–89	Science Museum
1989–2012	National Museum of Science and Industry
2012–Present day	Science Museum Group
Display	
1862–84	Patent Office Museum, South Kensington, London
1884–Present day	Science Museum, South Kensington, London
Summary Details	
Plateway/railway gauge:	5ft (1524mm)
Wheel diameter:	3ft 3in (991mm)
Cylinder diameter:	9in (229mm)
Piston stroke:	39in (991mm)
Boiler length:	8ft 10¾in (2711mm)
Boiler diameter:	4ft 0in (1219mm)
Flue tube heating surface:	77ft^2 (7.15m^2)
Grate area:	6ft^2 (0.56m^2)
Working pressure:	50lbf/in^2 (3.4bar)
Valve gear:	Valve handle tappet change
Weight in working order:	8¼ tons

Side view of *Puffing Billy*, showing the Freemantle 'grasshopper' driving motion. Photograph taken at the Science Museum in 1876. (Science and Society Picture Library)

Detail of *Puffing Billy*, showing the driving gear train. (Author)

to desired direction. Vertical tappet rods, fitted to the motion beams, struck the valve handle ends to redirect the valves.

Separate regulator slide valves serve the two steam pipes inside the rear boiler ring, operated by a common vertical turn rod. The two safety valves are both later fittings, a Salter spring balance served a valve mounted in a round funnel, forward of which is an oval funnel enclosing a six-leaf 'Hackworth' type spring valve (Chapter 6). A whistle was also a later addition. Photographic evidence shows that the boiler feed pump on the left side, which was operated by a vertical drive rod from the motion beam, was raised slightly towards the end of the locomotive's operating life.

The oak frame, just under 1ft (305mm) deep and 5in (127mm) wide, is formed of two planks, bolted and stayed to three equally robust cross-members. On their underside trunnion, bearing blocks are fitted for the two axles, the crankshaft and the two intermediate gear shafts. The axles and shafts were forged square with turned journals. The gearwheels were correspondingly cast with square hub-centres. The 32-teeth driving gearwheel is 20¼in (514mm) diameter, the 30-teeth intermediate gears are 19in (482mm) and the 17-teeth axle gears are 10¾in (273mm) diameter.

The wheels may well be the third set, having wrought-iron segmental 'petal' form spokes cast into the hubs and secured with wrought-iron rims. They probably date from the *c.* 1830 rebuild, and may be compared with the leading wheelset on *Invicta* (Chapter 5).

The tender has a robust wooden-framed truck and rectangular tank, unlike the smaller vehicle depicted in its early plateway configuration. It has four cast-iron wheels with flat radial spokes, each wheel being cast in halves and secured with wrought-iron rings shrunk onto the hub ends. In conjunction with the raised water pump, the tank was raised slightly towards the end of the locomotive's life.

PUFFING BILLY
MUNICH OPERABLE REPLICA AND TENDER

In 1905, plans to establish the Deutsches Museum in Munich were met with enthusiasm by the Union of German Railway Administrations, which offered to assist in providing railway exhibits. On the union's behalf, the Bayerischen Staatseisenbahnen (Bavarian State Railways) offered to build a replica of *Puffing Billy*. A team from the railway's central workshops visited the South Kensington Museum in the spring of 1906. They carried out a detailed survey of the locomotive and prepared working and arrangement drawings.

Above: 'Munich' replica of *Puffing Billy* built in 1906. (Author)

Right: Close-up of 'Munich' replica of *Puffing Billy*, showing cylinder plate and rivet detail. (Author)

Puffing Billy Munich operable replica and tender

Built

1906	Zentralwerkstätte, Bayerischen Staatseisenbahnen (Bavarian State Railways, Central Workshops), Munich, Germany

Ownership

1906–Present day	Deutsches Museum, Munich

Display

1906–25	Deutsches Museum (original site)
1925–Present day	Deutsches Museum (present site)

(Static exhibit – motion occasionally activated by compressed air)

Summary Details

As shown for original locomotive

The team's work was very thorough and required some dismantling to reveal hidden components and construction detail.

Fifty-eight working drawings were prepared, covering every component of the locomotive and tender. All dimensions were taken in metric units. The railway's central workshops completed construction of the replica in December 1906. Every effort was made to replicate the materials and construction methods without compromise, and the exhibit is undoubtedly the most accurate locomotive replica yet made. Attention to detail included the original locomotive's imperfections, distortions, cracks and patches.

Before being handed over to the new museum, the replica was steamed on a specially prepared track and pulled 40 tons at 6mph (10kph), comparing well with records of the original hauling 50 tons at 5mph (8kph). The replica was then placed on static display in the new museum. In 1925, the Deutsches Museum moved to its present site on a large island in the River Isar. The move provided the opportunity to steam the replica again. A length of 5ft (1524mm) gauge track was laid in a military camp south of the city, and the locomotive's operation was recorded on moving film. The replica remains on display in the Deutsches Museum, supported on jacks to allow the motion to be turned by compressed air.

PUFFING BILLY
BEAMISH OPERABLE REPLICA AND TENDER

This second replica of *Puffing Billy* was completed in 2006 at Beamish – The Living Museum of the North, under the supervision of Jim Rees, the museum's special projects manager.

Copies of the Munich drawings were used, the replica having been designed and built as a close representation of the original in its end-of-service form, whilst adopting available materials and meeting safety requirements for passenger operations. It was erected with components contracted out to several British companies. The replica operates on the Pockerley waggonway within the museum's extensive complex.

Puffing Billy Beamish operable replica and tender	
Built	
2006	Beamish – The Living Museum of the North, Co. Durham
Ownership	
2006–Present day	Beamish – The Living Museum of the North
Display	
2006–Present day	Pockerley waggonway, Beamish Museum
Summary Details	
As shown for original locomotive	

WYLAM DILLY
STATIC ORIGINAL AND REPLICA TENDER

It is remarkable that two of Hedley's earliest locomotives on the Wylam waggonway have both survived. *Wylam Dilly* was also completed around 1814, to an arrangement very similar to that of *Puffing Billy*. As with the latter, its initial weight caused it to be rebuilt onto four axles, on which it ran until the waggonway's conversion to heavier section edge-rails in around 1830.

The Wylam coals were hauled along the waggonway to Lemington for tipping into keels for transhipment to ships further down the River Tyne. In 1822, a keelmen's strike threatened to disrupt movement of coal, and Hedley adapted one of the keels as a steam tug by placing the wheelless *Wylam Dilly* on board and fitting 8ft (2.4m) diameter paddle wheels. It resumed work as a locomotive shortly afterwards.

From around 1830, *Wylam Dilly* worked as a four-wheeled edge-rail locomotive on the waggonway until 1868, when the colliery closed. Crompton's survey (2003) showed that its boiler barrel was made in much the same form and period as that of its earlier sibling, with the exception of its front barrel ring which was 5½in (140mm) shorter. The boiler's flat end plate and return flue were renewed during its operational life. The replacement flue was longer, requiring a sixth barrel ring, and, together with the end plate, the material and workmanship are clearly of a later period.

Otherwise, the two locomotives are similar in arrangement, with the notable exception of the piston stroke which is 3in (76mm) shorter. It is most likely that the wooden frame and 'petal' form wheels, and the 'grasshopper' driving motion also date from its *c.* 1830 conversion. New tyres were fitted to the wheels late in its career, their profiles remaining in excellent condition.

Wylam Dilly, the second oldest steam locomotive. Displayed at the National Museum of Scotland, Edinburgh. (Author)

Detail of *Wylam Dilly*, showing the replacement end plate, flue end plate and fire hole door. (Author)

Detail of *Wylam Dilly*, showing the return flue and egg end interior. (Author)

Wylam Dilly Static original and replica tender

Built

c. 1814	? Wylam Colliery workshop

Ownership

1814–69	Wylam Coal Co.
1869–82	William and George Hedley
1882–1904	Museum of Science and Art, Edinburgh (accession No. 1882.1)
1904–85	Royal Scottish Museum
1985–Present day	National Museum of Scotland (accession No.T. 2002.38)

Display

1869–82	Craghead Colliery, Co. Durham
1882–1904	Museum of Science and Art, Edinburgh
1904–85	Royal Scottish Museum
1985–Present day	National Museum of Scotland

Summary Details

Plateway/railway gauge:	5ft (1524mm)
Wheel diameter:	3ft 4in (1016mm)
Cylinder diameter:	9in (229mm)
Piston stroke:	36in (914mm)
Boiler length:	8ft 10in (2692mm) + 1ft (305mm) for convex end
Boiler diameter:	4ft (1219mm)
Flue tube heating surface:	77ft² (7.91m²)
Grate area:	6ft² (0.56m²)
Working pressure:	50lbf/in² (3.4bar)
Valve gear:	Valve handle tappet change
Weight in working order:	8.3 tons + *c.* 4 tons for the tender

In 1869 there was a sale of equipment from the closed colliery, including *Wylam Dilly* which was purchased for £16 10/- (£16.50) by William Hedley's two sons, William and George, who took it to their Craghead Colliery in County Durham to be preserved. There is no evidence that the Hedley brothers also acquired a tender at this time. A number of photographs were taken by R.H. Bleasdale in 1881 at Craghead on a length of 5ft (1524mm) gauge track. The sons were proud to endorse the side and end of the locomotive 'William Hedley Wylam 1813', a reference to their father's initial experimentation and patent.

Liffen's research (2006) strongly suggests that the tender shown in the photographs is a replica dating from 1881, which remains coupled to the locomotive. It has a wooden barrel for its water reservoir rather than a rectangular iron tank as on *Puffing Billy*'s tender.

In 1882, the Hedley brothers exhibited *Wylam Dilly* at the North East Coast Exhibition for Naval Architecture, Marine Engineering, Fishery & Co. at Tynemouth. Following the exhibition the locomotive was acquired by the Museum of Science and Art in Edinburgh and taken directly to the Scottish capital where it remains on exhibition.

STEAM ELEPHANT

OPERABLE REPLICA

(See p.98 for colour image.) One of the most notable replicas to be constructed in recent years is the six-wheeled *Steam Elephant*. Research into the history of the locomotive was carried out by Jim Rees at the Beamish Museum and elsewhere in the 1990s (Rees, 2001). Although vignettes of the locomotive had been known for many years, the re-emergence in a local school of an oil painting, and its loan to the museum in 1995, stimulated the notion to design and build a replica. Rees headed up the project which was carried out at Beamish and completed in 2001.

The research concluded that the original locomotive was built by John Buddle (1773–1843) and William Chapman (1749–1832) in 1815 to draw coals along the approximately 4ft 8in (1422mm) gauge Wallsend edge-rail waggonway. It had been erected at Wallsend, with machined components being supplied by Hawks of Gateshead. Both engineers referred to it as the *Steam Elephant* but there is no evidence of it carrying the name.

The design of the replica is largely based on the oil painting, but reference was also made to other illustrations and component detail of other surviving locomotives. It combined the features of both Murray's and Hedley's locomotives, having two in-line cylinders set into the boiler top, and gear drive, in this case providing 2:1 reduction drive to all three axles. The cylinder centres are in line with two gearwheel shafts, the cranks at the end of which are driven by the piston rods via crosshead beams, working in vertical slide bars fitted to the boiler top, and connecting rods.

The crankshafts have been fitted with tentering (adjusting) gear to maintain optimum mesh, a feature which is apparent on *Puffing Billy* and *Wylam Dilly*. A top speed of 4–4.5mph (6.4–7.2kph) would be possible assuming a maximum crankshaft speed of about 80rpm, a reasonable estimate for this type of vertical engine with no apparent balancing.

The valve gear arrangement is based on that latterly adopted by Timothy Hackworth, an example of which may be seen on his *Sans Pareil* and its replica at the Locomotion Museum in Shildon (Chapter 6). The rear axle mounted slip-eccentric drives the steam inlet valves, with which they communicate via a vertical boiler end link and horizontal boiler top extension that trips the valve levers. Adjustment of the slip-eccentric alters the steam valve trip sequence for reversal.

In accordance with the oil painting and other illustrations of *Steam Elephant*, the wheels are formed with reverse 'S'-spokes. The use of such spokes on the original locomotive would have reduced the risks of failure during casting, but their relationship to the patent taken out by George Stephenson and William Losh in 1816 for this type of wheel is uncertain (Chapter 3). The frame is formed from two baulks of timber, one above the other, resulting in different buffing heights front and rear.

A distinctive feature is the feed pump, located beneath the tapering chimney, which supplies the boiler with water heated by the exhaust gases from the flue tube. Improved thermal efficiency by the use of feed-water heaters was sought after by a number of early locomotive engineers, but with only limited success.

The *Steam Elephant* would only have been used for short-distance banking or marshalling work as none of the illustrations of it show it with a tender,

Steam Elephant Operable replica

Built

2001	Beamish Museum, Co. Durham

Ownership

2001–Present day	Beamish Museum

Display

2001–Present day	Pockerley waggonway, Beamish Museum

Summary Details

Track gauge:	4ft 8½in (1435mm)
Wheel diameter:	2ft 9in (838mm)
Cylinder diameter:	8in (203mm)
Piston stroke:	24in (609mm)
Boiler diameter:	4ft (1219mm)
Boiler length:	8ft (2438mm)
Flue tubes number:	31
Flue tubes diameter:	2¼in (57mm)
Total heating surface:	79ft^2(7.4m^2)
Grate area:	7ft^2(0.7m^2)
Working pressure:	55lbf/in^2 (3.8bar)
Valve gear:	Hackworth

Detail of *Steam Elephant*, showing frame, wheels and driving gear shafts. (Author)

and the limited water capacity of the boiler could not have sustained continuous running for any distance. It operated at least until the mid-1820s when it was rebuilt, perhaps extending its life for a further decade.

The replica operates frequently on the Beamish Museum's Pockerley waggonway.

THE GEORGE STEPHENSON TYPES 1820s

The name of George Stephenson (1781–1848) has been immortalised over the last two centuries as being the engineer who introduced successful and economic steam railway locomotion to become the 'Father of Railways'. Such a label unfairly dilutes the all-important work of his contemporaries, but Stephenson's simultaneous improvements to both locomotives and track in the mid-1810s and 1820s provided a good economic case for railway expansion by colliery and public railway investors.

Stephenson's first locomotive, *My Lord*, acknowledging his employer, Lord Ravensworth, was completed in 1814 and operated on the upgraded Killingworth Colliery edge-rail waggonway in Northumberland. He made further improvements to locomotives and track over the next 13 years, some of which were jointly patented with his collaborators, Ralph Dodds (1792–1874) and William Losh (1770–1861).

Some of his locomotives were described and illustrated in contemporary publications (notably Wood, 1825 and 1831). He selected the 'Murray' and *Steam Elephant* arrangement of two in-line cylinders set into the boiler top with transverse crossheads and vertical connecting rods (Chapter 2). Instead of their geared drive, Stephenson adopted wheel cranks and coupling chains with which to propel the six-wheel locomotives. As experience was gained, however, the chain drive was replaced by coupling rods and fly cranks, whilst stronger rails allowed him to introduce four-wheeled locomotives. Two examples of his locomotives survive, albeit very much rebuilt, and two replicas, one operational, serve to illustrate his developing designs during the first half of the 1820s.

BILLY 0-4-0

STATIC ORIGINAL AND TENDER

(See p.99 for colour image.) The oldest example of a surviving Stephenson locomotive is this four-coupled example affectionately known as *Billy*. Whilst it has been well known on Tyneside since its preservation in 1881, its origins remain uncertain. Rees (2003) has sought to relate *Billy* to a list of locomotives built by Stephenson, drawn up from the best evidence currently available, but it is not yet possible to confirm its origin. Although substantially rebuilt, some characteristics provide clues as to its original form, but a detailed artefactual and archival study would allow a more complete history to be determined.

Billy latterly worked on the Killingworth waggonway in north Tyneside, and was last modified at its workshops in 1867. Together with other collieries and their attendant railways, the Killingworth system had been acquired in 1850 by John Bowes & Partners from the previous owners, Lord Ravensworth & Partners (the 'Grand Allies').

Billy, displayed at the Stephenson Railway Museum, Tyneside. (Author)

Billy's arrangement is very much that of a Stephenson locomotive of the late 1810s and early 1820s, which has been rebuilt on at least two, and probably three, occasions with a number of further improvements effected from time to time. The periodical replacement of worn-out components with new parts, or those cannibalised from other locomotives, reflected the frugal policy of providing cheap motive power in a very competitive industry. Of particular significance, therefore, is the retention of the early driving and valve motion geometry.

There are alternative possibilities for *Billy*'s origin. It either operated on the Killingworth waggonway throughout its career, or it was one of two locomotives that originally operated on the Springwell Colliery line in County Durham, also acquired from the 'Grand Allies' in 1850. One of the latter was said by Warren (1923) to have been transferred to Killingworth in 1863, but no source for this assertion was quoted.

Both Forward (1941–42) and Mountford (1966/76), whilst acknowledging the lack of evidence, also suggest that *Billy* was one of the Springwell Colliery locomotives. These locomotives, one of which was photographed by R.E. Bleasdale about 1862, were made in the Newcastle factory of Robert Stephenson & Co. in 1826 ('Travelling Engines' nos. 1 and 2). Rees (2003) has questioned this presumption, identifying differences between the survivor and the 'Springwell' locomotive.

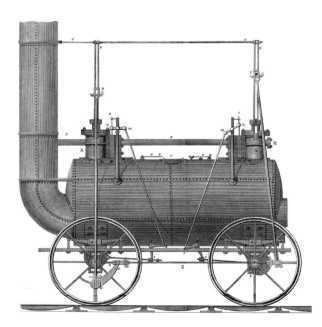

Early view of a George Stephenson Killingworth locomotive with a 6ft 4in (1931mm) wheelbase. (Nicholas Wood, *A Practical Treatise on Rail-Roads &c*, second edition, London, 1831, Plate VII)

Indeed, there are fundamental differences between the two locomotives. Forward's study suggests that the 'Springwell' locomotive had a wheelbase of 5ft 8in (1727mm), and close examination of Bleasdale's photograph seems to confirm this. *Billy*'s wheelbase, however, is 6ft 4in (1931mm), which is the same as one of the original Killingworth locomotives, shown in Wood (1831). This drawing shows a modification, with a frame and plate springs, and might, itself, be an earlier view of *Billy*. This may have given rise to the belief that it had been built in 1830, being so captioned for some of its museum display life.

It is evident that *Billy* underwent successive rebuildings. To have replaced the boiler and the frame wheelsets at the same time would have resulted in virtually a new locomotive, and thus there would have been no point in perpetuating the 1820s driving and valve motion arrangement and wheelbase. The drive motion, which has the same geometry as that shown on the Wood drawing, has vertical piston/crosshead/connecting rod arrangements for each driving wheelset, the two sets being linked only by the coupling rods and fly cranks. Each valve is driven by vertical connecting rods linked to slip-eccentrics, and hand shifted to permit reversing.

The surviving wheels and substantial timber framing and springs post-date the Wood drawing. Indeed, the wheelsets have probably been replaced on at least two occasions, one of which resulted in a decrease in diameter from 4ft (1219mm) to the surviving 3ft 7in (1092mm), possibly to accommodate the more substantial frame. The piston stroke has remained constant at 24in (609mm).

Billy's boiler was probably fitted in the early 1850s. When the boiler was blast cleaned in the 1980s, it revealed a plate size commensurate with that decade. In spite of this late period, it retains two vertical cylinders partly sunk into the barrel top, their 6ft 4in (1931mm) centre line separation corresponding with the wheelbase. This allowed for the retention of the driving motion, frame, horns, springs and boiler brackets. The form of boiler, with an oval firebox containing the grate leading to a combustion chamber, tube plate and multiple tubes, is similar to that fitted to the 'Hetton' and *Nelson* locomotives (p.33 and Chapter 17). This form of boiler was patented by Fossick & Hackworth of Stockton in 1847.

The balance of probability is that *Billy* began life on the Killingworth waggonway, either as an early (*c.* 1815) example of Stephenson's work, or as a previously unknown example from perhaps 1820. It was probably erected at Killingworth, and subsequently rebuilt and modified there during its working life, until it was retired in 1881.

In June of that year it travelled under its own steam for the last time in the procession of historic locomotives to commemorate the centenary of George Stephenson's birth. *Billy* was then presented to the city of

Firebox interior of *Billy*, showing fire grate, combustion chamber and tube plate. (Author)

Billy 0-4-0 Static original

Built

c. 1815–20	? Killingworth Colliery workshop

Ownership

c. 1820–50	?Lord Ravensworth & Partners (the 'Grand Allies')
1850–81	John Bowes & Partners
1881–1974	Corporation of Newcastle-Upon-Tyne
1974–81	Newcastle-Upon-Tyne City Council
1981–Present day	Tyne & Wear Archives and Museums Service

Display

1881–96	Plinth, High Level Bridge, Newcastle-Upon-Tyne
1896–1945	Plinth, Newcastle Central Station
1945–81	Municipal Museum of Science and Industry, Newcastle
1981–Present day	Stephenson Railway Museum, Middle Engine Lane, North Shields

Summary Details

Track gauge:	4ft 8½in (1435mm) (originally 4ft 8in (1422mm))
Wheel diameter:	3ft 7in (1092mm)
Cylinder diameter:	c. 9in (229mm)
Piston stroke:	24in (609mm)
Boiler length:	10ft (3048mm)
Boiler diameter:	4ft 6in (1371mm)
Tubes:	66
Tube diameter:	2¼in (57mm)
Tube length:	5ft 2in (1575mm)
Heating surface:	c. 235ft^2 (21.85m^2)
Grate area:	c. 10.5ft^2 (1m^2)
Working pressure:	Not recorded, but c. 50lbf/in^2 (3.4bar)
Valve gear:	Slip-eccentric for each valve

Newcastle-Upon-Tyne by Sir Charles Palmer, the managing partner of John Bowes & Partners, and began its retirement on display at the north end of the city's High Level bridge.

In 1896 it was removed and placed on a plinth inside Newcastle Central Station. At this time cosmetic restoration was undertaken, mahogany cladding being added to the boiler and the chimney top was cut away. The tender, the earlier history of which is unknown, was rebuilt with springs and an early form of wheel. *Billy* was painted in a livery similar to the standard North Eastern Railway locomotive livery, but later repaintings by the LNER concluded with a 'gas-lamp' green livery.

In 1945, *Billy* was moved to Newcastle's Municipal Museum of Science and Industry, in Exhibition Park, where it was displayed until the site was closed in 1981. It is now displayed at the Stephenson Railway Museum in North Shields, being maintained in movable condition through the lubrication of pistons, crossheads and connecting rods, although the drive from the slip-eccentrics is disconnected.

'HETTON' LOCOMOTIVE 0-4-0
STATIC REPLICA (ORIGINALLY NAMED '*LYON*')

The 'Hetton' locomotive is the oldest replica locomotive in the world, having been completed in 1852. It is to a design purporting to be that of a George Stephenson locomotive of 30 years earlier that had been used on the Hetton Railway in County Durham. As Rees (2003) has discussed, it was designed and built at Hetton Colliery by W. Moor, its chief engineer, assisted by Thomas Harle, second engineer and James Young, the foreman. It was apparently named *Lyon*, presumably as it worked at Hetton's Lyon Colliery. That this, and another similar replica locomotive, were built as working examples for use on the colliery's railway, apparently arose from a strong interest by Sir Lindsay Wood (1834–1920), one of the colliery's principal owners, who was the son of Nicholas Wood (1795–1865), the one-time viewer and later manager of Killingworth Colliery. The second example was destroyed in an explosion in 1858/9.

The 'Hetton' locomotive was built as a 'lookalike' rather than as an accurate portrayal of its forebear. Wood apparently arranged for the replica to be built out of sentiment for his father's and George Stephenson's endeavours 30 years earlier, presumably to demonstrate that the basic design was still economical and 'fit for purpose' in the latter part of the nineteenth century. It is thus unique as being the only replicated locomotive to have

The 'Hetton' locomotive at the Pockerley Waggonway shed, the Living Museum of the North, Beamish. (Author)

Detail of the 'Hetton' locomotive, showing the three-position link motion. (Author)

'Hetton' locomotive (*Lyon*) 0-4-0 static replica

Built

1851/2	Hetton Colliery workshop

Ownership

1852–1911	Hetton Coal Co. (Hon. A. Cochrane & Partners)
1911–23	Lambton & Hetton Collieries Ltd
1923–26	Lambton, Hetton & Joicey Collieries Ltd
1926–47	London & North Eastern Railway
1948–62	British Transport Commission
1962–74	British Railways Board
1974–2012	National Museum of Science and Industry (Accession No. 1978-7009)
2012–Present day	Science Museum Group

Display

1912–26	Hetton (Lyon's Colliery), Hetton-le-Hole, Co. Durham
1926–41	York Railway Museum
1941–47	Reedsmouth (in store – war safety measures)
1947–74	York Railway Museum
1974–Present day	Beamish – The Living Museum of the North

Summary Details

Track gauge:	4ft 8½in (1435mm)
Wheel diameter:	3ft (914mm)
Cylinder diameter:	10¼in (260mm)
Piston stroke:	24in (610mm)
Boiler length:	10ft 2in (3099mm)
Boiler diameter:	4ft 4in (1321mm)
Fire tube:	5ft long x 2ft 1½in (1524mm x 647mm)
Small tubes:	58 tubes, 5ft 2in long x 2in diameter (1575mm x 51mm)
Heating Surface:	157.5ft^2 (14.65m^2)
Grate area:	7.9ft^2 (0.74m^2)
Working pressure:	80lbf/in^2 (5.5bar)
Drive motion:	Freemantle parallel motion
Valve gear:	Three-position link motion replaced slip-eccentrics in 1882
Weight in working order:	9 tons 15cwt (9.9 tonnes)

worked industrially for many years, rather than be constructed for museum or heritage purposes.

The replica's design incorporated a number of mid-nineteenth century features, which are more related to *Billy*'s rebuilt form than to the original 'Stephenson' form. Its boiler barrel contained an oval firebox, the grate leading to a combustion chamber, tube plate and multiple flue tubes. It is not known if this arrangement was similarly influenced by the 1847 Fossick & Hackworth patent (Chapter 17). It was correspondingly fitted with a smokebox and smaller chimney. It also had a manhole door in the side of the boiler closed by a brass cover. Its two in-line cylinders were partially set into the boiler top, with crosshead and vertical connecting rods to the wheel cranks. However, unlike *Billy*, the replica was originally fitted with Freemantle's parallel motion.

It was probably in 1881, when it appeared at the Stephenson centenary celebrations in Newcastle, that the first suggestions arose that it had been rebuilt from an original 1822 locomotive. This reputation had stuck for many years, but the evidence is strong for its replicated form and date. It was rebuilt in 1882 and fitted with a three-position link motion to replace its original slip-eccentrics, its reversing lever being on the left-side running board. Often described over the years as being a type of Stephenson link motion, the quadrant action actually allows for simple reversing rather than cut-off options. 'Gifford' type injectors were fitted, made possible by its working pressure of 80lbf/in^2 (5.5bar). It was also fitted with a primitive but prominent enclosure for the driver above the left-side running board, but this has been removed in preservation.

The 'Hetton' locomotive was retired from service by Lambton and Hetton Collieries Ltd in 1912, after a remarkable sixty-year career. It was preserved by the company, next coming to prominence in July 1925 when it led the parade, in steam, commemorating the centenary of the Stockton & Darlington Railway. A year later, it was donated to the London & North Eastern Railway for preservation in its York Railway Museum. It has subsequently passed to the National Collection.

LOCOMOTION 0-4-0
STATIC ORIGINAL AND TENDER

(See p.99 for colour image.) Robert Stephenson & Co. was established by George and Robert Stephenson, with other partners, in Newcastle-Upon-Tyne in 1823. It was set up to manufacture locomotives and other railway and mining equipment. Its first locomotive was *LOCOMOTION*, completed in September 1825 for the Stockton & Darlington Railway (SDR). It was later given the railway's running 'No. 1'. This public railway was principally for the conveyance of coal from the West Durham coalfield to the ship loading staithes on the River Tees.

George Stephenson determined the locomotive's arrangement but, whilst supervising the building of the SDR, he left responsibility for its construction and fitting to James Kennedy (1797–1886) and Timothy Hackworth (1786–1850). Kennedy later became Edward Bury's superintendent in

Liverpool (Chapter 11), whilst Hackworth became locomotive superintendent of the SDR, and later a notable locomotive builder (Chapters 6 and 17).

LOCOMOTION worked on the SDR for 16 years. It could haul typically 80–90 tons at 5–8mph (8–13kph). It was rebuilt on several occasions, and was involved in several accidents, the worst being in October 1839 when it was 'much broke'. Although withdrawn from service in 1841, it was steamed again in June 1846 for the opening of the Middlesbrough and Redcar Railway. In 1850, it was acquired by the Pease family business for pumping water at their west Durham colliery. It was 'restored' in 1857, and further restored in 1961. Very few, if any, of its surviving components are original, being a mixture of those replaced in service, those put on when first restored for preservation, and those put on in 1961.

Such is the extent of the rebuilding that its original form can only be speculated upon, but in 1941, E.A. Forward, the London Science Museum curator, and author of early railway history, produced a drawing of the *LOCOMOTION* type in its original form. This has provided the most reasoned view of its likely appearance, including alternative views of the earliest wheels.

In common with the earliest Stephenson locomotives, the original boiler barrel would have had convex ('egg'-ended) end plates, with a single fire tube. It was, however, often unable to generate sufficient steam for normal operations, and drivers occasionally increased the weight on the safety valve to operate at a higher pressure. Failure to release the weights when stationary caused the fire tube to collapse in July 1828. Indeed, its fire tube was changed several times. By 1833, Hackworth had remade the boiler to accommodate a main fire tube dividing into two return flues. By 1840, the boiler was described as having a single return flue. The date of the surviving flat-ended boiler, which has a single non-return flue, with horizontal lap-riveted plates, 'U'-form support brackets and riveted drawbar brackets, is unknown but may date from 1850.

LOCOMOTION's original eight-spoked cast wheels broke easily in the absence of springing, on the SDR's uneven track. Hackworth replaced them with robust two-piece cast-iron plug wheels. The rim castings were fitted to the hub castings by oak plugs, and aligned by four bolts and nuts. The outer castings, subjected to occasional breakage, were more cheaply replaced than a complete wheel, although the hub castings were also occasionally replaced. *LOCOMOTION*'s wheels were probably replaced several times, one of the survivors being of a different pattern from the others.

To overcome the difficulty of keeping all four wheels on the undulating track, the rear axle was originally fitted inside a 'cannon box' or tube, centrally pivoted under the boiler to maintain wheel contact. This meant that neither

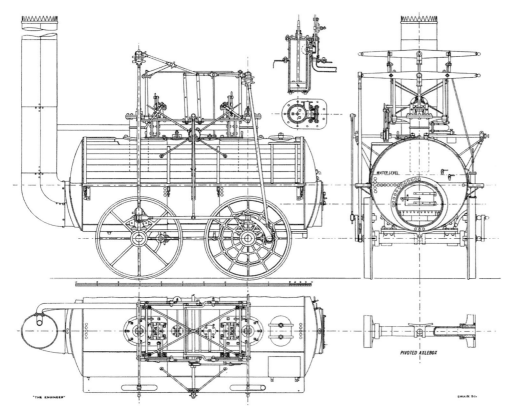

Above: Detail of underside of *LOCOMOTION* showing rear axle, horn assemblies and draw arm. (Author)

Left: Speculative drawing of the *LOCOMOTION* type as built. (Prepared by E.A. Forward, published in *The Engineer*, 17 October 1941)

gear nor chain drive could be used, and coupling rods were therefore fitted. As preserved, however, there is no evidence of the tube, nor has it a frame and springs as were later fitted to the Killingworth locomotives, including *Billy*. The bearing assemblies are fitted within horn blocks, potentially to work with springs, but are now secured in place by wooden blocks.

The cylinders are set into the boiler top, their centre lines over the axle centres, similar to *Billy* and the 'Hetton' locomotive. It is fitted with a more compact form of Freemantle's 'grasshopper' parallel motion than that seen on *Puffing Billy* (Chapter 2). The front and back crankpins on each side are at 90 degrees to each other, and fly cranks are fitted on the right-side front wheel and left-side rear wheel. The fly-cranks were originally curved, but were later replaced by straight ones. The single boiler-feed pump, on the right side, was operated by a horizontal lever, pivoted on a boiler bracket, and driven by a drop arm from the crosshead.

The regulator valves were controlled by a common vertical rod through the boiler top just in front of the rear cylinder. At its bottom was a double crank, working rods forwards and backwards to slide valves at the bottom of each steam chest, offering difficult access in case of failure. Two common exhaust pipes are fitted, one either side of the boiler centre line, leading into either side of the chimney.

The presence of the one-time rear axle 'cannon box' required the valve gear to be operated by a single slip-eccentric, fitted between the axle bearing and nave of the left-side front wheel. It has a semicircular flange making contact with a lug on the wheel which provided an angular advance of 19 degrees for both forward and reverse, providing a cut-off of about 90 per cent. The valve travel was only 2in (51mm). The long eccentric rod for the leading valve rocking shaft lever above the boiler is gab-ended. The eccentric strap also has a horizontal rod (broken and replaced in preservation) which drove a bell crank

Detail of *LOCOMOTION* showing eccentric rod, bell crank and vertical operating rod for the rear valve. (Author)

and vertical operating rod, also with a gab end, for the rear valve rocking shaft lever. Reversal by the driver, standing on the left-side running board, required disengagement of the gabs and manual repositioning of the valves.

The tender is a simple wooden truck with a rectangular water tank and wrought-iron flat-spoked wheels. It is not known if it worked with the locomotive or was attached at the time of preservation.

In 1857, *LOCOMOTION* was presented for preservation to the SDR, which placed the locomotive and tender on a plinth outside North Road Station, Darlington. In 1892, the North Eastern Railway, successor to the SDR, moved it to a plinth on Darlington's main Bank Top station. It remained there, accompanied by *DERWENT* (Chapter 17), for 83 years until it was moved in 1975 back to North Road Station, newly established as the Darlington Railway Centre and Museum, now 'Head of Steam', where it remains on display.

LOCOMOTION has participated as a stationary exhibit in several commemorative events, namely 1875 (SDR Jubilee), 1876 (Philadelphia), 1881 (Newcastle-Upon-Tyne), 1883 (Chicago), 1886 (Liverpool), 1887 (Newcastle-Upon-Tyne), 1889 (Paris), 1890 (Edinburgh) and 1924 (London). In 1925, it appeared in the procession of locomotives for the SDR Railway Centenary in Darlington, albeit driven by a petrol engine in the tender.

LOCOMOTION 0-4-0 Static original and operable replica

ORIGINAL

Built

| 1825 | Robert Stephenson & Co. (Travelling Engine No. 3) |

Ownership

1825–50	Stockton & Darlington Railway
1850–57	Messrs. Pease & Partners
1857–63	Stockton & Darlington Railway
1863–1922	North Eastern Railway
1923–47	London & North Eastern Railway
1948–62	British Transport Commission
1963–74	British Railways Board
1974–2012	National Museum of Science and Industry (Accession No. 1978–7010)
2012–Present day	Science Museum Group

Display

1857–92	Plinthed – North Road Station, Darlington
1892–1975	Plinthed – Bank Top Station, Darlington
1975–Present day	Darlington Railway Museum (Head of Steam)

REPLICA

Erected

| 1974 | ICI's wagon repair shop at Billingham, Teesside |

Ownership and Display

| 1974–2009 | The Locomotion Trust (based at Beamish Museum) |
| 2009–Present day | Beamish – The Living Museum of the North |

Summary Details

	As Built	As Preserved	Replica
Track gauge:	4ft 8in (1422mm)	4ft 8½in (1435mm)	4ft 8½in (1435mm)
Wheel diameter:	4ft (914mm)	4ft (914mm)	4ft (914mm)
Cylinder diameter:	9in (228mm)	9.5in (241mm)	9.5in (241mm)
Piston stroke:	24in (610mm)	24in (610mm)	24in (610mm)
Boiler diameter:	4ft 6in (1372mm)	4ft (1219mm)	4ft (1219mm)
Boiler length:	11ft 6in (3505mm)	10ft 4in (3149mm)	10ft 4in (3149mm)
Fire tube:	c. 18in x c. 132in (457mm x 3352mm)	22in x 120in (558mm x 3048mm)	25in x 138in (635mm x 3505mm)
Heating Surface:	c. 52ft^2 (4.8m^2)	58ft^2 (5.4m^2)	72ft^2 (6.7m^2)
Grate area:	c. 4.5ft^2 (0.4m^2)	4.5ft^2 (0.4m^2)	6ft^2 (0.6m^2)
Working pressure:	50lbf/in^2 (3.4bar)	50lbf/in^2 (3.4bar)	50lbf/in^2 (3.4bar)
Drive motion:	Freemantle parallel motion		
Valve gear:	Single loose eccentric – manual reversing		
Weight in working order:	c. 7.75 tons	8.4 tons	

LOCOMOTION 0-4-0
OPERABLE REPLICA AND TENDER

(See p.100 for colour image.) This replica is a close copy of *LOCOMOTION* in the form in which it has been preserved. It was built between 1973 and 1975, as a voluntary and co-operative project by many commercial, industrial and educational organisations in the north-east of England, involving a substantial amount of apprentice training. The project was undertaken under the initiative and leadership of the late Michael Satow OBE, through the specially formed 'Locomotion Trust'. Components were designed to meet modern safety requirements, together with proscribed performance and construction specifications, and to provide for a reasonable working life in museum service. They were manufactured by many engineering companies in the north-east, and erection was undertaken in ICI's wagon repair shop at Billingham on Teesside.

The boiler is of welded steel construction with cosmetic rivet heads. To overcome some of the original weaknesses, additional stays were fitted, notably to strengthen the top and bottom of the fire tube. The boiler's flat end plates were subject to unacceptably high stress loadings by today's safety codes, and the replica's plates have been stiffened. Eighteen cross-tubes were fitted through the fire tube, alternately left and right inclined at 45 degrees, to increase the heating surface. The boiler is accompanied by a water gauge, two lock-up spring safety valves and a pressure gauge.

As the geometry of the original locomotive's parallel motion was retrofitted in preservation in a non-operable state, the replica's motion was redesigned from first principles. The problems of achieving an accurate straight line with the parallel motion were resolved to within ±0.030in (0.75mm) throughout the 24in (610mm) stroke, compared to ±0.25in (6.35mm) or more of the original.

Although there is no trace of springing on *LOCOMOTION*, springs have been incorporated on the replica, in the horn assemblies of all four wheels. Vertical oscillation and axle box travel have been limited, and this has provided a steady ride on modern track.

As the loose-eccentric and valves on the original are badly worn, their detailed layout for the replica was again designed from scratch, whilst maintaining the 2in (51mm) valve travel. The lap was set at ⅛in (3.2mm) and eccentric travel to 4½in (104mm) with steam cut-off thereby reduced to 80 per cent. The difficulties of maintaining the regulator valves on the original locomotive has been resolved by the use of a 3-part progressive disc valve, made integral with the steam branches to the valve chest. This was inserted before the cylinders were fitted, the joints being made within the valve chests.

The *LOCOMOTION* replica has attended several major commemorative events, most particularly leading the Grand Steam Cavalcade at the 150th anniversary celebrations for the Stockton & Darlington Railway in 1975, as well as many local and regional events throughout Great Britain. It has also been displayed at other major events in Britain and overseas. In 2009 the Locomotion Trust was wound up and ownership of the replica passed to the Beamish Museum. The replica is permanently based at Beamish, where it frequently operates in steam.

JOHN RASTRICK'S LOCOMOTIVES 1828–29

John Urpeth Rastrick (1780–1856) was a leading civil and mechanical engineer of his generation. During the first decade of the nineteenth century he was appointed the 'Engineer' and a partner in the Bridgnorth Foundry, in Shropshire, with John Hazledine and two of his brothers. It was here in 1808 that the foundry manufactured Richard Trevithick's *Catch Me Who Can* (Chapter 1). He left the foundry in 1817 to become a consulting engineer, some of his clients pursuing a number of early railway projects.

In 1819, Rastrick formed a partnership with James Foster (1786–1853) as proprietors of a large manufacturing firm and foundry at Stourbridge, Worcestershire. Foster, Rastrick & Co.'s works built machinery and steam engines, including four locomotives constructed in 1828 and 1829. There has been speculation over many years regarding the sequence in which the locomotives, all of similar design, were constructed. However, Crompton (1998) has argued that *THE AGENORIA* was the first to be built, for use on the Shutt End Railway in the Black Country district of the West Midlands, preceding the locomotives exported to Pennsylvania, USA.

Crompton's extensive surveys of the surviving locomotive components shows that *THE AGENORIA* has survived largely as built, indicating that some innovatory features can be attributed to Rastrick . These are the spring safety valve, wheel-mounted balance weights and a mechanical lubricator. Evidence of a fusible plug suggests priority with this feature as well.

In the 1820s, both George Stephenson (Chapter 3) and Timothy Hackworth (Chapter 6) were seeking to improve the performance of their locomotives through greater heating surface to increase steam generation. Rastrick, too, sought this objective, but chose a bifurcated mid-section to the flue tubes, rather than adopting a return flue. Whilst having the desired effect, the maintenance of such flues would have been time consuming and expensive.

In spite of the innovatory features, which continued to be adopted by other manufacturers for many years, no more locomotives were built by Foster, Rastrick & Co. From the 1830s Rastrick pursued a successful career in railway engineering.

THE AGENORIA 0-4-0
STATIC ORIGINAL WITHOUT TENDER

James Foster (1786–1853) was a driving force in the exploitation of the mineral wealth of the Black Country in Britain's West Midlands. The district became a major exporter of pig iron, manufactured goods and bricks, in addition to coal, for which the region's canal system was an essential means of transport.

By agreement in 1827 between Foster and Lord Dudley, who held major land and mineral rights in the small communities of Pensnett, Kingswinford and Shutt End, a railway was constructed to convey materials to the Staffordshire & Worcestershire Canal at Greensforge. The 3¾-mile Shutt End Railway, which opened in June 1829, had inclined planes at each end. Between was a gradient of 1 in 330 for 1⅞ miles (3km), in favour of the load, over which a locomotive provided the motive power.

Construction of the Shutt End Railway's locomotive was probably commenced in 1828, or even 1827. The American engineer, Horatio Allen, visited Stourbridge in the summer of 1828 and apparently saw the locomotive under construction. If it had been completed in 1828, it could have helped in the line's construction, but evidence is lacking.

The locomotive was later named *THE AGENORIA*, which translates from the Greek as 'courage' or 'valour', qualities ascribed by Homer to a lion pursued by hunters. This is an interesting juxtaposition with its contemporary locomotive, *Stourbridge Lion*, described below. The name, carried on cast-iron cover plates for the rear wheel balance weights, includes the definite article, although the locomotive is often referred to without it. The plates, probably

THE AGENORIA displayed at the National Railway Museum, York. (Author)

Left: Detail of *THE AGENORIA* showing the right-side driving wheel with balance weight and cast name/works plate. (Author)

Below: Interior of *THE AGENORIA*'s boiler showing the fire grate and divided flue tube. (Author)

fitted later in the locomotive's career, also record the railway's opening in 1829.

After the opening of the line, *THE AGENORIA* was given a series of trials, none more spectacular than when people gathered to travel in eight carriages, on twelve loaded coal wagons, and the tender. 920 people were conveyed (with perhaps another 300 hanging on), an all-up weight of 131½ tons, a load which it moved at nearly 3½mph (5.6kph). With engine and tender alone, but still carrying twenty passengers, it attained 11mph (17.7kph) over the same downhill stretch.

THE AGENORIA worked on the Shutt End Railway until about 1865, when it was replaced. William Foster (1814–99), who took on his uncle's financial assets including *THE AGENORIA*, probably retained it out of sentiment. In 1885, he presented it to the South Kensington Museum, where it resided, until being loaned to the York Railway Museum in 1936. Apart from its wartime evacuation, *THE AGENORIA* remained at York, being transferred to the National Railway Museum in 1975.

Much of the locomotive remains as built. The three-ring boiler, lap-riveted with hand-closed rivets, has convex end plates. The rear end plate is bolted to the barrel allowing removal of the fire tubes for maintenance. The 29in

(737mm) diameter fire tube divides into two 18in (457mm) diameter flues, rejoining at the forward end into a chamber, above which a vertical tube directed the hot gases into the chimney. The latter is perhaps the tallest ever used on a locomotive, its top being nearly 22ft (6.7m) above rail level to encourage a greater draw on the fire.

THE AGENORIA originally had two safety valves. That over the rear boiler ring has been replaced by a steam dome, set into the top of which is a safety valve served by a spring balance. The second safety valve, over the middle ring, has been removed, the hole now serving as an inspection hole with a bridge and stud-tightened door.

The contemporary drawing of *Stourbridge Lion* (p.42) shows it to have had a 5in x 1½in (127mm x 38mm) iron bar frame, and it is possible that *THE AGENORIA* was at first similarly fitted. This has been replaced by an inside wood and wrought-iron sandwich frame, joined only by front and rear beams. Its underside includes axle box guides, braced to the frame ends. The boiler is supported by three brackets on each side, bolted to the frame. The leading wheelset is fitted with leaf-springs above the frame, the driving set being springless.

The cast-iron wheels have wrought-iron tyres. Balance weights on the driving wheels would seem to be original, as evidence from *Stourbridge Lion* strongly suggests that it, too, was fitted with balance weights. The axle boxes are unusual as they incorporate a shaft gear driven off the axle, to drive leather oil-throwers, the earliest example of mechanical lubrication.

Two vertical cylinders are mounted on brackets at the rear on either side of the boiler, the left-side one being cracked. The 36in (914mm) stroke pistons are guided by 'grasshopper' parallel motions, the arrangement being similar to that of *Puffing Billy* and *Wylam Dilly* (Chapter 2). The motion beams are located at their leading ends by an iron frame bolted to the middle boiler ring and braced back to a cylinder-mounted framework. The two motions are cross braced, both between the cylinders and at the leading end.

Left: Rear view of *THE AGENORIA* showing left-side cylinder, slide valve and motion. (Author)

Below: Top view of *THE AGENORIA* showing arrangement of the 'grasshopper' parallel motion. (Author)

Detail of *THE AGENORIA* showing sandwich frame, boiler bracket and leading axle spring set. (Author)

THE AGENORIA 0-4-0 Static original without tender

Built

1828/9	Foster, Rastrick & Co., Stourbridge, Worcestershire

Ownership

1828/9–53	James Foster
1853–84	William O. Foster
1884–99	Department of Science & Art
1899–1909	Board of Education (Science Division, Victoria & Albert Museum)
1909–83	Science Museum
1983–2012	National Museum of Science and Industry (Accession No. 1884-92)
2012–Present day	Science Museum Group

Display

1884–86	Patent Office Museum
1886–1936	London Science Museum
1936–41	York Railway Museum (on loan)
1941–47	Reedsmouth (in store – war safety measures)
1947–74	York Railway Museum (on loan)
1975–Present day	National Railway Museum, York

Summary Details

Track gauge:	4ft 8½in (1435mm)
Wheel diameter:	4ft ¾in (1238mm)
Cylinder diameter:	8½in (216mm)
Piston stroke:	36in (914mm)
Crank travel:	27in (686mm)
Boiler length:	10ft (3048mm)
Boiler diameter:	4ft (1219mm)
Furnace tube diameter:	29in (737mm)
Heating flues diameter:	18in (457mm)
Total heating surface:	c. 85ft² (7.9m²)
Grate area:	8.5ft² (0.79m²)
Working pressure:	c. 50lbf/in² (3.4bar)
Valve gear:	Slip-eccentrics, hand-operated valve change
Weight in working order:	c. 8 tons

The rear axle is driven by connecting rods from the motion beams. There is a single boiler feed pump on the left side operated by a drive rod from the motion beam, and an adjustable lever arm. The slide valves, facing the footplate, are driven from the rear axle by slip-eccentrics. The valves and eccentrics were moved by hand for change of direction, regularly undertaken on the short Shutt End line.

Exhaust steam from the cylinders was fed through tubes along the underside of the boiler, uniting at the front end and fed into the base of the chimney, but with little or no blast effect. The iron-bodied tender has not survived.

STOURBRIDGE LION 0-4-0
ORIGINAL COMPONENTS

Stourbridge Lion was one of three locomotives built by Foster, Rastrick & Co. for the Delaware & Hudson Canal Company (DHCC) in Pennsylvania, USA. They were ordered in 1828 by the American engineer, Horatio Allen (1802–1889), who was authorised by John B. Jervis (1795–1885), the company's chief engineer, to procure locomotives for the line. Together with a fourth locomotive, *Pride of Newcastle*, built by Robert Stephenson & Co. (Chapter 5), they were the first locomotives to be tried out in the United States. A contemporary engraving of the locomotive was published (Renwick, 1830).

The DHCC built its 108-mile (174km) canal from Honesdale, in north-east Pennsylvania, to Rondout on the Hudson River to export anthracite from the new Carbondale Mine, destined for New York City. Between Carbondale and Honesdale lay the 1900ft (580m) Farview Mountain, over which a

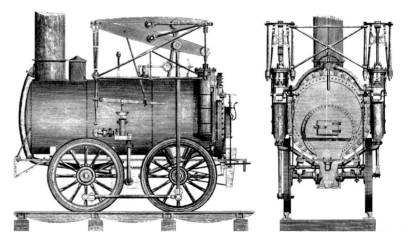

Contemporary engraving of *Stourbridge Lion*. (James Renwick LL.D., *Treatise on the Steam Engine*, Carvill, New York, 1830, Plate IX)

waggonway was built, motive power being winding engines to the top, and a 'Gravity Railroad' down to Honesdale's canal basin. Three stretches of the latter had gradients appropriate for locomotive haulage.

Allen had been instructed that the locomotives should weigh less than the maximum 5½ tons specified for the DHCC's wooden track. However, the three locomotives, built directly after *THE AGENORIA*, were all similar to its construction and weight. He had been aware of the Stephensons' success in adopting direct transmission, using compact crossheads and slide bars between piston and wheel cranks, which obviated the need for parallel motion (Chapter 5). Although the price of the locomotives was 20 per cent less than the Stephensons' engine, it is not known why Allen ordered three examples of a superseded design.

Stourbridge Lion apparently left Stourbridge with a fearsome lion's head painted on the front boiler end plate, an interesting extension of *THE AGENORIA* theme. The adoption of the name *Stourbridge Lion* is less certain, however, as the Renwick drawing does not show it. It arrived in New York in May 1829, and was demonstrated in steam at West Point Foundry.

The trials of the Rastrick and Stephenson locomotives were extraordinary, particularly as they were the United States' first steps into commercial steam railroading. The waggonway was made of 6in x 12in (152mm x 304mm) hemlock 'stringer' rails set on edge. The timbers were 20–30ft (6.1–9.1m) long and capped by ½in (12.7mm) thick wrought-iron straps, which avoided the high cost of rolled iron rails.

With a big audience of townspeople, *Stourbridge Lion* was steamed on 8 August 1829 and ran several successful trips from the centre of Honesdale. The iron strap was depressed into the timber rails under the locomotive's

weight, however, whilst the track itself became distorted. Although Jervis allowed a further trial a month later, the expense of track upgrading was too great and all the locomotives were laid aside.

America's first experience with revenue-earning locomotives had therefore ended in expensive failure. Jervis had specified to Allen a maximum weight, in working order, of 5½ tons for a four-wheel locomotive (or 6–7 tons if on six wheels). At about 8 tons in working order, *Stourbridge Lion* weighed half as much again. Jervis later wrote that Allen had been misled by Foster, Rastrick & Co., but this overlooks the similarly overweight *Pride of Newcastle*. Jervis concluded '[...] I was disposed to consider the failure as attributable to the want of knowledge on the subject, though I could not have been more particular than I had been on the question of weight […] It was clear the agent had not carried out my instructions.'

Stourbridge Lion was laid up in a shed at Honesdale and unsuccessfully offered for sale in 1834. About 1845, the locomotive was dismantled, components being removed by various people for various uses. The boiler provided steam for a works engine in the Carbondale foundry of John Simpson. This was closed in the early 1850s and reopened, in 1856, by Messrs John Stuart and William Linsay. From 1869, the foundry proprietors were Patrick Early and William Linsay, who retired the boiler in 1871.

In 1883, the Delaware & Hudson Canal Co. borrowed the boiler to show at the Exposition of Railway Appliances in Chicago, Illinois. Early and Linsay later donated it to the National Museum in Washington DC in 1888.

The boiler and flues are similar to *THE AGENORIA*'s, although the balance weight safety valve was mounted on the middle, rather than the rear boiler ring. The leading safety valve was mounted on the leading ring, just

Boiler, motion beams and cylinder of *Stourbridge Lion*. (Peter Davidson)

Interior of *Stourbridge Lion*'s boiler showing divided flue tube. (Author)

behind the chimney. The 'grasshopper' motion, boiler feed-pump drive and valve motion were also similar to *THE AGENORIA*'s. The chimney was shorter, however, its top being 15ft (4.6m) above rail level.

Also in 1888, one of the locomotive's motion ('walking') beams was donated to the museum by the Delaware & Hudson Canal Co., and was remounted above the boiler. In 1901, the right-side cylinder, reportedly used by the railroad to operate a pumping engine, was added to the museum's collection and, finally, in 1913, the other motion beam was donated from a private owner.

The feed-water pipe under the boiler passed through a simple preheating box, through which the exhaust steam was fed. A single outlet pipe from the box fed the exhaust steam to the front of the locomotive and up to the base of the chimney.

Stourbridge Lion's frames, depicted on Renwick's engraving, shows a light bar-iron construction. Small leaf-springs, located under the frame, acted directly on simple bearing blocks for the leading axle. The wheels were of wooden construction, except the spokes containing the crank bosses which were probably iron. Of particular note was the inclusion of balance weights on the driving wheels, probably confirming that *THE AGENORIA* was similarly fitted, and both therefore being the earliest examples of locomotive balancing.

The reunited components were continuously displayed at the Smithsonian Institution until 2000, from which date they have been exhibited at the Baltimore & Ohio Railroad Museum.

Right-side cylinder of *Stourbridge Lion*.
(Peter Davidson)

Stourbridge Lion 0-4-0 Original components

Built

1829	Foster, Rastrick & Co., Stourbridge, Worcestershire

Ownership

1829–c.1852	Delaware & Hudson Canal Company

Boiler

c. 1852–56	John Simpson Jr
1856–69	John Stuart and William Linsay
1869–88	Patrick Early and William Linsay
1888–Present day	United States National Museum (Catalogue TR*180149)

Right-side Cylinder

c. 1852–1901	G.T. Slade
1901–Present day	United States National Museum (Catalogue TR*209826)

1st Motion Beam (Walking Beam)

c. 1852–88	Delaware & Hudson Canal Company
1888–Present day	United States National Museum (Catalogue TR*180030-A)

2nd Motion Beam (Walking Beam)

?–1913	Mrs Townsend Poore
1913–Present day	United States National Museum (Catalogue TR*277700)

Display

1888–2002	Smithsonian Institution, Washington DC (boiler, cylinder and 1st walking beam)
1901–2002	Smithsonian Institution (cylinder)
1913–2002	Smithsonian Institution (2nd walking beam)
2002–Present day	Baltimore and Ohio Railroad Museum

Summary Details

Track gauge:	4ft 3in (1295mm)
Cylinder diameter:	8½in (216mm)
Piston stroke:	36in (914mm)
Boiler length:	10ft (3048mm)
Boiler diameter:	4ft (1219mm)
Total heating surface:	c. 85ft^2 (7.9m^2)
Grate area:	8.5ft^2 (0.79m^2)
Working pressure:	50lbf/in^2 (3.4bar)

STOURBRIDGE LION 0-4-0
OPERABLE REPLICA AND TENDER

In 1927, the Delaware & Hudson Railroad began planning the manufacture of a working replica of *Stourbridge Lion* for completion by its centenary 2 years later. The railroad's superintendent of motive power, George Edmonds, visited England and, with the assistance of the London Science Museum, obtained much information about *THE AGENORIA*. Design and construction work was undertaken in the railroad's Colonie workshops, near Albany, New York. In supervising the preparation of arrangement and working drawings, Edmonds incorporated all known facts from the surviving components, Renwick's engraving, as well as from *THE AGENORIA*. Although steel rather than wrought iron was used, the hand forged components were carefully reproduced, and the minor variations of the boiler's hand-closed rivets were duplicated. The replica locomotive and tender took much longer than anticipated to build, and were not completed until 1933.

Although only infrequent operations have taken place due to track availability, some changes have been made to aid handling and safety. The slip-eccentrics were correctly reproduced, and the valves were changed by

Stourbridge Lion replica displayed at the Wayne County Historical Society's Museum, Honesdale. (Author)

Stourbridge Lion 0-4-0 Operable replica and tender

Built

1933	Delaware & Hudson Railroad, Colonie Workshops, Albany, New York

Ownership

1933–68	Delaware & Hudson Railroad
1968–76	Delaware & Hudson Railway (subsidiary of Dereco)
1976–84	Delaware & Hudson Railway
1984–88	Delaware & Hudson Railway (subsidiary of Guilford Rail System)
1988–91	Delaware & Hudson Railway (in bankruptcy)
1991–Present day	Delaware & Hudson Railway (subsidiary of C.P. Rail)

Display

1933–40	Delaware & Hudson Railroad (occasional public display)
1940–Present day	Wayne County Historical Society, Honesdale, Pennsylvania

Summary Details

Track gauge:	4ft 3in (1295mm)
Wheel diameter:	4ft (1219mm)
Cylinder diameter:	8½in (216mm)
Piston stroke:	36in (914mm)
Crank stroke:	27in (686mm)
Boiler length:	10ft (3048mm)
Boiler diameter:	4ft (1219mm)
Total heating surface:	*c.* 85ft^2 (7.9m^2)
Grate area:	8.5ft^2 (0.79m^2)
Working pressure:	50lbf/in^2 (3.4bar)
Valve gear:	Slip-eccentrics, hand-operated valve change
Weight in working order:	*c.* 8 tons

hand. Valve clearances have, however, been increased slightly. The steel frame has an additional intermediate cross-member, which also serves to secure the eccentric rocking shaft mechanism. No water sight glass was fitted, reliance being placed on two back plate try-cocks, and the boiler is fitted with a pressure gauge. A lever-operated band brake is fitted round the rear axle.

The tender is speculative, no contemporary drawing having survived. It has a wooden frame and body, full-length drawbar, and rectangular water tank. The wheels have curved spokes.

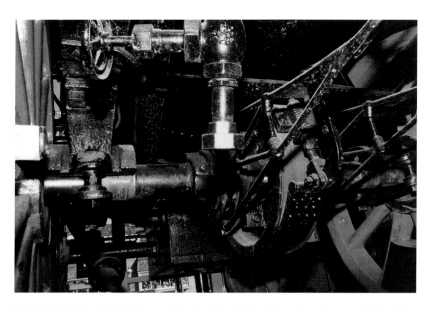

Underside of *Stourbridge Lion* replica, showing the leading axle, valve eccentric and band brake. (Author)

The *Stourbridge Lion* replica was first exhibited at the 'Century of Progress Exposition' in Chicago in 1933. It took part in the railroad pageant at the New York World's Fair in 1939 and 1940. Later in 1940, the replica was permanently loaned to the Wayne County Historical Society. In 1948, the Delaware & Hudson Company borrowed the replica for exhibition at Chicago's Railroad Fair. In 1973, the railroad again borrowed the locomotive, which was loaded onto a flat car and toured the system as part of the sesquicentennial celebrations of its incorporation.

The replica, complete with lion's head, is the centrepiece of the Wayne County Historical Society's museum, which was relocated in 1993 to Honesdale's Main Street, just a few yards from where the events of August 1829 took place.

THE LOCOMOTIVE COMES OF AGE – ROBERT STEPHENSON'S DESIGNS 1828–30

Extraordinary progress was made in locomotive design in the late 1820s. George Stephenson's passionate belief in the potential for locomotive development was strongly expressed to the railway's directors. However, his commitments in supervising the building of the Liverpool and Manchester Railway (LMR), the world's first main-line route, made him dependent upon his son, Robert Stephenson (1803–59), to pursue a programme of incremental component improvements.

Stimulated by the building of the LMR, the intense development programme undertaken under Stephenson's supervision, at his works in Newcastle-Upon-Tyne, was one of the quickest and most successful programmes in engineering history. Between early 1828 and the completion of the prototype *PLANET* in 1830, innovation was added to innovation in quick succession. In just thirty-three months, the slow and cumbersome designs of George Stephenson (Chapter 3) and John Rastrick (Chapter 4) were superseded by a fleet of fast lightweight locomotives suitable for regular, timetabled passenger and goods services.

During the development period, Robert Stephenson & Co. received orders for several locomotives from customers in Britain, France and the United States, which provided the opportunity for testing the innovatory features. These included steel plate springs, and the replacement of vertical cylinders with outside sloping cylinders, allowing direct transmission between piston and wheel crank. The preparations for the Rainhill Trials of October 1829 added stimulus to Stephenson's endeavours, culminating in the completion of *ROCKET* which famously won the competition.

The trials were the Stephensons' opportunity to demonstrate that they could provide the best locomotive fleet for the LMR, against competing designs from other engineers, notably *Sans Pareil* and *Novelty* (Chapter 6). By far the most important innovation was the adoption of multiple flue tubes and a separate firebox. Whereas heat transfer by conduction was

relatively small with single-flue boilers, radiant heat transfer from the firebox significantly increased steam-raising capability. The multiple tubes, with their increased heating surface and increased speeds of flue gases through them, were also beneficial in improving heat transfer to the water.

Other innovations included an axial-movement 'slip-eccentric' valve gear, allowing drivers to reverse direction more readily, and described by Stephenson as being 'as simple as I can make it and I believe effectual'.

Building on *ROCKET*'s success, Stephenson's development programme continued at an even quicker rate for several more months through 1830. In these busy months he introduced a steam dome, allowing drier steam to reach the cylinders, adopted smokeboxes to increase fire drawing, and boilers that incorporated rectangular fireboxes. With each innovation leading to greater efficiency and fuel saving, his work culminated with internal steam pipes serving centrally located cylinders under the smokebox, whose pistons drove cranked driving axles. In this form, Robert Stephenson's *PLANET* class (Chapter 7) was the progenitor of main-line locomotives.

PRIDE OF NEWCASTLE 0-4-0
ORIGINAL COMPONENTS

In the spring of 1828, Robert Stephenson & Co. built *Lancashire Witch*, the first to incorporate steel plate springs, and angled cylinders with direct drive between piston and wheel crank. It was fitted with a twin-flue boiler and a trial variable steam cut-off valve. It was to have been used for building the LMR line, but was diverted by agreement to be used for similar purposes on the Bolton & Leigh Railway.

A replacement locomotive was being built for the LMR in July 1828, when it was seen by Horatio Allen during his visit on behalf of the Delaware &

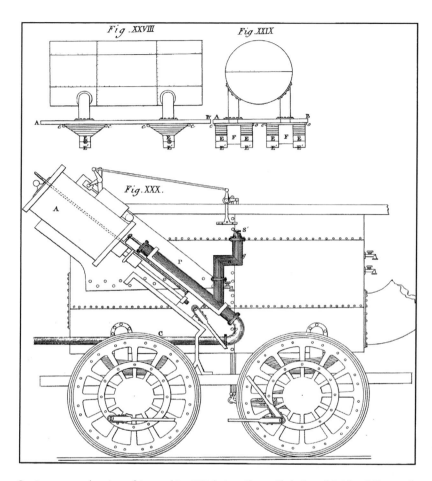

Contemporary drawing of *Lancashire Witch*, together with boiler of *Pride of Newcastle* showing variation in suspension arrangement. (L. Coste and A.A. Perdonnet, *Machine Locomotives*, Annale Des Mines, VI, 1829)

Hudson Canal Company (DHC – Chapter 4). Allen was aware of *Lancashire Witch*'s successful operation when he met the Stephensons and ordered a locomotive for the DHC. They obligingly diverted the LMR engine to this company. However, Allen had been authorised by John B. Jervis, the DHC's chief engineer, to procure a locomotive with a maximum weight in working order of 5½ tons. Allen apparently exceeded his authority as he must have been aware that, like the Rastrick locomotives, the Stephenson engine exceeded this weight by about 2½ tons.

The locomotive was also seen, under construction, by the French engineers, Coste and Perdonnet, who recorded details about it and *Lancashire Witch* (Coste and Perdonnet, 1829). Unlike the latter, with leaf-springs above its light iron frame, they were mounted on the underside of the frame on the new locomotive. The boiler, also supported by four tubular brackets, was made slightly larger.

It was completed in October 1828 and shipped to New York, arriving in January 1829. It was there referred to as *Pride of Newcastle,* but it is doubtful that a name was ever carried. Poor weather prevented immediate dispatch upriver, the opportunity being taken to set it up on blocks and demonstrate it in steam. In July, the *Pride,* accompanied by the Rastrick locomotives, was shipped up the Hudson River to Rondout and transhipped there for the canal journey to Honesdale, Pennsylvania. Following *Stourbridge Lion*'s unsuccessful trial, being too heavy for the line's light track, the company abandoned use of locomotives, and in 1834 tried unsuccessfully to sell them.

Left: Wheel believed originally to have been fitted to *Pride of Newcastle*. Now retained in the collection of the Smithsonian Institution. (Author)

Below left: The left-side cylinder assembly from *Pride of Newcastle* erroneously displayed as the inverted right-side assembly at the Smithsonian Institution. (Author)

Below right: Piston fitted to the left-side cylinder assembly of *Pride of Newcastle*. (Author's collection)

Pride of Newcastle 0-4-0 Original components

Built

1828	Robert Stephenson & Co. ('Travelling Engine No. 12')

Ownership

Wheel tyres and crank rings

1829–88	Delaware & Hudson Canal Co.
1888–Present day	United States National Museum (Catalogue TR*180030-b & c)

Cylinder and piston

1829–?	Delaware & Hudson Canal Co.
?–1890	P. Early and W. Linsay
1890–Present day	United States National Museum (Catalogue TR*180922)

Display

1888/90–2002	Smithsonian Institution, Washington DC
2002–Present day	Smithsonian Institution (in store)

Summary details

Track gauge:	4ft 3in (1295mm)
Wheel diameter:	4ft (1219mm)
Cylinder diameter:	9in (228mm)
Piston stroke:	24in (609mm)
Working pressure:	c. 50lbf/in² (3.4bar)

In 1876, four wrought-iron tyres and three crank rings, now accepted as having been from *Pride of Newcastle*, were exhibited at the Centennial Exhibition in Philadelphia. In 1888, DHC donated the tyres and crank rings to the US National Museum. The museum fitted them to replica wooden wheels which were originally placed under *Stourbridge Lion's* boiler in the mistaken belief that they originated from that locomotive.

In 1890 the Carbondale-based foundry of Linsay & Early donated *Pride of Newcastle's* left-side cylinder and piston to the National Museum. The assembly includes the valve chest, valve, spindle and spindle-guide, and lever arm rocking shaft brackets. For many years these were displayed in the Smithsonian Institution. They were, however, erroneously displayed as being the right-side assembly, but should have been rotated and displayed as being for the left side.

The 9in (228mm) diameter piston is 5in (127mm) deep and fitted with two compression rings with splits cut at an angle of 60 degrees to the edges of the rings. The rings were packed with hemp which, when wet, would cause the rings to expand against the cylinder wall.

From the 1890s, the locomotive was erroneously referred to as '*America*', which was perpetuated by authors for several years. The name had been taken from the Stephenson Company's delivery book entry, being a clear reference to its destination rather than a name.

Independent researches by Messrs Bob Thayer (1998) and Ray State (2001) have led them to pursue the theory that *Pride of Newcastle* blew up after arrival in Honesdale in July 1829. This theory was prompted by the discovery in the 1980s of a small coffin-shaped box, which depicts an early train, with the words 'Blew up July 26, 1829' and 'John B. Jervis – D & H Canal Company'. Their work remains incomplete and, in the absence of any provenance for the box, there is insufficient evidence to relate it to the demise of the locomotive.

ROCKET 0-2-2
STATIC ORIGINAL WITHOUT TENDER

ROCKET is perhaps the most iconic of all surviving locomotives, famous the world over as being the progenitor of main-line locomotion. Its fame as winner of the Rainhill Trials has, however, obscured its true place in the story of the rapid evolution of locomotive design in the late 1820s. Building on the suggestion by Henry Booth, the LMR's secretary, Robert Stephenson and his team developed *ROCKET's* multi-tubular boiler and separate firebox. It was thus the first locomotive to be so fitted, although Marc Seguin had earlier patented an example in France which he subsequently installed on his first locomotive (Chapter 6).

ROCKET's success at the trials was afterwards celebrated by a 'light engine' run past the spectators at the extraordinary speed of 35mph (56kph). After the trials, it was acquired by the LMR and assisted in the construction of the line. As each stretch was completed, it was used as a test track, and during this time *ROCKET* hauled 42 tons at an average 14mph (22.5kph) on level track. Up the 1½-mile long (2.5km), 1 in 96 Whiston incline, it hauled 16 tons at an overall 12½mph (20kph).

The remarkable events of the railway's opening day in September 1830, when *ROCKET* ran over and killed William Huskisson, the former president of the Board of Trade, have been well recorded. However, it suffered three further accidents during its career, all resulting in modifications as well as repairs (Bailey and Glithero, 2000). These modifications explain the very different appearance of the surviving locomotive from its original arrangement.

The introduction of 'Planet' class locomotives from the end of 1830 saw ROCKET relegated to secondary duties. In 1833/4 it was used as an experimental vehicle, firstly as a dynamic test bed for an 'undulating railways' project and latterly to test a prototype 'rotary engine'.

In 1836, ROCKET was sold to the Earl of Carlisle, whose agent, James Thompson (1795–1851), operated his Naworth Colliery railways near Carlisle. The collieries and railways were leased to Thompson from 1838. ROCKET worked on the 4-mile (6.5km) line until 1840, before being laid aside and subsequently stripped of most of its non-ferrous components. These included the copperplate firebox and its brass (formerly copper) tubes.

It remained derelict until 1851, when it was returned to the Stephenson works for 'restoration' pending display at the Great Exhibition in London. This would have been the first occasion that a historic locomotive had been restored, but the arrangements were cancelled. ROCKET was left, partly dismantled, at the works after Thompson died. Ownership passed to his wife's company, set up in 1852 with two of her sons.

In 1862 the Thompson family donated ROCKET to the newly established Patent Office Museum in London as an artefact of national importance. Although incomplete, it was 'restored' by the Stephenson Company, unfortunately incorporating several erroneous replica components. It was displayed at the museum for more than 60 years with erroneous exhaust pipes and chimney, quite unlike those used in service. They were removed in 1923, and another replica chimney added. The carrying wheels are straight-spoked, cast-iron replicas put on by the Science Museum in 1892, replacing a wagon wheelset dating from 1862.

ROCKET has thus received several modifications, restorations and replicated replacements during its long career which has made it difficult to interpret. A detailed archaeological examination of the locomotive's remains, accompanied by a full archival investigation, was therefore carried out in 1999 by the author and John Glithero (Bailey and Glithero, 2000).

ROCKET has a 1in by 4in (25mm x 102mm) bar frame, which supports the boiler by curved pedestals ahead of the firebox, and rectangular brackets above the driving axle. The two-ring boiler barrel is original. The rings are lap-riveted, whilst the plates are butt- and strap-riveted along the horizontal centre line. The examination determined that ROCKET was not fitted with a dome when first made. After experience with Invicta (p.54), and later locomotives, its dome and internal steam pipe were fitted in 1830.

Although the boiler tubes, copper firebox and other non-ferrous fittings are missing, the wrought-iron firebox back plate remains. This is a self-contained water jacket assembly, added in the first few months of service to replace the original dry back plate. A smokebox, replacing the original tube cover plate, was added in 1830. It included a large ashbox below frame level.

In 1831, ROCKET's cylinders, originally inclined at 38 degrees, were lowered to 8 degrees, to provide a more stable ride. New cylinder carrying frames were bolted to the boiler sides, and braced across the firebox back plate. To simplify the valve motion, the cylinders were swapped over, side for side, and inverted, with the valve chests uppermost. The valve rocking shaft was relocated across the upper face of the firebox back plate, fouling the upper part of the firehole which was correspondingly reduced in size. The diamond-profile slide bars, secured to the cylinder frames by short brackets, maintained the alignment of the pistons using bronze crossheads.

The ROCKET displayed at the London Science Museum. (Science and Society Picture Library)

Detail of ROCKET showing boiler tube plate and firebox back plate. (Peter Davidson)

ROCKET 0-2-2 Static original without tender

Built
1829	Robert Stephenson & Co. ('Travelling Engine No. 19')

Ownership
1829	Henry Booth, George Stephenson, Robert Stephenson
1829–36	Liverpool & Manchester Railway
1836–38	Earl of Carlisle
1838–51	James Thompson
1852–62	M. Thompson & Sons
1862–84	Commissioners of Patents
1884–99	Department of Science and Art
1899–1909	Board of Education
1909–89	Science Museum
1989–2012	National Museum of Science and Industry (Accession No. 1862-5)
2012–Present day	Science Museum Group

Display
1862–76	Patent Office Museum
1876–84	South Kensington Museum (on loan)
1884–1909	South Kensington Museum
1909–Present day	Science Museum, London

Summary Details
Track gauge:	4ft 8½in (1435mm)
Driving wheel diameter:	4ft 8½in (1435mm)
Cylinder diameter:	8in (203mm)
Piston stroke:	16½in (419mm)
Boiler length:	6ft (1828mm)
Boiler diameter:	3ft 4in (1016mm)
25 tubes diameter:	3in (76mm)
Total heating surface:	138ft² (12.8m²)
Grate area:	6ft² (0.6m²)
Working pressure:	50lbf/in² (3.4bar)
Valve gear:	Slip-eccentric, manual valve change
Weight in working order:	4 tons 5cwt (4.3 tonnes)

The adoption of 'slip-eccentric' valve gear for easier reversal of *ROCKET* was successful, and incorporated on subsequent locomotives by the Stephenson Company, including the early *Planet* types (Chapter 7). The two eccentrics were fitted to a loose sleeve on the left side of the driving axle. At the two ends of this assembly are cheekplates with slots to receive

Detail of *ROCKET* showing the lowered rearrangement and inversion of the cylinder on the left side. (Peter Davidson)

either forward or reverse dogs clamped to the driving axle at the appropriate angular orientations. These 'drivers', as they were known, were fixed to provide a cut-off of 90 per cent. When a change of direction was required, the eccentric assembly was slipped axially using a 'yoke', engaged by a foot pedal, to allow engagement of the opposite dog.

To achieve alignment with the other dog however, the engine had to be driven manually, for partial rotation of the axle. The eccentric rods, hinged to their straps, drove a combination rocking shaft just ahead of the firebox, the left side motion being via a hollow tube loose-sleeved over the main shaft. Drive to the valve motion rocking shaft was by side rods with gab ends which engaged pins on the valve change hand levers. For reversal, therefore, the gabs were disengaged with levers, allowing the driver to rotate the rocking shaft and valves, when light steam was admitted to the cylinders.

The oak driving wheels are splendid survivors of the type adopted between 1828 and 1832, pending the development of reliable iron wheels. They date from the early 1830s being similar replacements for the originals following one of the accidents. The cast-iron naves incorporate sockets, into which the spokes are fitted, and the crank pin boss. Small brass works plates screwed into the axle ends were probably added in 1862.

ROCKET 0-2-2
'DEARBORN' OPERABLE REPLICA AND TENDER

The iconic reputation of *ROCKET* has led to several operable and dummy replicas being made over the years, all purporting to show the locomotive as it was originally made and operated at the Rainhill Trials. The centenary

Detail of *ROCKET* showing driving axle, slip-eccentric cluster, driving dogs and adjusting yoke. (Peter Davidson)

Works plate from *ROCKET* screwed into the driving axle end, probably dating from 1862. (Author)

'Dearborn' replica of *ROCKET* displayed outside St George's Hall, Liverpool in 1929. (Author's collection)

of the Trials in 1929 prompted the Henry Ford Museum in Dearborn, Michigan, to contract with Robert Stephenson & Co. to build an operable replica at its Darlington works. It was to be a close representation of its Rainhill form, using the same materials and construction, as well as design.

The Stephenson Company carried out significant research with the assistance of J.G.H. Warren, its former chief draughtsman and author of its centenary history, and the London Science Museum. Sixty-eight working drawings of the locomotive and eight of the tender were prepared, plus arrangement drawings, these forming the best judgement of *ROCKET*'s 'as-built' appearance. The drawings, used to build the 'Dearborn' replica, were later used for three further replicas during the 1930s.

After completion in May 1929 the replica was operated in steam within the Stephenson works yard. It was exhibited, principally in London, during the summer, and at Liverpool in September, before being shipped to Dearborn. The replica has since been on static display at the Henry Ford Museum.

ROCKET 0-2-2
'NEW YORK' SECTIONED REPLICA AND TENDER

Publicity surrounding the construction of the 'Dearborn' replica stimulated the interest of the New York City Museum of Science and Industry, part of the city's Museums of Peaceful Arts. In 1930, it ordered a duplicate replica from Robert Stephenson & Co., which was, however, to be sectioned for display. The 'Dearborn' drawings were used, and similar materials adopted.

The sectioned replica was completed at Darlington in 1931 and shipped directly to New York. It remained on exhibition at the museum until around 1955, when it was acquired at auction by a private owner. Ownership has remained in private hands since that time, the last change being in 2004 when it was acquired by a private collector in Southern California.

ROCKET 0-2-2
'CHICAGO' OPERABLE REPLICA AND TENDER

The 'Dearborn' replica also stimulated interest from the newly established Museum of Science and Industry in Chicago, Illinois. An operable replica was ordered from Robert Stephenson & Co. in 1931. The 'Dearborn' drawings were again used, and similar materials adopted. The replica was completed at the Darlington works in September 1931 and shipped directly to Chicago.

'Chicago' replica of *ROCKET* displayed at the Museum of Science and Industry, Chicago, Illinois. (Author)

The replica has been on permanent exhibition at the museum, and is raised slightly above its display track to allow wheels and motion to be turned by electric power. The slip-eccentrics have, however, been rigidly fixed to the driving axle, and the reversing yoke and pedal linkage removed.

ROCKET 0-2-2
'LONDON' SECTIONED REPLICA AND TENDER

In 1934, the London Science Museum ordered a sectioned replica of *ROCKET* from Robert Stephenson & Co. Again, the 'Dearborn' drawings were used, and original materials and construction methods adopted. As with the 'New York' replica, it was made as a gallery demonstrator, being 'sectioned' on the right side.

'London' replica of *ROCKET* displayed at the National Railway Museum, York. (Author)

It was completed at the Stephensons' Darlington works in early 1935 and unveiled at the Science Museum in April. It remained at the museum, alongside the original *ROCKET* until 2000 before being transferred to the National Railway Museum, York.

ROCKET 0-2-2
'YORK' OPERABLE REPLICA AND TENDER

Anticipating the 150th anniversary of the Rainhill Trials in 1979, the National Museum of Science and Industry asked Michael Satow, the project leader for the recently completed *LOCOMOTION* replica (Chapter 3), to construct an operable replica of *ROCKET*. Locomotion Enterprises Ltd, based at Springwell Workshops in County Durham, was established to undertake this and other replica projects, including *Novelty* (Chapter 6).

The replica was to incorporate the surviving locomotive frame, carrying and tender wheelsets, upper chimney and other smaller parts from a full-size non-operable replica that had been built by the London & North Western Railway at Crewe in 1881. This had latterly been displayed on a plinth outside the former British Transport Museum at Clapham, south London, but its wooden components had decayed.

Locomotion Enterprises prepared the specification and carried out the design work. Although the 'Dearborn' drawings were consulted, new drawings were required to reflect material availability and latter-day health and safety

'York' operable replica of *ROCKET*, based at the National Railway Museum, York. (Author)

ROCKET 0-2-2 Replicas and tenders

'DEARBORN' OPERABLE REPLICA

Built

1929	Robert Stephenson & Co. Ltd, Darlington (Works No. 3992)

Ownership and Display

1929–Present day	Henry Ford Museum, Dearborn, Michigan

'NEW YORK' SECTIONED REPLICA

Built

1930	Robert Stephenson & Co. Ltd, Darlington (Works No. 4071)

Ownership and Display

1930 – *c.* 1955	New York Museum of Peaceful Arts
c. 1955–Present day	Private owners

'CHICAGO' OPERABLE REPLICA

Built

1931	Robert Stephenson & Co. Ltd, Darlington (Works No. 4072)

Ownership and Display

1931–Present day	Chicago Museum of Science and Industry

'LONDON' SECTIONED REPLICA

Built

1935	Robert Stephenson & Co., Darlington (Works No. 4089)

Ownership and Display

1935–89	Science Museum
1989–2000	National Museum of Science and Industry (Accession No. 1935-87)
2000–Present day	National Railway Museum, York

'YORK' OPERABLE REPLICA

Built

1979	Locomotion Enterprises, Springwell Workshops, Co. Durham

Rebuilt

2009	The Flour Mill Ltd, Gloucestershire

Ownership

1979–89	Science Museum
1989–2012	National Museum of Science and Industry (Accession No. 1979–7002)
2012–Present day	Science Museum Group

Display

1979–Present day	National Railway Museum, York

Summary Details

As original above

---

requirements. The replica, which closely followed the 1929 drawings, was first steamed in 1979 and appeared at the 'Rainhill 150' celebrations the following year. It thereafter acted as an ambassador for the National Railway Museum, appearing at national and international events in several countries.

After 30 years of operation, the condition of the boiler and firebox had deteriorated and the National Railway Museum arranged for them to be replaced. Following the archaeological work on the original *ROCKET*, undertaken by the author and John Glithero, the opportunity was taken to replicate precisely the locomotive's original design characteristics. The replacement boiler was made without a dome and with twenty-five copper tubes. The firebox saddle was made of copper plate and followed closely the formation of the original box. The work was carried out at the Flour Mill works in Gloucestershire. Completed in 2010, the replica resumed operations at York, with occasional visits to other operating centres.

INVICTA 0-4-0
STATIC ORIGINAL WITHOUT TENDER

Invicta is the world's longest-preserved locomotive, having been withdrawn from service in 1839, before many of the locomotives in this volume had been built. Its 1830s components have thus survived, providing a good opportunity to study design and material progress by that time.

It was completed by Robert Stephenson & Co. in April 1830, being a further advancement in its rapidly improving design programme. It was built for the Canterbury & Whitstable Railway (CWR) in Kent, a 6-mile (9.5km) line built by the Stephensons, which opened the following month as the world's first steam powered general service railway. Stationary winding engines operated the trains on the steeply graded line from the cathedral city, with *Invicta* adopted for the 2-mile stretch up from Whitstable Harbour.

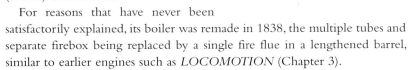

Invicta displayed in the Canterbury Heritage Museum. (Author)

Invicta, during its restoration by the York Railway Circle, in the workshops of the National Railway Museum York in 1977, showing its rear boiler extension. (National Railway Museum)

This included a 1080 yard (1km) stretch with a 1 in 50/57 gradient. *Invicta*'s original layout, with four coupled wheels and a boiler top manifold to ensure a higher water level to protect the firebox crown on the gradient, differed from the successful *ROCKET* arrangement. However, its limited load-hauling capability proved to be uneconomic and it was later restricted to just 1-mile (1.6km) of level track.

For reasons that have never been satisfactorily explained, its boiler was remade in 1838, the multiple tubes and separate firebox being replaced by a single fire flue in a lengthened barrel, similar to earlier engines such as *LOCOMOTION* (Chapter 3).

The rebuilding was unsatisfactory and *Invicta* was unsuccessfully offered for sale in 1839, described as a 12hp (9kW) locomotive in good repair. Rather than scrap it, the CWR directors stored it under cover in Whitstable, where it remained for 14 years. Following the railway's acquisition by the South Eastern Railway in 1853, *Invicta*, by then an object of historic interest, was moved to the paint shop of Ashford Locomotive Works.

Invicta participated in the Darlington Railway Jubilee in 1875 (for which event it was 'restored'), the 1881 Stephenson Centenary in Newcastle, and the Paris Exhibition of 1900. In 1906 the railway donated it to the Canterbury City Corporation, who placed it on a plinth just outside the city walls. Apart from attendance at the Railway Centenary in Darlington in 1925, it remained there until 1968, when it was relocated inside the walls.

Similar to *ROCKET*'s construction, *Invicta*'s original three boiler rings are butt- and strap-riveted at waist level, the rings being lap-riveted to each other. The additional ring added to the rear of the barrel in the 1838 rebuilding was similarly constructed, although the later rivets are a smaller and more spherical type.

The 1in x 4in (25mm x 102mm) bar frame, similar to that used for *ROCKET*, also steps down at the rear, as made for the original firebox. The rear of the boiler is secured to the lower frame by two vertical stays. A makeshift stretcher bar, formed from a length of fish-bellied rail, has been added between the frame's step-down verticals. A brace is fitted between this and a square drawhook on the frame's rear crossbeam to help carry the train load.

An unusual rectangular smokebox, fitted over the flue exit, serves as a base for the chimney. With no opening for ash clearance, however, the box was probably fitted for convenience at some stage during preservation. A cast-iron dome is fitted to the leading boiler ring, on top of which a steam pipe feeds a manifold regulator valve, linked back to a control handle over the centre of the boiler. With the extension of the boiler, the driving position was displaced from the rear to the left side of the boiler, footboards being provided for the driver.

Invicta's cylinders are mounted on wrought-iron frames bolted to the side of the boiler, with a slope of 30 degrees, 8 degrees less than for *ROCKET*. The slide bars and crosshead assemblies are similar to those on *ROCKET*.

In common with all the Stephenson locomotives in 1830, *Invicta* would have been delivered with wooden wheels. The surviving, unmatched iron wheelsets were clearly substituted on different occasions. The rear wheels have tubular cast-iron spokes, with wrought-iron tyres, whereas the leading wheels have wrought-iron flat 'petal' spokes, similar to those used on *Puffing Billy* (Chapter 2).

Invicta's valve gear is similar to that used on *ROCKET*, albeit with the pedal and yoke arrangement, and valve handles rearranged for the driver's

Detail of *Invicta* showing the cast-iron dome, steam pipe and manifold regulator valve. (Author)

Detail of *Invicta* showing the left-side leading wheel with wrought-iron flat 'petal' spokes. (Author)

Detail of *Invicta* showing the slip-eccentric cluster, and one of the driving dogs disengaged from the cheek plate slot. The adjusting yoke is to the rear. (Author)

Invicta 0-4-0 Static original without tender

Built

1830	Robert Stephenson & Co. (Probably works No. 6 (2nd list))

Ownership

1830–53	Canterbury & Whitstable Railway
1853–1906	South Eastern Railway
1906–77	Canterbury City Corporation/City Council
1977–Present day	Transport Trust

Display

1853–1906	Ashford Locomotive Works
1906–68	Canterbury: plinth outside city walls
1968–77	Canterbury: plinth in Dane John Gardens
1980–Present day	Canterbury Heritage Museum

Summary Details

Track gauge:	4ft 8½in (1435mm)
Wheel diameter:	4ft (1219mm)
Cylinder diameter:	10½in (267mm)
Piston stroke:	18in (457mm)
Boiler length (original):	8ft (2438mm)
(from 1838):	9ft 6in (2895mm)
Boiler diameter:	3ft 3in (991mm)
Total heating surface (as built):	192ft² (17.9m²)
Grate area (as built):	c. 6ft² (0.6m²)
Working pressure:	50lbf/in² (3.4bar)
Valve gear:	Slip-eccentric, manual valve change
Weight in working order (as built):	6 tons 5cwt (6.35 tonnes)

left-side position. This rearrangement saw the eccentric rods drive long-reach valve rods via bell cranks. The valve rods are fitted between the left-side crosshead and cylinder frame, to a boiler top rocking shaft, adjacent to the driving position. The slip-eccentrics on the rear axle are less robust than the replacements now seen on *ROCKET*, and apparently date from its construction in 1830. The eccentric plates have only small rectangular slots to engage the driving dogs, thus providing limited opportunity for valve change before the engine came to rest.

In 1977, *Invicta* was purchased by the Transport Trust, prompted by its worsening condition from prolonged exposure. In the workshops of the National Railway Museum, York, it was restored by the York Railway Circle, a voluntary group headed by the trust's vice chairman, Michael Satow, who was also chairman of Locomotion Enterprises (p.53). After the 150th anniversary celebrations in Canterbury in 1980, *Invicta* was returned on long-term loan to the city council and displayed in the Canterbury Heritage museum.

ROCKET'S RIVALS 1828–1830

Robert Stephenson's locomotive programme in the late 1820s stimulated other engineers to develop new designs. These included Timothy Hackworth, who had experience of locomotive building both at Wylam Colliery, with *Puffing Billy* and *Wylam Dilly* (Chapter 2), and at the Stephenson works with its first locomotives (Chapter 3). In 1826 he was appointed as locomotive superintendent of the Stockton & Darlington Railway (SDR), with the opportunity to develop his own ideas of reliable locomotion.

The French engineer, Marc Seguin (1786–1875), also took an early interest in locomotive development. He formed, with his four brothers, the firm of Seguin Frères which was responsible for railway development in the coal-rich St Étienne region of France. On visits to England, Seguin saw the SDR locomotives at work, and acquired two later examples from Robert Stephenson & Co. in 1828 with which to conduct trials. He subsequently built his own prototype with a multi-tubular boiler which challenged precedence with *ROCKET*.

The Rainhill Trials of October 1829 on the Liverpool & Manchester Railway (LMR) encouraged entries from four engineers, in addition to the Stephensons. Only two of the entrants competed with *ROCKET*, however, the *Sans Pareil*, designed and built under Hackworth's supervision, and *Novelty*, entered by John Braithwaite (1797–1870) and his Swedish partner, John Ericsson (1803–1809).

The three Rainhill locomotives, together with Seguin's first locomotive, completed just after the trials, demonstrated extraordinary innovation, making 1829 a most significant year in the history of locomotive development. It is therefore fitting that, in addition to the surviving locomotives and relics, operable replicas of each one have been made to demonstrate their respective operating characteristics.

ROYAL GEORGE 0-6-0
SURVIVING SAFETY VALVE

Timothy Hackworth's appointment as the SDR's superintendent, gave him daily experience of keeping locomotives in working order, together with modifications for their improvement. His *Royal George* locomotive in 1828 was a significant step forward in the reliability and load haul capability for the railway's coal operations.

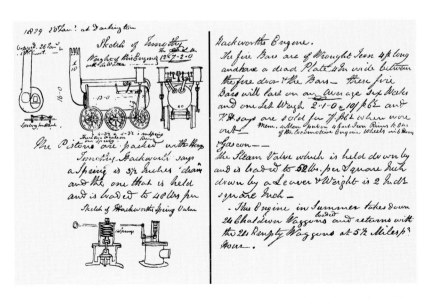

Entry in John Rastrick's 1829 notebook showing his sketches of Timothy Hackworth's *Royal George*, including the novel leaf-spring safety valve. (Senate House Library, University of London)

An early example of Timothy Hackworth's leaf-spring safety valve, sometimes attributed to that fitted to *Royal George*, and retained in the Locomotion Museum, Shildon. (Science and Society Picture Library)

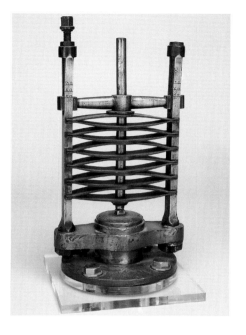

One of Hackworth's innovations was a form of safety valve which he used on his locomotives until the late 1830s. It overcame the valve-lifting problems due to motion-induced bouncing of the balance weight lever arm valves hitherto used. He replaced the balance weight by a set of individual spring leaves, mounted back to back, which were formed into a pack within an adjustable frame and secured by a bridge. An early example of the valve survives and is on display in the Locomotion Museum.

It was believed to have been the original one used on *Royal George*, but its form varies from that shown in the sketch by John Rastrick, engineer of *THE AGENORIA* (Chapter 4), who witnessed a number of the early locomotives. It may therefore have been modified, or originated on a later locomotive. Tests carried out on the valve in 1998 (Gibbon, 2001) showed that its form offered no operational benefits over the coil-spring safety valves developed by the Stephensons and others. A smaller valve of the same type, probably of later manufacture, also survives (Chapter 17).

SANS PAREIL 0-4-0
STATIC ORIGINAL WITHOUT TENDER

The Rainhill Trials offered Hackworth the opportunity to demonstrate his abilities in new locomotive design and construction. His entrant, proudly called *Sans Pareil* ('Without Equal', or possibly 'Without Parallel', to reflect the use of slide bars and crossheads instead of parallel motion), was built in the SDR's Shildon works during the summer of 1829.

Royal George 0-6-0 Surviving safety valve

Built

1828	Stockton & Darlington Railway workshops, Shildon, Co. Durham

Ownership

1828–63	Stockton & Darlington Railway
1863–1923	North Eastern Railway
1923–47	London & North Eastern Railway
1948–62	British Transport Commission
1962–75	British Railways Board
1975–2012	National Museum of Science and Industry (Accession No. 1978-7349)
2012–Present day	Science Museum Group

Display

1928–75	York Railway Museum
1975–94	National Railway Museum, York
1994–2003	Timothy Hackworth Victorian and Railway Museum, Shildon
2004–Present day	Locomotion Museum, Shildon

Sans Pareil displayed in the Welcome Building, Locomotion Museum, Shildon. (Author)

Detail of *Sans Pareil* showing the fire grate extension and flue tube interior. (Author)

was not made, however, and although the early boiler brackets survived, additional vertical brackets were added above the four axle boxes. These were turned over at the top and bolted to the boiler. No springs were fitted.

The barrel of *Sans Pareil*'s original return flue boiler is made of eight horizontal rows of lap-riveted wrought-iron plates. The convex rear has eight flanged perimeter plates and a large circular end plate. The flat front end is built up of riveted plates and collars for the extensions to both ends of the return fire tube. Both the 2ft (610mm) long fire grate extension and the exhaust end of the return flue have saddle-form water jackets to increase heating surface whilst avoiding the weight of a longer barrel.

The rear-mounted vertical cylinders were bolted to bracket frames riveted to the barrel. These frames have slide bars bolted to their inner faces with countersunk bolts, which guided channel-section crossheads. The tops of the cylinders are cross-braced and secured to the boiler top by a vertical brace.

With four wheels, it needed to be within the stipulated weight limit of 4½ tons in working order, but was actually judged to be 5½cwt (279kg) overweight. This should have disqualified it, but it was allowed to participate, albeit dogged by failures. Its boiler feed pump failed on one run, quickly terminating it, whilst a crack in one of its cylinders allowed steam to escape and inhibited its performance. On one trial run, however, it achieved a top speed of 22.7mph (36.5kph) with a load of 19.1 tons, including the locomotive.

After the trials, *Sans Pareil* was purchased by the LMR, but in 1832 it was bought by John Hargreaves, lessee of the adjacent Bolton & Leigh Railway. In 1837, Hargreaves modified the locomotive, replacing Hackworth's 4ft 6in (1372mm) diameter wooden-spoked wheels with 4ft (1220mm) diameter cast wheels with oval-section spokes. He also replaced the 7in (178mm) diameter cylinders with others of 8in (203mm) diameter.

In 1844, *Sans Pareil* was withdrawn from railway service, but as Hargreaves needed a winding and pumping engine at his Coppull Colliery near Chorley, also in Lancashire, he relocated it there. The leading wheelset was removed, whilst a drive gear was fitted to the rear axle.

It ceased operation in 1863, and the following year Hargreaves gave the locomotive to John Hick, a partner with his son, William, in the Bolton firm of Hick, Hargreaves & Co. Hick 'restored' *Sans Pareil* and presented it to the Patent Office Museum in London (Liffen, 2003). The rear wheels were refitted, but the leading wheelset was lost and replaced by a pair of cast wheels replicated from the rear set. The left-side coupling rod was found, but the right-side rod was missing and not replaced.

The restoration provided other replica components for museum display, notably the chimney, exhaust pipe, fire grate and footplate. A replica frame

Detail of *Sans Pareil* showing the cylinders and boiler-top framework. (Author)

Detail of *Sans Pareil* showing the slip-eccentric cluster on the driving axle. (Author)

The tender and some boiler fittings, including safety valves, regulator and steam pipes, did not survive. The right-side boiler feed pump, although disconnected, remains *in situ* in the rear end plate, the left-side being blanked off.

The two adjacent slip-eccentrics were fitted over a sleeve clamped and keyed to the centre of the rear axle. Their alignment was restrained by rings towards the outer edges of the sleeve. The eccentrics were driven by dogs secured to the sleeve, semicircular gaps in flanges on the eccentrics allowing them to slip until the correct orientation for forward or reverse motion was achieved. The arrangement gave a cut-off of 90 per cent.

The long, upright eccentric rods were curved round the boiler end up to the driving position between the two cylinders. They have gabbed ends with release catches, which engaged with drive pins on the valve handles thus forming levers for the transverse valve rocking shafts. The valve spindles were driven by levers at the ends of the rocking shafts.

Sans Pareil was moved in 2004 to the Locomotion Museum at Shildon, where it remains on long-term display in the Welcome Building.

SANS PAREIL 0-4-0
OPERABLE REPLICA AND TENDER

(See p.100 for colour image.) Anticipating the 150th anniversary celebrations of the Rainhill Trials and the opening of the LMR in 1980, the Hackworth Locomotive Trust was formed by local authorities and industry in Shildon. Its purpose was to design and construct an operable replica of *Sans Pareil* that could be regularly steamed at the Timothy Hackworth Victorian and Railway Museum after the celebrations.

Design and construction was undertaken by British Rail Engineering Ltd (BREL), in consultation with Michael Satow, then also engaged on the construction of the *ROCKET* replica (Chapter 5). BREL students surveyed the original locomotive before working drawings were prepared.

Sans Pareil 0-4-0 Static original without tender

Built

1829	Timothy Hackworth, Shildon, Co. Durham

Ownership

1829	Timothy Hackworth
1829–31	Liverpool & Manchester Railway
1831–63	John Hargreaves
1863–64	John Hick
1864–84	Patent Office Museum
1884–1909	South Kensington Museum
1909–75	Science Museum
1975–2012	National Museum of Science and Industry (Accession No. 1864-45)
2012–Present day	Science Museum Group

Display

1864–1999	London Science Museum
1999–2004	National Railway Museum, York
2004–Present day	Locomotion Museum, Shildon

Summary Details

Track gauge:	4ft 8½in (1435mm)
Wheel diameter (as built):	4ft 6in (1372mm)
(as modified 1837):	4ft (1220mm)
Cylinder diameter (as built):	7in (177mm)
(as modified 1837):	*c.* 8in (203mm)
Piston stroke:	18in (457mm)
Boiler length:	6ft (1829mm)
Boiler diameter:	4ft 2in (1270mm)
Flue tube length:	14.6ft (4453mm)
Flue tube internal diameter:	19.5in (495mm)
Total heating surface:	90.3ft^2 (8.4m^2)
Grate area:	10ft^2 (0.9m^2)
Working pressure:	50lbf/in^2 (3.4bar)
Valve gear:	slip-eccentric, manual valve change
Weight in working order:	4.78 tons

SANS PAREIL replica operating at the Locomotion Museum, Shildon. (Author)

SANS PAREIL 0-4-0 Operable replica and tender

Built

1979	British Rail Engineering Ltd, erected Shildon, Co. Durham

Ownership

1980–2009	Hackworth Locomotive Trust
2009–12	National Museum of Science and Industry (Accession No. 2009-7054)
2012–Present day	Science Museum Group

Display

1980–2003	Timothy Hackworth Victorian and Railway Museum, Shildon
2004–Present day	Locomotion Museum, Shildon

Summary Details

Track gauge:	4ft 8½in (1435mm)
Wheel diameter:	4ft 6in (1372mm)
Cylinder diameter:	7in (177mm)
Piston stroke:	18in (457mm)
Boiler length:	6ft (1829mm)
Boiler diameter:	4ft 3in (1295mm)
Flue tube length:	14.6ft (4453mm)
Flue tube internal diameter:	18in (457mm)
Total heating surface:	84.2ft^2 (7.8m^2)
Grate area:	7.3ft^2 (0.7m^2)
Working pressure:	50lbf/in^2 (3.4bar)
Valve gear:	slip-eccentric, manual valve change
Weight in working order:	9.04 tons

Construction was undertaken at several BREL workshops, with erection carried out in the Hackworth Museum at Shildon. Final fitting work and testing was undertaken at BREL's Shildon wagon works, where the original locomotive had been made.

The *SANS PAREIL* replica is a compromise between *Sans Pareil* as built and as it is now preserved. Modern materials, construction methods and safety features were employed, including the adoption of air brakes fitted to the tender and charged by a portable compressor. Three safety valves are fitted, a 'Hackworth' leaf-spring, a 'pop' valve and a weighted lever valve. Springs are fitted within the boiler brackets, with axle boxes redesigned accordingly. In spite of these modifications, the replica well demonstrates the essential features of Hackworth's design.

SANS PAREIL took part in the re-enactment of the Rainhill Trials for the BBC's *Timewatch* programme, broadcast in 2003. Data obtained during the trial runs showed the boiler to be inefficient, and the replica frequently ran out of steam, although the optimum driving techniques were not pursued (Davidson and Glithero 2006).

In 2009 the replica passed to the National Collection and remained at Shildon. Apart from occasional steaming elsewhere, *SANS PAREIL* often operates in steam at the museum.

NOVELTY 2-2-0WT
NON-OPERABLE REPLICA WITH SURVIVING COMPONENTS

In 1828 John Ericsson designed a fire engine, with steam-driven pumps, which was built in John Braithwaite's London engineering works. The engineers belatedly heard about the Rainhill Trials and quickly built their locomotive, *Novelty*, with similar characteristics to the fire engine.

Living up to its name, *Novelty* was a lightweight machine with a two-part boiler. A vertical boiler, said to have been sheathed in copper, housed a firebox, whilst a narrow horizontal barrel housed a looped fire tube leading to a small chimney at the leading end. Water was carried in a wrought-iron under-frame tank, and coke was stored on the central platform.

The locomotive performed well on initial trials at Rainhill, but weaknesses in the boiler, probably due to hasty construction, cut short its trials and Ericsson withdrew it from the competition. It had been popular however and, after modifications, was allowed further trials on the LMR. Braithwaite and Ericsson made two larger locomotives of similar arrangement, but their performance, and that of *Novelty*, fell far short of *ROCKET* and the subsequent Stephenson locomotives. All three were later employed on the adjacent St Helens & Runcorn Gap Railway.

In 1833, *Novelty* was substantially modified by Robert Daglish Jr (1809–83) who was then engaged with Lee, Watson & Co., iron founders of St Helens. From this time it seems to have been used for railway construction purposes, until being withdrawn from service about 1840.

In the 1833 modification, Daglish replaced both cylinders and parts of the motion and gave the original sets to John Melling (1782–1856), the LMR's workshop foreman. Melling left the railway in 1840 and established the Rainhill Iron Works, taking the cylinders and motion with him. The site was later occupied by the Rainhill Gas & Water Co., which used one cylinder and

Novelty 2-2-0WT Original components

Built

1829	John Braithwaite's New Road Works, London

Ownership

LOCOMOTIVE:

1829–33	John Braithwaite and John Ericsson
1833–c.1835	St Helens & Runcorn Gap Railway (cylinders and motion parts replaced 1833 – given to John Melling)
c. 1835–c. 1838	Construction of North Union Railway
c. 1838–c. 1840	Construction of Preston & Longridge Railway

1st cylinder and motion:

1833–40	John Melling
1840–c. 1870	Rainhill Iron Works
c. 1870–1904	Rainhill Gas & Water Co.
1904–09	South Kensington Museum (Accession No. 1904-16)
1909–29	Science Museum

Wheels:

c. 1840–c. 1855	Owner(s) and location unknown
c. 1855–c. 1900	Owner(s) unknown based at Haydock, Lancashire
c. 1900–14	T.W. Ward Ltd of Sheffield
1914–29	Science Museum (Accession No. 1914-83)

Non-operable replica:

1929–Present day	Science Museum (Accession No. 1929-866)

2nd cylinder:

1833–40	John Melling
1840–c. 1870	Rainhill Iron Works
c. 1870–1929	Rainhill Gas & Water Co./Gas Co.
1929–30	Prescot & District Gas Co.
1930–47	London Midland & Scottish Railway
1948–62	British Transport Commission
1962–96	British Railways Board
1996–2012	National Museum of Science and Industry (Accession No. 1996-7035)
2012–Present day	Science Museum Group

Display

NON-OPERABLE REPLICA:

1929–80	Science Museum, London
1980–83	North Western Museum of Science and Industry
1983–Present day	Museum of Science and Industry in Manchester (long-term loan)

2nd cylinder:

1930–70	Rainhill Station booking office
1970–79	Liverpool Museum (stored)
1979–Present day	Rainhill Public Library

its pedestal, together with its piston, crosshead, slide bars, side rods and part of the valve gear to drive a lathe. Said to be largely in original condition, these were donated to the South Kensington Museum in 1904. The wheels were apparently fitted with wrought-iron tyres in 1833, but otherwise remained with the locomotive until 1840. They were set aside in unstated premises in Haydock, Lancashire until the site was acquired by the Sheffield steel firm of T.W. Ward Ltd. This firm donated the wheels to the Science Museum in 1914.

In 1929, the Science Museum put on a special LMR centenary exhibition, for which a non-operable replica of *Novelty* was built, incorporating the original wheels, as well as the cylinder and motion components mounted on the right side. The replica was later made available to the Museum of Science and Industry in Manchester, which restored it in 1988, and where it remains on display.

Non-operable replica of *Novelty*, incorporating original wheel sets and one cylinder assembly. (Museum of Science and Industry, Manchester)

Novelty had a wooden frame suspended above the axle bearings by leaf-springs. The wheels have fourteen 1in (25mm) diameter wrought-iron spokes slotted into conical holes in bosses cast into a 'T'-section rim. The spokes have a staggered 'bicycle' formation, a design patented by Theodore Jones in 1826, whose company in Vauxhall, London, may have supplied the wheelsets.

The firebox was fitted to the frame behind the rear axle, the grate being set well below frame level. A coke hopper, with top and bottom flaps, was fitted to the top of the firebox to avoid forced air ejecting hot coke particles each time fuel was added with the locomotive in motion. The hopper fed coke to a vertical feed tube which widened at frame level into a combustion chamber, the upper leading face of which led to a narrow tapering flue tube. The flue passed through the horizontal boiler, with an extended 'S'-return loop, to the chimney.

The fire was excited by air forced through the grate by a blower, fitted in a front end box, and driven by the driving motion, apparently a version of George Vaughan's 1820 patent (Lamb, 2006). As steam was raised in just 55 minutes during the trials, there was apparently a supplementary means of exciting the fire.

The two vertical cylinders were mounted on small pedestals bolted to the frame just behind the front axle. Two slide rods above each cylinder guided a crosshead coupled to two vertical drive rods. The indirect drive motion, via bell cranks, had long connecting rods passing under the leading axle, which drove the cranked rear axle. The crank axle notably preceded its adoption on *PLANET* (Chapter 7) by nearly a year.

Novelty's second cylinder and its associated components drove a winch at Rainhill Gas Works. However, in 1904, the South Kensington Museum noted that it had been substantially altered and its donation was declined. It remained in the gas works until 1930, when it was donated by the Prescot & District Gas Co. to the London, Midland & Scottish Railway and displayed in Rainhill Station as part of the LMR centenary celebrations. The cylinder and associated components now form part of the National Collection, but remain on long-term display in Rainhill library.

NOVELTY 2-2-0WT

OPERABLE REPLICA

(See p.101 for colour image.) Anticipating the 150th anniversary of the Rainhill Trials and the opening of the LMR in 1980, an independent company, Flying Scotsman Enterprises Ltd (FSE), contracted with Locomotion Enterprises (LE) to design and build an operable replica of *Novelty*. LE's chairman, Michael Satow, oversaw the work in addition to the *SANS PAREIL* and *ROCKET* (Chapter 5) replicas.

Working drawings were prepared by apprentices from British Steel, Teesside, based on the 1929 Science Museum drawings for the non-operable replica. The locomotive was erected at LE's workshops at Springwell, County Durham.

Contemporary arrangement drawings of *Novelty* omit illustration of the blower, so at first it was excluded. Considerable difficulty was experienced in both raising and maintaining steam, however, and in consequence, the replica was displayed as a stationary exhibit on a flat wagon for the 'Rainhill 150' celebrations.

Novelty subsequently went to the Museum of Science and Industry in Manchester, where the director, Dr Richard Hills, made modifications to improve its steaming. A steam blower was installed in the chimney and a conjectural flap-type blower fitted, worked off one of the bell cranks. This, however, delivered air on the outward stroke only, and a pipe was installed to direct the blast below the fire grate.

At the request of Sveriges Järnvägars (Swedish Railways), *Novelty* was shipped to the Sveriges Järnvägsmuseum (Swedish Railway Museum) in Gävle in May 1981, to participate in their 125th anniversary celebrations, with due recognition to John Ericsson. It was put into operable condition there by Dr Hills, but steam pressure could not be maintained, suggesting that a double

Novelty's second cylinder assembly displayed in Rainhill Library, Merseyside. (Author)

acting blower was required to excite the fire. It was also found necessary to keep the firing hole at the top of the boiler partially open to balance the draught between the chimney and boiler top. *Novelty* was afterwards purchased by the Swedish Railway Museum, and remained there as a static exhibit.

Novelty 2-2-0WT   Operable replica

Built

1979	Locomotion Enterprises, Springwell, Co. Durham

Ownership

1979–81	Flying Scotsman Enterprises Ltd
1981–Present day	Sveriges Järnvägsmuseum (Swedish Railway Museum)

Display

1980–81	North Western Museum of Science and Industry, Manchester
1981–98	Sveriges Järnvägsmuseum, Gävle, Sweden
1998–2002	Banmuseet, Ängleholm, Sweden
2002–Present day	Sveriges Järnvägsmuseum, Gävle, Sweden

Summary Details

Track gauge:	4ft 8½in (1435mm)
Wheel diameter:	4ft 2¾in (1289mm)
Cylinder diameter:	6in (152mm)
Piston stroke:	12in (305mm)
Vertical boiler:	
height:	5ft 6in (1676mm)
diameter:	2ft 6in (762mm)
Horizontal boiler:	
length:	10ft 6in (3200mm)
diameter:	1ft 1in (330mm)
Heating surface	
original:	42.5ft² (3.95m²)
replica:	36.3ft² (3.38m²)
Grate area:	
original:	1.8ft² (0.17m²)
replica:	1.1ft² (0.10m²)
Working pressure:	50lbf/in² (3.4bar)
Valve gear:	Fixed eccentrics, manual valve change
Weight in working order:	
original:	3.86 tons
replica:	5.24 tons

In order to take part in the BBC's 2003 *Timewatch* programme re-enacting the Rainhill Trials, the replica was returned to Britain and renovated at the National Railway Museum in York. Its performance still suffered from inadequate draughting and an air compressor was carried to maintain steam pressure. Firing was hazardous because of the firehole location and risks from carbon monoxide exhaust. However, from data obtained, Davidson and Glithero (2006) noted that the boiler had good heat transfer characteristics, giving a powerful cylinder output. The disadvantage was that much of the power was needed to drive the bellows, and residual power delivered to the wheels was only average for the size of locomotive.

MARC SEGUIN 0-4-0
OPERABLE REPLICA AND TENDER

(See p.101 for colour image.) Seguin Frère's railway interests included the 58km (36 miles) long Chemin de Fer de St Étienne à Lyon. The first part of this difficult route, with its extension to Andrézieux linking the rivers Loire and Rhône, opened in 1827 (Cowburn, 2001). Following Seguin's trials with the two Stephenson locomotives received in 1828, he began his own development programme anticipating the potential of multi-tubular boilers. His February 1828 patent for such a boiler was a year before completion of *ROCKET*'s boiler, although it was actually described as being for stationary engine use.

Seguin's first locomotive, equipped with a multi-tubular boiler, was constructed in the railway's Perrache workshops in Lyon, and tested in November 1829. Two years earlier, he had experimented with a stationary multi-tubular boiler, of similar size to his subsequent locomotives. Although this successfully raised plenty of steam, with the furnace excited by centrifugal fans, his first locomotive was more limited for steam, even after experimentation with fans fitted on the tender.

The prototype was tried out on the 16km (9.9 miles) section of the railway between Givors and Rive-de-Gier, and drew 24 tonnes up a 0.6 per cent gradient, and 45 tonnes on the level. The later experiments on one of the subsequent locomotives showed a capability of 30 tonnes up the gradient and 70 tonnes on the level.

Eleven similar locomotives were working on the railway by 1838, when they were seen by Jules-Albert Schlumberger (1804–92) and Émil Koechlin (1808–1883) of the Société Industrielle de Mulhausen (Mulhouse). They recorded arrangement details and performance achievements in a report to the society, which included arrangement drawings of one of the locomotives.

Detail of *Marc SEGUIN* replica, showing its under-slung water-jacketed firebox, fire hole door and chimney. (Author)

Detailed interior view of *Marc SEGUIN* replica, showing the fire grate and semi-cylindrical water-jacketed flue under the boiler. (Author)

A sixth-scale model of the type was presented to the Conservatoire Nationale des Arts et Métiers (National Museum of Arts and Crafts) in Paris in 1891 by Seguin's son, Augustin. The model, believed to have been made some years before, differs in some details from the Mulhausen drawings, emphasising that each locomotive incorporated design innovation. The 'Mulhausen' locomotive had a wooden frame resting on plate springs. The four wheels, of similar pattern to those of the two Stephenson locomotives, had cast-iron naves, wooden spokes and felloes hooped by plain iron bands, and wrought-iron tyres. Two flat iron rings were bolted to either side of the spokes, to which the crank pins were fitted.

The replica, named *Marc SEGUIN*, was designed and built over 6 years by the Association pour la Reconstitution et la Préservation du Patrimoine Industriel (ARPI – Association for the Reconstruction and Preservation of Industrial Heritage), and completed in 1987.

The project leader was Gaston Monnier, professor of mechanics at Ledru-Rollin Technical School in Paris. Although working drawings were based on the Mulhausen drawings, modern materials and construction methods were adopted to meet safety requirements and current practices.

ARPI obtained assistance from six major companies, and apprentices from twenty technical schools assisted with fabrication of the components.

At the rear of the unlagged boiler is an underslung water-jacketed firebox, the firehole door being under the chimney. The unstayed firebox walls, of 20mm (0.8in) thick cast iron, are linked at the front by a bridge connecting the water jacket with the boiler barrel. The hot gases pass under the boiler through a semi-cylindrical water-jacketed flue, which serves as a feed-water heater. The flue gases double back through forty-two boiler tubes of 42mm (1.6in) diameter to the chimney. A weighted lever safety valve is fitted.

There is no blast pipe, a large volume of low pressure air being forced via flexible pipes through the firebox from two four-bladed fans, 1625mm (5ft 4in) in diameter. The fans, mounted on either side of the tender, are worked by pulleys on the wheels, and sufficient air is provided at 300rpm. Echoing the limitations of *Novelty*, much of the engine's output is diverted to powering the fans and therefore limiting that available for traction.

Two vertical cylinders, either side of the boiler and midway between the wheels, are fitted to frame-mounted brackets. The cylinders exhaust to atmosphere, a speculative arrangement not shown on the contemporary

Marc SEGUIN 0-4-0 Operable replica and tender

Built

1980	Association pour la Reconstitution et la Préservation du Patrimoine Industriel

Ownership

1980–Present day	Association pour la Reconstitution et la Préservation du Patrimoine Industriel

Display

1980–Present day	Occasional display at special events

Summary Details

	Mulhausen	Replica
Track gauge:	1372mm (4ft 6in)	1435mm (4ft 8.5in)
Driving wheels:	1120mm (3ft 8in)	1240mm (4ft 0.75in)
Wheelbase:	1450mm (4ft 9in)	1600mm (5ft 3in)
Cylinders diameter:	230mm (9.1in)	230mm (9.1in)
Piston stroke:	600mm (23.6in)	600mm (23.6in)
Boiler length:	2750mm (9ft)	2790mm (9ft 2in)
Boiler diameter:	800mm (31in)	800mm (31in)
Tubes No. x diam.:	43 x 40mm ($1^9/_{16}$ in)	42 x 42mm ($1^5/_8$in)
Length:	Unknown	2819mm (9ft 3in)
Total heating surface:	21.19m^2 (228ft^2)	Unknown
Grate area:	0.86m^2 (9.2ft^2)	0.51m^2 (5.5ft^2)
Working pressure:	2.96bar (43lbf/in^2)	2.76bar (40lbf/in^2)
Valve gear:	Motion beam driven, manual reversal	
Weight in working order:	c. 6000kg (5.9 tons)	5993kg (5.9 tons)

drawings. The pistons are guided by parallel motion, the radius rod pivots of which are mounted on cast pillars standing on the frame and stayed to the boiler. Horizontal beams transmitted the piston action by connecting rods descending to the wheel crank pins. This copies the motion that had been used on the two Stephenson locomotives.

The valves are driven by vertical rods, engaged by the motion beams, with springs to dampen the action. Hand reversing levers reach the valves along the side of the boiler from the rear driving position. Steam to the valve chests is regulated by a manifold valve on the boiler top, between the cylinders.

The replica was first steamed in May 1987, and now operates from time to time around France, and occasionally further afield. At other times, it is stored at the railway depot at Villeneuve St Georges in Paris.

Detail of *Marc SEGUIN* replica, showing one cylinder and parallel motion, valve gear and water pump. (Author)

THE *PLANET* SUITE EARLY 1830s

Robert Stephenson's impressive programme to develop locomotives for main-line operations (Chapter 5) took advantage of the increasing length of the Liverpool & Manchester Railway (LMR) line as it became available during 1830. These trials led to improvements in design and performance, including a higher rate of steam generation, improved thermal efficiency, and better stability as speeds rose to over 20mph (32kph).

The programme culminated in September 1830 with the completion of *PLANET*, the prototype main-line locomotive. This was quickly followed by other examples of the type, but in the early months of operation, whilst the design was generally successful, serious component failures occurred. Material innovation and better construction methods were required to overcome these failures and replace prematurely worn components. This meant that each of the new *Planets* incorporated design and material improvements.

Otherwise, the success of the type in providing the speed and load haul capabilities for main-line operation led to further orders from railways in Britain, and several early railways in Continental Europe and North America. Robert Stephenson & Company made approximately forty of the 2-2-0 *Planets*, and a similar number of 0-4-0 variants. Other manufacturers, including some in the United States, built further examples.

The *Planets* provided significant increases in heating surface and grate area over earlier types, giving a higher rate of steam generation. The smokebox increased the benefits of the blast pipe in drawing air through the grate, exciting the fire and improving heat transfer. The firebox was integrated with the boiler to provide better heat circulation, a steam riser within a dome provided drier steam, whilst an internal steam pipe within the boiler and smokebox, together with inside cylinders in the bottom of the smokebox, minimised heat loss. These improvements in thermal efficiency correspondingly reduced fuel consumption.

Inside cylinders, whilst overcoming the oscillation of earlier outside cylinder locomotives, required crank axles which had an inherent structural weakness. Even with improvements to iron quality and forging and machining methods, reliable crank axles were hard to achieve.

Avoiding the unreliability of cast-iron wheels, the first *Planets* had wooden wheels, hooped with flanged iron tyres. The 0-4-0 type wheels had concentric iron rings on their outer face to which crank pins were fitted. From 1831 the Stephensons experimented with 'gas pipe' wheels, using lengths of iron pipe as spokes set into a cast-iron nave and rim. After several failures and modifications, wheels were developed with hollow, tapered wrought-iron spokes, alternately offset around the nave.

The boiler was supported by a substantial outside sandwich frame. The adoption of inside cylinders allowed the use of timber and iron plate sandwich frames, clamped together by multiple bolts. Provided the bolts were kept tight, the assembly was remarkably rigid, providing a primitive form of 'I'-beam. These members also provided locations for inner and outer horn plates, braced against each other by the axle box slides, allowing a good length of axle box and a symmetrical arrangement for the springs. Thus the gravitational and traction forces acted along the frame centre lines, avoiding bending or twisting forces. Finally, suspension-springs attached to the outside frames were very effective in controlling roll.

Supports for inside bearings, slide bars and crosshead-driven boiler feed pumps were provided by inner frame bars fitted between the smokebox back plate and the firebox front plate. Piston forces were symmetrically carried by these frames, with axle bearings tied back to the cylinders. The train load was taken by the boiler itself, the draw pin bracket being riveted to the firebox back plate.

The 'slip-eccentric' valve gear was similar to that used on *ROCKET* and *Invicta* (Chapter 5), but adapted for the leading cylinders. Two long eccentric rods, hinged to allow for the axial shift, passed between the two cylinder/valve

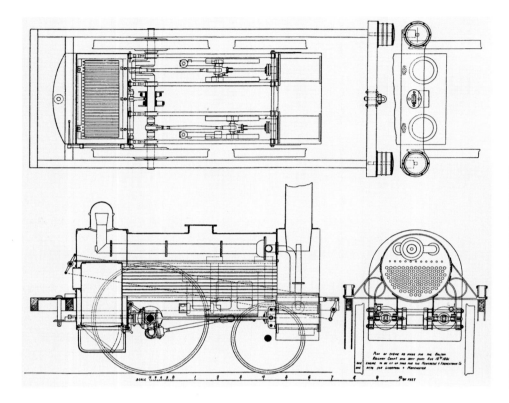

Left: Retraced drawings of original *Planet* type locomotive, dated 15 August 1831. (Reproduced in Warren, 1923, p. 300.)

Below: Replica *PLANET* and train on trials at the Great Central Railway, Loughborough, February 1993. (Frank Beard)

assemblies. Their gabs at the front ends, engaged with and drove the front end valve rocking shafts. They were alternatively engaged for reversing using levers fitted to long rods along the sides or top of the boiler. The valves were manually reversed using levers, fitted to rocking shafts on the firebox back plate, which communicated with the valve rocking shafts by rods along the boiler sides. The valve levers thus rocked backwards and forwards when the locomotive was in motion, causing a hazard to the driver, and the early upright levers were soon replaced by forward-directed curved levers.

PLANET 2-2-0
OPERABLE REPLICA AND TENDER

To fill a gap in the full-size locomotive story, a much needed operable replica of a typical early *Planet* locomotive was designed, fabricated and erected by an experienced engineering team from the Friends of the Museum of Science

and Industry in Manchester. The project, managed by the author, began in 1986 and the replica, named *PLANET*, was first steamed in September 1992.

Its design was based on surviving arrangement drawings of several *Planet* locomotives, together with contemporary component illustrations. Every endeavour was made to achieve an accurate design, but materials, construction methods and safety features were necessarily modified to suit the modern era. The boiler pressure was doubled to $100 \mathrm{lbf/in}^2$ (6.9bar) to ensure effective working of an injector, although a working crosshead feed pump was also fitted. The cylinder diameter was reduced from 11in (279mm) to 8in (203mm) to compensate for the higher pressure so that *PLANET*'s load hauling capability was comparable with the original class.

The sandwich frame and inner frames were connected to allow the train load to be taken through the frame rather than through the boiler. To allow for easier boiler removal, the smokebox was made in two parts, dividing above the valve chests. Cast-steel wheels were fitted to represent the tapered 'gas pipe' design.

PLANET 2-2-0 Operable replica and tender

Built

1992	Friends of the Museum of Science and Industry in Manchester

Ownership

1992–2012	Museum of Science and Industry in Manchester
2012–Present day	Science Museum Group

Display

1992–Present day	Museum of Science and Industry in Manchester

Summary Details

	Original Type	Replica
Track gauge:	Mostly 4ft 8½in (1435mm)	4ft 8½in (1435mm)
Driving wheel diam.:	Mostly 5ft (1524mm)	5ft (1524mm)
Cylinder diameter:	Mostly 11in (279mm)	8in (203mm)
Piston stroke:	16in (406mm)	16in (406mm)
Boiler length:	6ft–7ft 9in (1829–2362mm)	6ft 9¾in (2075mm)
Boiler diameter:	2ft 6in–3ft 1in (762–939mm)	3ft ½in (927mm)
Heating surface:	221.5–407.7ft² (20.6–37.9m²)	c. 435ft² (40.5m²)
Grate area:	5.37–7.31ft² (0.5–0.68m²)	6ft² (0.56m²)
Working pressure:	50lbf/in² (3.4bar)	100lbf/in² (6.9bar)
Valve gear:	Slip-eccentrics, manual valve change	
Weight in working order:	6.59 tons–9.56 tons	c. 8 tons

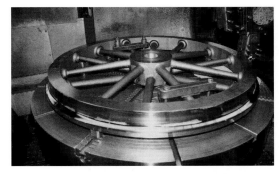

Cast-steel driving wheel for replica *PLANET* during machining. (Frank Beard)

Under boiler rear-facing view of replica *PLANET*, showing driving axle, illustrating restrictive space for driving and valve motion. (Author)

Its design and fitting illustrated well the restricted space available in the short wheelbase vehicle. Although the valve gear carefully followed early drawings, it was found that the slip-eccentric yoke required the insertion of a spring to ensure satisfactory engagement of the forward 'driver'.

An important finding of the project was that the original axles had been poorly designed. The replica's axles broke following a derailment, revealing an inherent weakness at the shoulder adjacent to the wheel seat. Further research confirmed that axles had been redesigned for the type in the early 1830s, suggesting similar failures had occurred in service.

Comprehensive performance and consumption trials were carried out, during which *PLANET* achieved 1,350lbf (6kN) of tractive effort (Bailey 1996–97). This compared well with the original class. *PLANET* is frequently steamed at the Museum of Science and Industry in Manchester.

JOHN BULL 2+2-2-0 (ORIGINALLY 0-4-0)
STATIC ORIGINAL AND REPLICA TENDER

John Bull is the only surviving example of a *Planet* type. It has never carried the name by which it is affectionately known, which reflects the personification of its British origins. It was built by Robert Stephenson & Co. to the order of Robert L. Stevens (1787–1856), president and chief engineer of the Camden & Amboy Railroad and Transportation Co. (CAR) in New Jersey. He was the son of Col John Stevens, who made the *Steam Waggon* in 1825 (Chapter 8).

After seeing the trial of the prototype *PLANET* in December 1830, Robert Stevens visited the Stephenson factory to see *SAMSON*, the first 0-4-0 variant, being assembled. He ordered a similar locomotive, although with a round firebox instead of the usual rectangular type. Actually 'D'-shape in plan, round fireboxes were a design feature of Edward Bury's locomotives (Chapter 11), and Stevens was probably persuaded of its merits by the trials of Bury's 0-4-0 prototype, *LIVERPOOL*.

John Bull on display at the US National Museum of American History, Smithsonian Institution. (US National Museum of American History)

The locomotive was shipped to the CAR's shops in Bordentown, New Jersey, and began trial operations, as the railroad's No. 1, in September 1831. The standard and curvature of the 4ft 10in (1473mm) gauge track did not suit the 0-4-0 wheel arrangement, however, causing derailments and axle failure. It was modified, probably in 1833, by the addition of a pilot truck and removal of the coupling rods, resulting in a 2+2-2-0 wheel arrangement.

The railroad, completed in 1834 to Camden, opposite Philadelphia on the Delaware River, offered a route for passengers and freight between New York and Philadelphia, in conjunction with a steamship service. No. 1 was generally reliable and by 1837 fifteen similar locomotives had been built by the railroad itself. No. 1 was relegated to occasional duties in the 1840s, and from 1849 it was used as a stationary boiler at the Bordentown shops, celebrated as *John Bull*.

After withdrawal from service in the mid-1860s, the CAR retained it as an historic artefact, passing it to the Pennsylvania Railroad (PRR) in 1871. In 1876 it was exhibited at the Centennial celebrations in Philadelphia, for which the Bordentown shops 'restored' it, replacing some of the modified components with others of more 'original' appearance. These features are retained, although some are erroneous and represent neither its original nor concluding features.

John Bull remained at the Bordentown shops until their closure in 1881, when temporary storage was found in Kearney, New Jersey. In 1883 it was exhibited at the National Railway Appliance Exposition in Chicago, Illinois, whilst in the following year the PRR donated it to the Smithsonian Institution, as the museum's first engineering exhibit. In readiness for the World's Columbian Exposition in Chicago in 1893, the PRR borrowed *John Bull* and reconditioned it in their Jersey City shops. It made a remarkable 1,800-mile round trip in steam to Chicago and back, at up to 30mph (48kph), with much publicity and apparently no mechanical problems.

In 1927, it was again in steam at the Baltimore & Ohio Railroad's 'Fair of the Iron Horse' centennial celebrations. In 1933–34, for the 'Century of Progress' Exposition in Chicago, and in 1939–40, for the New York World's Fair, it was displayed as a static exhibit. Apart from its move in 1964 into the National Museum of American History's new building, *John Bull* has remained on display in the Smithsonian.

In 1980, however, it made a remarkable return to steam, running successfully on the Southern Railway's Calverton branch, near Washington DC. This was a prelude to a 150th anniversary celebratory steam run on 15 September 1981, on the Baltimore & Ohio's Georgetown branch near Washington.

Although *John Bull* retains its Stephenson features, many changes were made during its career and in the 1876 'restoration'. However, the boiler barrel and firebox wrapper plates are original. The plates for each of the barrel rings are butt- and strap-riveted, similar to those of *ROCKET* (Chapter 5) – a practice not normally used on later *Planet* type locomotives. The five firebox wrapper plates are lap-riveted, as are the eight hemispherical shoulder plates and crown plate. The inner firebox crown plate is flat, but distorted from prolonged use. Eleven full-length boiler stays remain, but a replacement tube plate provides for eight fewer tubes than when first built.

A major alteration was the removal of the dome and regulator from above the firebox, a replacement dome (oval in cross section) being fitted to

Detail of *John Bull* showing the Bury type round firebox. (Author)

the front boiler ring. This contained a manifold regulator valve feeding two outside steam pipes, which were routed through the smokebox upper plates to the steam chests. Although allowing for ease of maintenance, this would have reduced thermal efficiency. The dome, surmounted with a safety valve and whistle, was removable for boiler inspection, the original hatch now being covered and topped by a bell.

John Bull was originally fitted with slip-eccentric valve gear, but the eccentrics were later fixed by keys to the driving axle. Each was fitted with two eccentric rods, one passing over, and the other under the leading axle. The rods passed between the cylinder/valve assemblies to a drive arm keyed to the front rocking shaft. The gab ends of the rods alternatively engaged pins at either end of the drive arm according to direction of travel. The original eccentric rod lifting-gear, to engage/disengage the pins, was adapted to lift the eccentric rod pairs. These lifting rods, keyed to cross shafts mounted on the top of the smokebox front plate, were raised and lowered using pull rods along the boiler top. Straight valve levers, pre-dating forward-arc levers, survive with the locomotive.

John Bull's original 9in (229mm) diameter cylinders were replaced by 11in (279mm) ones at an early stage. The Stephenson practice of fitting the cylinders in the bottom of the smokebox was abandoned. The smokebox was shortened above the cylinder line and a new bottom plate added, allowing the boiler to be lifted free from the cylinder/valve assemblies. The cylinders

Underside forward view of *John Bull*, showing right-side cylinder, drive motion and water pump. (Author)

Upward view of the leading end of *John Bull*, showing the valve-motion rocking shaft with the gab-ended eccentric rods and vertical lifting rods. (Author)

were secured to transverse bridge plates fitted to extended and strengthened inner frames. This work was probably carried out with the valve gear changes, as the bridge plates have vertical slots to accommodate the eccentric rods. Two boiler feed pumps, driven by curved drive arms keyed to the piston rods, are secured to the inner frames.

The wheels have been replaced at least twice, the cast-iron survivors having 'H'-section spokes, and tyres bolted to the wheels. The pilot wheels are fitted to the locomotive by a timber-framed 'yoke' which is bracketed to the axle ends of the front wheelset with allowance for small fore-and-aft movements. The pilot truck and wheelset could thus swivel in unison as a single four-wheel truck. A tripod suspension was obtained by the yoke-spring and the front wheelset springs. In the 1876 'restoration', the solid cast-iron pilot wheelset was replaced by spoked wheels.

Logs were used as fuel during its final years of operation, for which a spark arresting stack was fitted. This was replaced in 1876 by a fluted-top stack, mistakenly thought to represent the original appearance. The restoration also saw the removal of the locomotive's later wooden cab.

The four-wheel tender, matched with *John Bull* in 1876, and probably a rebuild of its eight-wheeled service tender, was a tall covered vehicle to keep the logs dry and free from sparks, and incorporating a vertical water cylinder. The condition of this tender had decayed by the early twentieth century, however, and it was dismantled, the surviving components being stored. For the 1927 'Fair of the Iron Horse', a replica tender was built by the PRR at

Left: Early driving wheel, thought to have been fitted to *John Bull*, on display at the US National Museum of American History, Smithsonian Institution. (Author)

Right: Early driving wheel, thought to have been fitted to *John Bull*, on display at the Railroad Museum of Pennsylvania. (Author)

John Bull 2+2-2-0 Static original and components

Built	
1831	Robert Stephenson & Co., Newcastle-Upon-Tyne (works No. 25, (2nd list))
Ownership	
1831–71	Camden & Amboy Railroad and Transportation Co.
Locomotive	
1871–84	Pennsylvania Railroad
1884–Present day	US National Museum of American History, Smithsonian Institution (Catalogue TR*180001)
Driving Wheel (1)	
1871–94	Pennsylvania Railroad
1894–Present day	US National Museum of American History, Smithsonian Institution (Catalogue TR*181194)
Driving Wheel (2)	
1871–1968	Pennsylvania Railroad
1968–Present day	Pennsylvania Historical and Museum Commission
Display	
Locomotive	
1866–81	Bordentown, NJ (in store), occasional exhibition display
1881–84	Kearney, NJ (in store), occasional exhibition display
1884–Present day	Smithsonian Institution, Washington DC
Driving Wheel (1)	
1830s–94	Storage unknown
1894–Present day	Smithsonian Institution, Washington DC
Driving Wheel (2)	
1830s–c. 1900	Storage unknown
c. 1900–1950s	Pennsylvania Railroad library, Philadelphia
1950s–1975	Storage unknown
1975–Present day	Railroad Museum of Pennsylvania
Summary Details	
(see replica panel)	

Altoona shops to operate with *John Bull*. In 1930 the shops built a second replica tender incorporating the 1876 tender's surviving components, for long-term display. This tender continues to be matched with the locomotive, but it has more recently been displayed without its timber body, with water barrels and open timber storage.

Two early wooden driving wheels, thought originally to have been fitted to *John Bull*, also remain in existence. The first, 4ft 6in (1372mm) in diameter, is displayed in the Smithsonian Institution, albeit missing its flanged tyre. It was donated to the museum by PRR in 1894. Its fourteen spokes and felloes are wooden, and have been strengthened by wrought-iron rings that are apparently replacements for the original crank rings.

The other surviving wheel is on display in the Railroad Museum of Pennsylvania. PRR retained it for many years until donating to the museum in 1983. It too is missing its flanged tyre, but is displayed with a wooden mock-up to illustrate its original appearance. The provenance of both these wheels cannot be confirmed through documentary evidence, but they have been associated with the locomotive since the mid-nineteenth century.

JOHN BULL 2+2-2-0
OPERABLE REPLICA AND TENDER

(See p.102 for colour image.) After *John Bull*'s static appearance at the World Fairs in the 1930s, the PRR was keen for a working exhibit and manufactured an operable replica for the 1940 New York World's Fair.

JOHN BULL 2+2-2-0 Operable replica and tender

Built

| 1940 | Pennsylvania Railroad, Altoona shops |

Ownership

| 1940–79 | Pennsylvania Railroad |
| 1979–Present day | Commonwealth of Pennsylvania Historical and Museum Commission |

Display

| 1940–76 | Northumberland, Pa. (in store), occasional exhibition operation |
| 1976–Present day | Railroad Museum of Pennsylvania |

Summary Details

	Original	Replica
Track gauge:		
Originally:	4ft 10in (1473mm)	
Subsequently:	4ft 8½in (1435mm)	4 ft 8½in (1435mm)
Driving wheel diameter:	4ft 6in (1372mm)	4ft 6in (1372mm)
Cylinder diameter:		
Originally:	9in (228mm)	
Subsequently:	11in (279mm)	11in (279mm)
Piston stroke:	20in (508mm)	20in (508mm)
Boiler length:	6ft 9in (2057mm)	6ft 9in (2057mm)
Boiler diameter:	2ft 6in (762mm)	2ft 6in (762mm)
Boiler tubes:		
Originally:	82 x 1⅝in (42mm)	
Subsequently:	74 x 1¾in (44mm)	74 x 1¾in (44mm)
Total heating surface:		
Originally:	296.5ft² (27.6m²)	
Subsequently:	287.7ft² (26.8m²)	291ft² (27.1m²)
Grate area:	10.07ft² (0.94m²)	10.07ft² (0.94m²)
Working pressure:	50lbf/in² (3.4bar)	60lbf/in² (4.1bar)
Valve gear:		
Originally:	slip-eccentrics, manual valve change	
Subsequently:	2 fixed-eccentrics	2 fixed-eccentrics
Weight in working order:		
Subsequently:	c. 11 tons	19.6 tons (including tender)

Carrying the name *JOHN BULL*, it was designed and built at Altoona shops to replicate the original locomotive as it has appeared since 1876, rather than attempt to reproduce its original arrangement. 1940s materials and construction methods were adopted. The 1927-built tender, matched with *John Bull* for the 'Fair of the Iron Horse' event, was coupled with the replica.

The replica was exhibited at the Chicago Railroad fair in 1948/49, but was otherwise stored at PRR's depot in Northumberland, Pennsylvania, where its condition deteriorated from neglect. In 1976, it was reconditioned and moved to the newly built Railroad Museum of Pennsylvania, where it remains on display.

In 1982–83 the replica was restored to operable condition. A large new stack was fitted, which, together with other cosmetic changes, served to display *JOHN BULL* closer to its mid-1830s appearance. In 1986, it operated at the Great Steam Exposition in Vancouver, British Columbia, but is now a static exhibit at the Railroad Museum.

ADLER (EAGLE) 2-2-2
1935 OPERABLE REPLICA AND TENDER

(See p.102 for colour image.) *ADLER* (*Eagle*, the German Empire's imperial symbol) was the first locomotive to operate in Germany from 1835. It was to operate on very light track restricting the axle load to 3.5 tons. It was therefore a *Planet* type with its weight distributed over a third, trailing axle, rather than being an early *Patentee* type (Chapter 10).

ADLER was one of a pair built by the Stephenson Company for the Bayerische Ludwigsbahn (Ludwig Railway of Bavaria). The 4-mile (6.5km) line, named after King Ludwig I, was a waggonway on which, for many years, horses had been used to haul goods between Nürnberg (Nuremberg) and its satellite town of Fürth. Although expensive for their limited use, both locomotives were used on passenger services to emulate British experience of railway travel.

It was scaled down to dimensions and weights that were less than the regular *Planets*. It had a 2ft 4in (711mm) diameter boiler, and its weight in working order was just 6 tons 12cwt (6.7 tonnes). *ADLER* worked on the Ludwigsbahn until scrapped in 1857.

Anticipating the railway's centenary in 1935, the Deutsche Reichsbahn (DR) designed and constructed, at its Kaiserslautern workshops, a replica of *ADLER* to operate in the commemorative parade in Nürnberg that December. The 1835 arrangement drawings for locomotive and tender had been preserved, and were used to design the replica, together with contemporary published illustrations and descriptions of *ADLER* and other locomotives.

Although the overall arrangement was correct, designs for several components were speculative. Springs were fitted above the frame for the crank axle and below the frame for the carrying axles. Cast-steel wheels simulated Stephenson's 'gas pipe' wheels, with strengthening collars around the spokes.

Crosshead-driven boiler feed pumps were fitted to both sides, water level being monitored by a single gauge glass and two try-cocks. The water level, fixed by DR regulations at a minimum 10cm (3⅞in) over the firebox crown, limited the amount of steam space. Two safety valves were fitted, a spring balance valve and a leaf-spring valve within a brass funnel. The dome and regulator valve were mounted on the forward boiler ring, whilst the inspection hole, with a whistle set into the cover plate, was fitted over the firebox crown.

The layout of the valve gear is speculative as the arrangement drawings provided insufficient detail. They showed that *ADLER*'s valve-drive rocking shafts were fitted immediately to the rear of the valve chests, instead of being ahead of them as for the early *Planets*. Alternative layouts were considered, but the resulting valve gear arrangement is uncharacteristic of Stephenson practice, and is apparently a 1935 solution to an 1835 problem.

Unlike the foot-pedal operation of earlier *Planets*, the eccentric cluster on the driving axle was moved sideways between forward and reverse dogs, by a yoke linked through a lever to a vertical rod up the left side of the firebox front plate. The rod was rotated by a turn handle on the firebox shoulder to select the required direction of travel.

For reversing, the leading, gabbed ends of the eccentric rods were lifted from the rocking shaft drive pins by a transverse shaft under the boiler fitted with 'cotton reel' lifting arms. The shaft was rotated by a lever rod and handle on the right side of the boiler.

As with earlier *Planets*, the valve reversing levers were fitted to firebox back plate rocking shafts, which communicated to the front rocking shafts by substantial side rods. However, unlike earlier designs, the leading ends of these side rods have gabbed ends that could be disengaged from the valve-drive

Detailed view of the 1935/2007 *ADLER* replica, showing the firebox back plate. (Author)

rocking shaft. This prevented the reciprocating action of the valve levers whilst the locomotive was in motion. Disengagement was by rotation of a further transverse rod (cranked under the boiler) to lift or lower the side rods, again by 'cotton reel' lifting arms. The rod was rotated by a lever, the handle for which was on the left side of the firebox.

ADLER was, for many years, based at the Nürnberg Verkehrsmuseum's Roundhouse at Nürnberg West depot where several locomotives were displayed. In 2005, however, a fire badly damaged it. The Deutsche Bahn (DB) agreed to build a new replica incorporating as much of the 1935 engine as could be salvaged. Fortunately the boiler was intact and was reused. The opportunity was taken to carry out detailed research into component design, and to correct some errors that the locomotive previously carried. The reconstruction was completed in 2007 and the replica is now frequently steamed in Nürnberg and elsewhere.

ADLER 2-2-2
1952 STATIC REPLICA AND TENDER

In 1951–52 a second full-scale replica of *ADLER* was built by DB's apprentices at its Kaiserslautern workshop. It was made using the same drawings as the 1935 replica, but completed to a higher standard of manufacture, many components being finished as 'bright' metal.

Left-side detailed view of the 1952 *ADLER* replica, showing the valve rocking shaft, gab-ended eccentric rod and cranked transverse shaft fitted with 'cotton reel' lifting arms. (Author)

ADLER 2-2-2 Static and operable replicas

STATIC REPLICA

Built

1952	Deutsche Bundesbahn – Kaiserslautern workshops

Ownership

1952–96	Deutsche Bundesbahn
1996–Present day	Deutsche Bahn AG

Display

1952–96	Verkehrsmuseum, Nürnberg
1996–Present day	DB Museum, Nürnberg

OPERABLE REPLICA

Built

2007	Deutsche Bahn – Meiningen workshops (incorporating boiler and other components from fire-damaged 1935 replica).

Ownership

2007–Present day	Deutsche Bahn AG

Display

2007–Present day	DB Museum – Nürnberg west locomotive depot

Summary Details

	Original	Replicas
Track gauge:	4ft 8½in (1435mm)	1435mm (4ft 8½in)
Driving wheel diameter:	4ft 6in (1372mm)	1372mm (4ft 6in)
Cylinder diameter:	9in (229mm)	229mm (9in)
Piston stroke:	16in (406mm)	406mm (16in)
Boiler length:	6ft 4⅜in (1940mm)	1940mm (6ft 4⅜in)
Boiler diameter:	2ft 4in (711mm)	711mm (2ft 4in)
Total heating surface:	196.37ft² (18.26m²)	18.20m² (195.8ft2)
Grate area:	5ft² (0.47m²)	0.48m² (5.2ft²)
Working pressure:	60lbf/in² (4.1bar)	6.3bar (91lbf/in²)
Valve gear:	Slip-eccentric, manual valve change	
Weight in working order:	*c.* 6.7 tonnes	8.25 tonnes

1952 *ADLER* replica on display at the Nürnberg Verkehrsmuseum. (See also p.102 for colour image.) (Author)

The replica has only been used for display purposes, initially as an exhibit at trade exhibitions, and has never worked in steam. It has been displayed within the *Adler* exhibition hall of the Nürnberg Verkehrsmuseum for many years.

'CHERAPANOV' LOCOMOTIVE 2-2-0
STATIC ½-SCALE REPLICA WITHOUT TENDER

This half-scale replica of the first locomotive to operate in Russia is worthy of inclusion as it was made during the nineteenth century from detailed knowledge of the original locomotive. It was made by students at St Petersburg's Institute of Engineers' Communication Networks, although the exact date of construction is unknown. It was a working research model used for educational purposes.

The original locomotive had been made under the supervision of Yefim Cherepanov (1774–1842) and his son, Miron (1803–49). They were serfs working for the Demidovs, a family of factory owners, and were renowned as engineers who developed machine tools and other machinery for use in blast furnaces, goldmines, iron and copper works, sawmills and flourmills. From 1822 until his death, Yefim Cherepanov had been chief mechanic of all the factories in the Urals town of Nizhny Tagil. In 1819 his son was appointed his deputy, and eventually replaced his father.

From 1820, the Cherepanovs built about twenty steam engines for pumping water in the mines. Their interest was aroused by development of 'road steam engines' in Britain, and Miron Cherepanov visited the country in around 1832 to learn more about them. There is no record of his meeting the Stephensons, but it would seem that he saw and made sketches of the *Planets* operating on the LMR.

½-scale replica of the 'Cherapanov' locomotive on display at the Central Museum of Railway Transport in St Petersburg. (Peter Davidson)

Detailed view of the front end of the 'Cherapanov' ½-scale replica, showing the valve rocking shaft and control rods. (Peter Davidson)

In 1833–34 the Cherapanovs built the first Russian steam locomotive, loosely based on the *Planet* design, for use in the Nizhny Tagil factory. In 1835 they built a second, more powerful locomotive that was sent to St Petersburg for technical evaluation. In spite of their achievements, including the building of Russia's first railway of about 2 miles (3km), their endeavours found no support outside of the factory and subsequently their locomotive was replaced by horses.

The replica thus seems to be a copy of the 1835 locomotive. Although the wheels copied the Stephenson 'gas pipe' design, they were much smaller than the *Planets*, probably due to limited machining capability. However, they offer an unusual opportunity to see 'gas pipe' wheels in their earliest form. The drawhook is fitted to the sandwich frame rather than the rear of the firebox.

The inside cylinders and cranked axle follow the *Planet* arrangement closely, confirming a skill for machining the axle. The valve gear also follows the *Planet* arrangement, but the lifting linkage that would have run along the top of the boiler is missing, although the smokebox mounted shaft and handle survive. The lack of any springs suggests limited opportunities for obtaining tempered steel, whilst the use of a weighted safety valve, instead of a spring balance valve, further suggests lack of manufacturing opportunity.

The replica has been on display at the Central Museum of Railway Transport in St Petersburg for many years.

THE AMERICAN PROGENITORS 1825–31

The potential for railways in North America was recognised from the 1820s, as intelligence was received about developments in Great Britain. The first requirement was for 'portage' railways linking navigable waterways or opening up areas poorly served by roads. However, the wider potential for longer distance railways using locomotive haulage was soon apparent, and several American engineers pursued locomotive development programmes. Early experimentation was not always successful, however, and some machines were technological 'blind alleys'. In contrast to Britain, a number of vertical boiler locomotives were tried out.

Although *Stourbridge Lion* and *Pride of Newcastle* had not been adopted because of inadequate track (Chapters 4 and 5), several other early railways imported locomotives from English manufacturers. However by copying the most reliable features of these imports, with improvements to meet the very different characteristics of the early lines from those in Europe, the American locomotive industry soon developed its own designs and quickly gained market share. By the late 1830s the nation had become self-sufficient in locomotive manufacturing (White, 1979).

STEAM WAGGON (4-WHEELED RACK VEHICLE)

SURVIVING COMPONENTS

Colonel John Stevens (1749–1838) was a distinguished lawyer, soldier, surveyor and businessman who also had a flair for invention and practical engineering. As early as 1788, he built a small marine steam engine served by a water tube boiler. After experimentation with marine engines and high-pressure boilers, he became a strong advocate of steam-powered railways.

In 1825, the Pennsylvania Society for Internal Improvements was evaluating transport options, prompting Stevens, at the age of 75, to build his '*Steam Waggon*', the first steam railed vehicle in the United States. He laid a 660ft (200m) long circular track on his estate, adjacent to the Hudson River in Hoboken, New Jersey, on which to test and demonstrate the vehicle. Stevens later made a number of alterations, to both vehicle and track, to improve performance, including a larger vertical boiler installed in 1828. A speed of 12mph (19kph) is said to have been achieved with passengers, higher speeds being achieved later on a straight test track.

No drawings or illustrations of the vehicle are known to exist. Although the vehicle was disposed of after Stevens' death, two components, the

View of the boiler-tube cluster of John Stevens' *Steam Waggon*, on display at the Smithsonian Institution, Washington DC. (Peter Davidson)

Steam Waggon (4-wheel rack tank) Surviving components

Built	
1825	Col John Stevens, Hoboken, New Jersey
Ownership	
1825–38	Col John Stevens
1838–70	Stevens' family
1870–88	Stevens Institute of Technology
1888–Present day	United States National Museum (Catalogue TR*180029)
Display	
1870–88	Stevens Institute of Technology
1888–2002	Smithsonian Institution, Washington DC
2002–Present day	Baltimore & Ohio Railroad Museum

original boiler tube cluster and safety valve, survived. They were exhibited occasionally at the Stevens Institute of Technology, set up in his Hoboken estate. Verification was provided in 1888 by Stevens' grandson, Dr Francis Stevens, when the components were donated to the US National Museum in Washington DC. Since 2002 they have been exhibited at the Baltimore & Ohio Railroad Museum. The second boiler had also been preserved at the Stevens Institute in the 1890s, but its present whereabouts are unknown.

The boiler tube cluster, to a design patented by Stevens in 1803, is made up of twenty wrought-iron water tubes set in a circle surrounding a grate. It is 4ft (1219mm) tall over the top and bottom headers, and is understood to have been enclosed by a jacket of sheet iron topped by a conical hood and stack. Wood fuel would have been fed through an opening in the hood, and ashes removed via a door at the base of the jacket. Steam was drawn from a 1in (25mm) pipe in the top header.

Working pressure was probably 50lbf/in^2 (3.4bar). The safety valve is formed by a disc suppressed by a 10in (254mm) lever. It was weighted by a 4lb (1.8kg) lead ball, which hung by a stirrup resting on one of several notches with different pressure release values.

JOHN STEVENS (4-WHEELED RACK TANK)

'CHICAGO' OPERABLE REPLICA

To celebrate the centenary of Stevens' successful Hoboken trials, the Pennsylvania Railroad (PRR) designed and built, at its Altoona shops in 1928, a working replica of the *Steam Waggon*, which it named *JOHN STEVENS*. It operated over a circular track in the grounds of the Stevens Institute of Technology, where it remained until 1932. In that year it was donated to the Museum of Science and Industry in Chicago, Illinois, where it remains on display.

The replica is speculative and based on the recollections of Stevens' grandson Francis who, as a teenager, had ridden on the *Steam Waggon*. His 60-year-old recollections of its arrangement became the basis of a conjectural 1:8-scale model made by the PRR for exhibition at the 1893 World's Columbian Exposition in Chicago, Illinois. In addition to the model and the surviving components, the PRR stated that it had used original drawings and manuscripts in the Stevens family possession to prepare working drawings for the replica, but later research failed to confirm this.

The wooden flat-bed platform, just over 16ft (4.9m) long, supports at one end the single cylinder and valve chest with their attendant drive motions, together with the vertical firebox/boiler and water barrel. At the other end are a fuel bin and two passenger bench seats.

The horizontal piston drove a simple crosshead, connecting rod and half crankshaft carrying a pinion mounted on the platform. The pinion in turn

'Chicago' replica of *JOHN STEVENS* on display at the Museum of Science and Industry in Chicago, Illinois. (Peter Davidson)

JOHN STEVENS 4-wheel rack tanks Operable replicas

'CHICAGO' REPLICA

Built

1928	Pennsylvania Railroad, Altoona shops, Pennsylvania

Ownership

1928–32	Pennsylvania Railroad
1932–Present day	Museum of Science and Industry, Chicago, Illinois (Catalogue No. 1932.443)

Display

1928–32	Stevens Institute of Technology
1932–Present day	Museum of Science and Industry, Chicago, Illinois

'PENNSYLVANIA' REPLICA

Built

1939	Pennsylvania Railroad, Altoona shops, Pennsylvania

Ownership

1939–68	Pennsylvania Railroad
1968–79	Penn Central Transportation Co.
1979–Present day	Pennsylvania Historical and Museum Commission

Display

1940–41	Pennsylvania Station, New York City
1941–43	Stevens Institute of Technology
1943–50s	PRR's Trenton Engine House (in store)
1950s–60	PRR's Northumberland, Pa., depot (in store)
1960–64	Strasburg Rail Road
1964–76	William Penn Memorial Museum in Harrisburg, Pa.
1976–Present day	Railroad Museum of Pennsylvania

Summary Details

Track gauge:	4ft 11in (1498mm)
Pinion wheel diameter:	2ft 4in (711mm)
Carrying wheel diameter:	4ft 9in (1448mm)
Cylinder diameter:	5in (127mm)
Piston stroke:	12in (305mm)
Water tube boiler height:	4ft (1219mm)
diameter:	2ft (609mm)
Water tubes:	20 x 13/16in (30mm)
Heating surface:	25ft^2 (2.33m^2)
Grate dimension:	9.5in (241mm)
Working pressure:	
original:	c. 50 lbf/in^2 (3.4bar)
'Chicago' replica:	100lbf/in^2 (6.9bar)
'Pennsylvania' replica:	150lbf/in^2 (10.3bar)
Weight in working order:	5125lb (2.327 tonnes)

Detailed view of the 'Chicago' replica of *JOHN STEVENS*, showing the cylinder and valve chest. (Peter Davidson)

drove a gearwheel, mounted below the platform, which engaged with a track-centre rack rail. A slide valve above the cylinder was driven by an eccentric on the crankshaft. There is no valve change mechanism, the vehicle being unidirectional.

The vertical boiler barrel, with its tube cluster, is 2ft (609mm) in diameter. Steam at 100lbf/in^2 (6.9bar) was drawn from the top header of the cluster via a regulating valve. Water from the barrel was pumped by hand into the bottom header. Water gauge, try-cocks and steam pressure gauge are fitted, which made possible the successful steaming in 1928. Since then, *JOHN STEVENS* has not been steamed.

JOHN STEVENS (4-WHEELED RACK TANK)
'PENNSYLVANIA' OPERABLE REPLICA

Anticipating New York's World's Fair in 1939/40 featuring a major railroad pageant, PRR sought unsuccessfully to borrow the 1928 replica from the Museum of Science and Industry in Chicago. However, wishing to take advantage of the 'Railroads on Parade' pageant and attendant publicity opportunities, the railroad's Altoona shops looked out the 1928 drawings and made a second *JOHN STEVENS* replica. It was similar to the first one, but with a working pressure increased to 150lbf/in^2 (10.3bar).

Both replicas display the four flangeless carrying wheels of 4ft 9in (1448mm) diameter. Guidance was provided by small guide wheels, fixed to upright wooden posts bolted onto the platform, which ran on the inside of

wood and strap-iron rails. The original had run on reversed tramway track, the 5in (127mm) guide wheels running on the inside of the vertical flange.

It is unlikely that it operated during its 2 years at the World's Fair, even if the boiler was steamed. In the absence of appropriate track, it was probably towed across the pageant's large arena. After the fair, *JOHN STEVENS* alternated between display and storage for long periods. In 1976 it was moved to the newly built Railroad Museum of Pennsylvania where it remains on display. There is no record of it having worked in steam.

TOM THUMB 0-2-2

OPERABLE REPLICA

TOM THUMB is a loose representation of the first locomotive tried out on the Baltimore & Ohio Railroad (B&O) in 1830, which has become legendary in American railroad history. The B&O's initial 13-mile (21 km)

route between Baltimore and Ellicott's Mills, Maryland, included many tight curves to avoid major civil works and, although horses were used, the railroad was unprofitable.

Peter Cooper (1791–1883) was a successful New York industrialist, whose Baltimore investments would have depreciated if the railroad had been abandoned. To prove that steam locomotives could operate around tight curves, he erected a simple steam propelled vehicle using a wooden platform set up on two wheelsets in his Baltimore ironworks. From his New York factory, he brought a 5ft (1524mm) high x 21in (533mm) diameter vertical boiler, with iron gun-barrel tubes, and a cylinder of probably 3¼in bore x 14¼in stroke (82mm x 362mm).

Cooper adopted a chain drive but soon converted to a geared drive. The vertical cylinder, supported by an 'A'-frame, had top-mounted slide bars and crosshead. The connecting rod and crankshaft operated a gearwheel which drove a pinion on the driving axle, giving about one and a quarter wheel revolutions to one of the crankshaft. Cooper used anthracite, and in order to maintain sufficient steam he fixed a belt-driven rotary fan blower to the top of the stack. A water barrel and anthracite box were mounted on the platform.

After trials and modifications, Cooper invited the B&O's president and others to take part in a trial in August 1830. He attached his 'engine', with six people on board, to a carriage carrying another thirty-six people, and drove to Ellicott's Mills in 72 minutes, holding down the safety valve to avoid steam wastage. The legendary return journey, with a more favourable gradient, was a race with a horse drawn vehicle, achieved in 57 minutes averaging nearly

14mph (22kph). It lost the race, however, because the blower belt slipped, and steam pressure dropped.

Although Cooper's vehicle demonstrated the feasibility of locomotives, it was little used afterwards, although the boiler remained in his shops for some years. Impressed by the demonstration, the directors encouraged improvements through a locomotive competition in June 1831 (p.82).

In 1893, forming part of the World's Columbian Exposition in Chicago, Illinois, the B&O prepared a major exhibition, called 'The World's Rail Way', which was organised by Major Joseph Pangborn (1845–1914). A number of replica locomotives were made, including a wooden replica of Cooper's engine. Although Cooper himself had described it (Brown, 1875), and data had appeared in the B&O's 1830 annual report, Pangborn reinterpreted and enlarged the replica, contradicting his quest for realism.

Unfortunately, in 1926 the B&O used Pangborn's vehicle as the model on which to base the design for an operable replica. This was constructed by the railroad for Philadelphia's sesquicentennial International Exposition, and its own 'Fair of the Iron Horse' the following year. It was called *TOM THUMB*, although there is no evidence that Cooper's machine was so named.

The boiler was increased in size to accommodate thirty-eight tubes. The top of the stack reached 12ft 9in (3.9m) above rail level, compared to perhaps

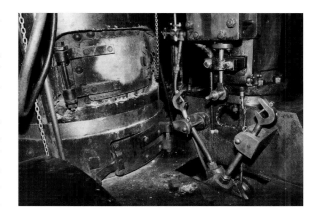

Detailed view of the *TOM THUMB* replica, showing bottom of vertical boiler and cylinder, and valve motion. (Author)

10ft (3m) on the original. A manifold in the boiler top served the safety valve, whistle and a water injector. A water gauge glass and three try-cocks were provided, whilst the regulator valve was located in the steam pipe. As well as a feed pump, driven from the crosshead via a pump arm, an injector was added. Another change was the relocation of the blower from the stack to the platform, from where air was blown directly under the fire grate. The four-vane blower was pulley driven from the non-driving axle.

TOM THUMB 0-2-2 Operable replica

Built

1927	Baltimore & Ohio Railroad, Mount Clare shops, Baltimore, Maryland

Ownership

1927–63	B&O Railroad
1963–72	Chesapeke & Ohio (C&O)–Baltimore & Ohio (B&O) Railroad
1972–80	Chessie Systems, Inc.
1980–87	CSX Corporation
1988–Present day	B&O Railroad Museum, Inc.

Display

1935–50	Bailey's Roundhouse, Baltimore (in store) – occasionally displayed
1950–53	Mount Clare, Baltimore (in store)
1953–58	Baltimore & Ohio Transportation Museum, Baltimore
1958–64	Mount Clare, Baltimore (in store)
1964–Present day	Baltimore & Ohio Railroad Museum, Baltimore

Summary Details

	Original	Replica
Track gauge:	4ft 6in (1372mm)	4ft 8½in (1435mm)
Wheel diameter:	2ft 6in (762mm)	2ft 6¼in (768mm)
Cylinder diameter:	3¼in (82mm)	5in (127mm)
Piston stroke:	14¼in (362mm)	27in (685mm)
Crankshaft pinion diameter:	21in (533mm)	33in (838mm)
Driving axle gear diameter:	15in (381mm)	27in (685mm)
Boiler height:	c. 5ft (1524mm)	5ft 6in (1676mm)
Boiler diameter:	c. 1ft 9in (533mm)	2ft 3in (685mm)
Total heating surface:	Not known	39.92ft^2 (3.7m^2)
Grate area:	Not known	2.7ft^2 (0.25m^2)
Working pressure:	c. 90lbf/in^2 (6.2bar)	90lbf/in^2 (6.2bar)
Valve gear:	Not known	2 fixed-eccentrics, manual valve change
Weight in working order:	c. 1 ton	c. 5 tons

The cylinder is larger than Cooper's original, and was mounted on a small plinth braced to the boiler side. A form of valve gear was devised, although it is not known what form this took on the original. Two eccentrics were fitted to the crankshaft, the short eccentric rods having gabbed ends. The valve rod was manually adjusted for change of direction, enabling the relevant gab to be engaged with the valve rod pin. The gab was held in place by a taper pin, and the unused gab secured in a small recess. Two band brakes were provided on the non-driving axle, activated by a hand-operated quadrant lever brake.

The vehicle was occasionally demonstrated in the 1930s and 40s and, when not being used, was stored in Baltimore. In the early 1950s, the B&O moved its historic rolling stock collection to its Mount Clare site, where *TOM THUMB* remains on display.

YORK 0-4-0
OPERABLE REPLICA AND TENDER

In 1831, the B&O directors announced a competition to find the best American-built locomotive to take place that summer, with a $4,000 prize.

The railroad was no doubt encouraged by its Assistant of Machinery, Ross Winans (1796–1877), who had been to England and knew about the 1829 Rainhill Trials (Chapter 5). British-built locomotives were excluded after the B&O's first locomotive, an unsuitable six-wheeled design made by Robert Stephenson & Co. in Newcastle-Upon-Tyne in 1829, was lost in a shipwreck.

The five locomotives entered for the competition could burn coke or coal but, as at Rainhill, they were required to 'consume their own smoke'. They were limited to 3½ tons, carried on four wheels and with springs. Steam pressure was to be no greater than 100lbf/in² (6.9bar), double that of regular English practice. Two safety valves were required, as was a mercurial pressure gauge. The locomotives were to undertake thirty days 'regular work', with the capability of achieving 15mph (24kph) on level track whilst hauling a 15-ton gross load.

The winner, *YORK*, was designed and built by Phineas Davis (1809–35) in his workshop in York, Pennsylvania. Formerly a watchmaker, Davis became a skilled engineer, helping to build the first American iron-hull vessel in 1825. Following his success with *YORK*, he went on, in conjunction with Ross Winans, to build other locomotives for the B&O, including *ATLANTIC*, one of the later 'grasshopper' type locomotives (Chapter 9).

Replica of *YORK* on display at the Museum of Science and Industry in Chicago, Illinois. (Author)

Detailed view of the *YORK* replica, showing the boiler back head, vertical cylinders, manifold and steam pipes. (Author)

Underside view of the *YORK* replica, showing the leading axle with pedal-shifted cam frame and cam pairs. (Author)

YORK 0-4-0 Operable replica and tender

Built

1926	Baltimore & Ohio Railroad, Mount Clare shops, Baltimore, Maryland

Ownership

1926–34	Baltimore & Ohio Railroad
1934–Present day	Museum of Science and Industry, Chicago, Illinois

Display

1934–Present day	Museum of Science and Industry, Chicago, Illinois

Summary Details

	Original	Replica
Track gauge:	4ft 6in (1372mm)	4ft 8½in (1435mm)
Wheel diameter:	2ft 6in (762mm)	2ft 6in (762mm)
Cylinder diameter:	Unknown	9in (228mm)
Piston stroke:	Unknown	12in (305mm)
Boiler height:	Unknown	5ft 6in (1676mm)
Boiler diameter:	Unknown	3ft 6in (1067mm)
Total heating surface:	Unknown	c. 137ft² (12.7m²)
Grate area:	Unknown	6.87ft² (0.64m²)
Working pressure:	c. 100lbf/in² (6.9bar)	115lbf/in² (7.9bar)
Valve gear:	Not known	Cam-operated, manual valve change
Weight in working order:	c. 3½ tons	c. 6½ tons

In 1927, anticipating its 'Fair of the Iron Horse' centenary, the B&O designed and built an operable replica of *YORK* at its Mount Clare shops in Baltimore. It was, however, conjectural, as only a vague description was recorded in 1831. With only this description and a rudimentary sketch published in 1868 to guide them, the B&O's designers 'regressed' some of the features of the preserved 'grasshoppers', including *ATLANTIC*. After the Chicago World's Fair in 1933/34, it was presented to the Museum of Science and Industry in that city, and remains on permanent display there.

YORK is a four-wheeled coupled vehicle with a vertical tubular boiler, seated on and bracketed to a composite wood and iron frame. The original boiler had been a water jacket cylinder, but the replica's domed boiler has 108 x 2in (51mm) diameter flue tubes.

Steam was fed from the leading face of the dome through a square section steel pipe to a cylinder-height manifold, containing the regulator valve, from which two copper steam pipes fed the cylinders. The two vertical cylinders were bracketed on the sides of the boiler. The downward piston action, using crossheads (with slide bars bracketed to the frame) and connecting rods, was to the centre of the trussed coupling rods. A weighted lever safety valve was fitted in the steam pipe. Copper exhaust pipes fed a common pipe exhausting to atmosphere rather than routed to the stack.

The type of boiler on the original *YORK* would have required some form of blower, as fitted to *TOM THUMB*, but none was fitted to the replica. A crosshead driven boiler feed pump was fitted to the right side of the boiler, which shared a common entry with a steam injector. Three try-cocks and a water sight glass were fitted.

The replica's valve gear used cams rather than eccentrics. The forward and reverse cam arrangement, shifted axially on the leading axle by yokes or cam frames, was modelled on the surviving 'grasshopper' locomotives. The cam pairs for each valve were at either end of the axle, shifted from the footplate by a cross shaft rotated by a foot pedal. The valves were shifted by hand levers, which advanced or retarded the cam frames, which were coupled to the valve spindles. The yokes reciprocated with the cams, in turn driving the valve spindles.

A simple two-axle flat wagon served as a tender, with two water barrels and coal box.

Although awarded the prize, and acquired by the B&O as its first operating locomotive, the original *YORK* was soon rebuilt with a tubular boiler to meet Winans' requirements. The cylinders were moved to the leading face of the boiler, the drive being redirected to the front axle only using a geared transmission. This arrangement became the forerunner of the 'grasshopper' locomotives. *YORK* operated successfully over the extended, 40-mile (64km) B&O route, between Baltimore and Parr's Ridge. It was credited with achieving 30mph (48kph) on level track but with an unspecified load.

BEST FRIEND 0-4-0
OPERABLE REPLICA AND TENDER

(See p.103 for colour image.) *Best Friend* (of Charleston), the first locomotive built in the United States to enter revenue-earning service, was built for trial operation on the South Carolina Canal & Rail Road (SCCR). The 5ft (1524mm) gauge line connected Charleston with Hamburg, across the Savannah River from Augusta, Georgia, to meet growing competition from the port of Savannah. Its name reflected the belief that a steam railroad could regain the commercial initiative for the Augusta traffic. It was built in New York City, by the West Point Foundry Association, which had tested *Stourbridge Lion* in 1829 (Chapter 4).

The railroad's chief engineer, Horatio Allen, had imported *Pride of Newcastle* and *Stourbridge Lion* from England. One of the railroad directors, Ezra Miller (1784–1847), funded *Best Friend*, the locomotive being designed by himself, Allen and a German immigrant, Christian Detmold. With echoes of the Rainhill Trials, the board specified that the locomotive should achieve 10mph (16kph) while pulling three times its own weight.

The components were delivered to Charleston in October 1830, with erection, trials and modifications taking about eight weeks. The locomotive achieved 30mph (48kph) when running light, and 12mph (19kph) hauling three times its own weight of around 4½ tons. The SCCR purchased *Best Friend* for passenger operations on the first 6 miles of its line from Charleston. Six months later, however, the boiler exploded, the fireman having suppressed the safety valve. The leading wheelset, cylinders, and some of the motion were salvaged and incorporated into a new locomotive called *Phoenix*.

The standard gauge replica, named *BEST FRIEND*, was designed and built by the Southern Railway, successor to the SCCR, at its shops in Birmingham,

Alabama, to commemorate the centenary of the SCCR's incorporation in 1928. The tender was made at its Hayne (SC) shops. Surviving general arrangement drawings were used to prepare working drawings, but 1928 materials and construction practices were adopted.

After the centenary celebrations, the replica was exhibited on the station concourse in Chattanooga, Tennessee. It often appeared at special events, including the World's Fair in New York in 1939–40 and the Railroad Fair in Chicago in 1948–49. A new boiler was fitted in 1948, and in 1969 it was further refurbished prior to the South Carolina tricentennial celebration.

BEST FRIEND has a 'bottle-shaped' vertical boiler carried at the rear of its timber frame. This 1948 replacement boiler, reaching 15ft 2in (4.6m) above rail level, is much larger than the original, to provide more steam for popular rides.

The original 'porcupine' boiler allowed hot gases to pass through small tubes around the firebox into an outside jacket, to pass up the smokestack. The firebox, particularly the crown, was well stayed, alternately from the sides and top. The 1928 boiler had fire tubes, as has the 1948 boiler, coal being used instead of timber. A weight-loaded safety valve has been augmented by two latter-day safety valves either side of a manifold, also serving as a blower control valve and whistle. A pressure gauge and sight glass were provided, although three dummy try-cocks simulate the original arrangement.

A water tank was placed under the frame at the forward end. The two inside cylinders, also at the front end, were angled down at 15 degrees towards the rear, cranked axle. It is noteworthy that the West Point Foundry forged and turned the cranked axle at the same time as the construction of *PLANET* (Chapter 7) in England.

The original wheels were similar to those of *Pride of Newcastle*, with iron hubs and wooden spokes and rim, hooped with iron. Two flat iron rings were bolted to either side of the spokes, to which were fitted the coupling rod crank pins. The 1928 replica wooden-spoked wheels failed during trials, and were replaced by steel 'lookalike' wheels.

The steam pipe, drawing steam from the top of the boiler cone, was routed down the boiler and along the left-side inner frame to a manifold serving the two steam chests above the cylinders. The driver sat between the cylinders, and above the steam pipe. The two exhaust pipes were routed through the water tank to provide preheating, before combining into a single pipe running along the right-side frame and up the side of the boiler into the base of the stack.

The original locomotive had slip-eccentrics, similar to those on *Stourbridge Lion*, but the replica has two fixed-eccentrics and no reversing gear. For short

Detailed view of *BEST FRIEND*, showing driver's seat, steam pipe, regulator, cylinders and driving motion. (Author)

In January 1863, Isaac Hazard of Newport, Rhode Island, donated to the city's Redwood Library: 'wheel of first locomotive used on first railroad of any length in America – Charleston, South Carolina, to Augusta, Georgia, 1835'. There is no reliable provenance for the wheel, but the suggestion was that it was once employed on *Phoenix*. Efforts to confirm the provenance have been unsuccessful, however, and despite enquiries to the library, it is not known if it continues to exist.

reversing movements the valves were manually operated by disengaging the gab-ended eccentric rods from the valve spindles. For longer reversals, however, a petrol engine installed in the tender operated a chain drive whilst also powering an air brake compressor for the tender wheel brakes.

The eccentrics also worked a rocking shaft, set above the frame at its mid-point, which drove two vertical water pumps feeding water through a single clack valve near the base of the boiler. Two small injectors have also been added, served by valves off the main steam pipe.

In 1987, *BEST FRIEND* was withdrawn by the Norfolk Southern Corporation, successors to the Southern Railway, and stored at the Hayne shops. In July 1993, the corporation presented it to the City of Charleston for permanent display in a building close to the site of the SCCR's 1830 terminus, which now forms the Best Friend of Charleston Railway Museum.

In 1831, some of *Best Friend*'s surviving components were reused in the construction of *Phoenix* which was placed in service in October 1832. Knowledge about *Phoenix* is based on an 1869 statement by Nicholas Darrell, engineer of *Best Friend* and later SCCR's superintendent of machinery.

BEST FRIEND 0-4-0 Operable replica and tender

Built

1928	Southern Railway, Birmingham shops, Alabama

Ownership

1928–82	Southern Railway
1982–93	Norfolk Southern Corporation
1993–Present day	City of Charleston, South Carolina

Display

1928–30s	Touring exhibit
1930s–69	Chattanooga Station, Tennessee
1969–93	Charleston/Spartanburg, South Carolina (in store), occasional operations
1993–Present day	Visitor Reception and Transportation Center in Charleston, South Carolina

Summary Details

	Original	Replica
Track gauge:	5ft (1524mm)	4ft 8½in (1435mm)
Wheel diameter:	4ft 6in (1372mm)	4ft 8in (1422mm)
Cylinder diameter:	6in (152mm)	6in (152mm)
Piston stroke:	16in (407mm)	17in (432mm)
Boiler height:	c. 6ft (1828mm)	7ft 10¾in (2407mm)
Boiler diameter:	c. 3ft (914mm)	3ft 3½in (1003mm)
Total heating surface:	Unknown	c.250ft² (23m²)
Grate area:	c. 6ft² (0.56m²)	6.1ft² (0.57m²)
Working pressure:	c. 50lbf/in² (3.4bar)	100lbf/in² (6.9bar)
Valve gear:	Slip-eccentric, manual valve change	Fixed-eccentrics (forward)
		Ford V8 petrol engine (reverse)
Weight in working order:	c. 4½ tons	c. 4½ tons

DEWITT CLINTON 0-4-0
DRIVING WHEEL

DeWITT CLINTON was built for the Mohawk & Hudson Rail Road Company (MHR). Its chief engineer was John Bloomfield Jervis, formerly with the Delaware & Hudson Canal Company, which had ordered *Stourbridge Lion* and *Pride of Newcastle* (Chapters 4 and 5). The MHR was chartered in 1826 to build a 17-mile (27km) line between Albany and Schenectady in New York State. The locomotive was named as a memorial to DeWitt Clinton (1769–1828), the state governor in the railroad's formative years.

The locomotive, built by the West Point Foundry Association, was the first American-built locomotive with a horizontal boiler. It was completed in June 1831 under the supervision of David Matthew, a young mechanic, and shipped up the Hudson River to Albany. It made a trial run in August, the journey being completed within an hour. Jervis tried unsuccessfully to burn 'hard' coal, and wood was thereafter selected. The locomotive hauled 8 tons at 30mph (48kph), and a train with 125 passengers at 25mph (40kph).

DeWITT CLINTON and an English-built locomotive faced problems on the poor track, prompting Jervis to introduce a leading swivel truck for later locomotives. It was infrequently used for just a few months before being withdrawn and dismantled. In 1891 a wheel, believed to be from the locomotive, was deposited in the United States National Museum by William Buchanan, superintendent of motive power of the railroad's successor, the New York Central and Hudson River Railroad Company (NYC).

The 4ft 4½in (1333mm) diameter iron wheel contains fourteen 1in (25mm) diameter wrought-iron spokes, staggered around the cast-iron hub and rim, similar to those used on *Novelty* (Chapter 6). There is no evidence to confirm suggestions that other components survive and were incorporated into the operable replica.

DEWITT CLINTON 0-4-0
OPERABLE REPLICA AND TENDER

Completed in 1892, the replica *DeWITT CLINTON* was designed and built by the NYC at its West Albany shops for exhibition at the 1893 World's Columbian Exposition in Chicago. Thereafter, it was exhibited, with replica passenger cars, at several national expositions and locations. For many years

Replica of *DeWITT CLINTON* displayed at The Henry Ford Museum, Dearborn, Michigan. (Peter Davidson)

Driving wheel thought to have originated from the *DeWITT CLINTON* displayed at the Smithsonian Institution, Washington DC. (Author)

Detailed view of the *DeWITT CLINTON* replica, showing left side of driving axle with slip-eccentric and dog pin, together with driving crank. (Peter Davidson)

DeWITT CLINTON 0-4-0 Operable replica and tender

Built

1893	New York Central & Hudson River Railroad Company (West Albany shops, NY)

Ownership

1893–1914	New York Central & Hudson River Railroad Company
1914–35	New York Central Railroad Co.
1935–Present day	Henry Ford Museum (Accession No. 35.788.1)

Display

1893–1920	Karner, West Albany, NY (in store)
1920–35	New York Grand Central Terminal
1935–Present day	Henry Ford Museum, Dearborn, Michigan

Summary Details

Track gauge:	
Original:	4ft 9in (1447mm)
Replica:	4ft 8½in (1435mm)
Wheel diameter:	4ft 6in (1372mm)
Cylinder diameter:	5½in (140mm)
Piston stroke:	16in (406mm)
Boiler diameter:	2ft 8in (813mm)
30 boiler tubes, length:	6ft (1829mm)
Total heating surface:	c. 144ft^2 (13.4m^2)
Grate area:	c. 4.3ft^2 (0.4m^2)
Working pressure:	50lbf/in^2 (3.4bar)
Valve gear:	Slip-eccentrics, manual valve change
Weight in working order:	
Original:	c. 4 tons
Replica:	c. 6 tons

it was displayed on the balcony in New York City's Grand Central Terminal. In 1935, the whole replica train was donated to the Henry Ford Museum in Dearborn, Michigan, where it remains on display. It was given a major overhaul in 1956, but has not been steamed for many years.

Although the replica was based on general arrangement drawings prepared by David Matthew in 1831, some changes were made. The boiler and dome were formed of small wrought-iron plates, lap-jointed with hand-closed rivets. It was unlagged, although wooden lagging had originally been used. The original firebox had two firehole doors, but only one is fitted to the replica.

The wooden frame supports the boiler by three brackets on each side, the centre ones incorporating braces to either side of the dome. The rear of the frame is bracketed down to a lower footboard, to which is bolted the draw pin bracket. Leaf-springs are fitted beneath the frame. The horn assemblies, bolted to the sides of the frame, are braced at the bottom by flat bars, the front and rear lengths sloping up to the main frame.

The wheels, copied from the surviving wheel, have several welded repairs. As first built, the coupling rods were double-trussed flat bars, but replacement round coupling rods are now fitted. The front axle has rectangular crank webs.

Two rear-mounted cylinders, with upper valve chests, are bolted to the frame sloping down at 15 degrees. The connecting rods pass between the frame and firebox sides to the cranked leading axle. Ungainly displacement lubricators have been added to the valve chests.

Slip-eccentrics were fitted, similar to those on *Stourbridge Lion*. Dog pins, secured to each eccentric, engaged in either end of a slot, the assemblies for which were bolted to the axle to allow for change of direction. Round bar eccentric rods drove the valve motion, the gab ends of which were

Detailed view of the *DeWITT CLINTON* replica, showing upper boiler, dome, regulator manifold and right-side valve levers. (Author)

lifted from drive pins on the valve levers to allow the valves to be manually moved when reversing until the eccentrics had slipped. The valve levers have knuckle connections to the short valve spindles, allowing easy repositioning of the valves.

The right-side drive pin also drove, via a bell crank, the single boiler feed pump fitted below the frame, adjacent to the leading wheel. A manual feed pump was also provided, on the left side of the footboard. The water pipes from both pumps served a common clack valve on the underside of the boiler.

A manifold regulator valve, serving external steam pipes, was fitted on the rear boiler ring. There are two try-cocks on the firebox back plate and no sight glass. A weighted safety valve fed steam, via an external pipe, into the chimney. A second safety valve, together with a whistle and steam gauge, have been added to the dome at different stages of the replica's career.

The tender, which carries the locomotive's name, has a wooden cross-braced frame to which the draw gear is attached. The body, covered by a canopy, is a flat-topped riveted wrought-iron tank, on top of which fuel was stacked, together with supplementary water barrels.

THE GRASSHOPPER TYPE 1830s

The success of the *YORK* in the Baltimore & Ohio (B&O) Railroad's 1831 trials (Chapter 8), encouraged further development of anthracite-burning vertical boiler locomotives. The work was initially undertaken by Phineas Davis and his partner Israel Gartner (sometimes Gardner) at their shops in Mount Clare, Baltimore, Maryland, and by Charles Reeder. Following separate accidental deaths for both Davis and Reeder, the shops were taken over by Ross Winans (1796–1877) and George Gillingham who continued development of the type. Winans became a strong advocate of vertical boilers and pursued their development until as late as 1843, before turning to horizontal-boilered locomotives (White, 1979).

In addition to their vertical boilers, the four-wheeled locomotives were characterised by two vertical cylinders bracketed to the leading face of the boiler, the crossheads operating in slide bars above the cylinders, motion beams pivoted on top of the boiler, and two long connecting rods driving a cranked axle at the leading end. A gearwheel on this axle in turn drove a smaller gear on a leading 'jack shaft' which drove both wheelsets by outside coupling rods. The insect-like movement of the motion beams and connecting rods gave rise to the 'grasshopper' nickname. Of the eighteen such locomotives built for the B&O, three have survived, albeit with many service and post-service modifications.

The first of the type, completed in 1832, was *ATLANTIC*. In that year, this locomotive, or a sister one, hauled a 30-ton train at an average speed of over 13mph (21kph), for 82 miles (132km) over gradients of between 1 in 93 and 1 in 165 (White, 1979). The tractive force was calculated at 1570lbf

(7kN) at 15mph (24kph). However *ATLANTIC*, with its lightweight and single driving axle, was soon unable to cope with increasing train loads. It was withdrawn in 1835 and replaced by larger 'grasshoppers' with improved traction from four wheels.

On these later examples, the exhaust steam rotated a turbine blower, bolted to the frame adjacent to the firebox, the forced air stimulating combustion of anthracite. It would seem to have been the first application of a steam powered turbine, and followed Winans' patent of 1834. Although innovative, the blower, developed from the belt-driven fan used on *Tom Thumb*

One of the three altered 'grasshopper' locomotives, *JOHN HANCOCK*. Displayed at the Baltimore & Ohio Railroad Museum, Baltimore. (Hays T. Watkins Research Library, Baltimore & Ohio Railroad Museum)

Operable replica of *Novelty*, photographed during the filming of the BBC *Timewatch* programme about the Rainhill Trials. (Peter Davidson)

Operable replica of *MARC SEGUIN*. (Gaston Monnier, Association pour la Reconstitution et la Préservation du Patrimoine Industriel)

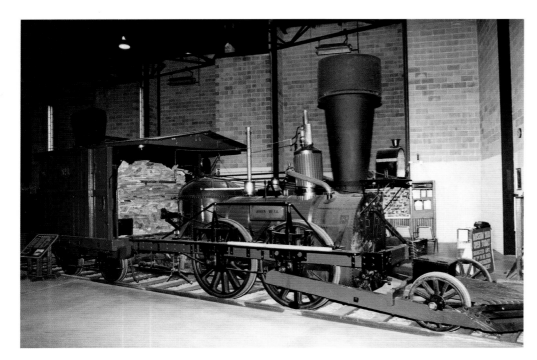

Left: *JOHN BULL* replica on display at the Railroad Museum of Pennsylvania. (Author)

Below left: 1935/2007 replica of the Nürnberg Verkehrsmuseum-based *ADLER*. (Author)

Below: Left-side rearward view of the 1952 *ADLER* replica, showing the slip-eccentric vertical control rod and turn handle. (Author)

Replica of *BEST FRIEND*, displayed at the Engine House, Best Friend of Charleston Railway Museum, Charleston, South Carolina. (Tommy Burkhalter, Best Friend of Charleston Railway Museum)

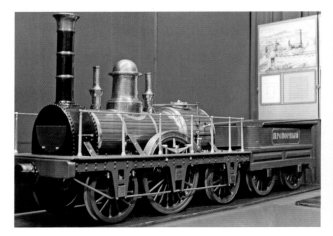

¼-scale replica of *PROVORNY*, displayed at the Central Museum of Railway Transport, St Petersburg. (Peter Davidson)

Forward view of ¼-scale replica of *PROVORNY*, from the footplate. (Peter Davidson)

Operable replica of *BAYARD*, displayed at Museo Nazionale Ferroviario, Pietrarsa,
Naples. (Museo Nazionale Ferroviario)

Left: Operable replica of *FIRE FLY* at the Great Western Railway site at Didcot. (Author)

Below left: Forward-facing right-side view of the Gothic firebox and boiler of the *FIRE FLY* replica. (Author)

Below right: The preserved *ROCKET* displayed at the Franklin Institute, Philadelphia, Pennsylvania. (Peter Davidson)

Replica of *SAXONIA* operating at the 1995 Dresdner Dampflokfest. (Author)

Right-side view of *LIMMAT*, showing the quadrant regulator handle and control rod to the regulator valve in the base of the smoke box, and the Stephenson link valve gear quadrant lever and reversing rod. (Author)

Above: Preserved *COPIAPÓ* locomotive on display at Universidad de Atacama (North Campus), Copiapó, Chile. (Crystal Green)

Right: Preserved *L'AIGLE* displayed at the Cité du Train Museum, Mulhouse. (Cité du Train Museum)

Preserved *ST PIERRE*, displayed at Cité du Train Museum, Mulhouse. (Cité du Train Museum)

LION 0-4-2 Static original

Built

1838	Todd, Kitson and Laird, Leeds

Ownership:

1838–45	Liverpool & Manchester Railway
1845–46	Grand Junction Railway
1846–59	London & North Western Railway
1859–1928	Mersey Docks & Harbour Board
1928–31	Liverpool Engineering Society
1931–47	Liverpool Engineering Society (Leased to London, Midland & Scottish Railway)
1948–62	Liverpool Engineering Society (Leased to the British Transport Commission)
1962–67	Liverpool Engineering Society (Leased to the British Railways Board)
1967–70	Liverpool Engineering Society (Loaned to City of Liverpool Museums (Accession No. 1967.41))
1970–74	City of Liverpool Museums
1974–86	Merseyside County Museums
1986–Present day	National Museums & Galleries on Merseyside

Display:

1930	Liverpool & Manchester Centenary Event, Wavertree, Liverpool
1930–41	Lime Street Station, Liverpool
1941–67	Crewe locomotive works (in store)
1967–70	Cosmetic restoration in Princes Half Tide Dock running shed
1970–87	City of Liverpool Museum
1987–90	Operational tour around Britain
1990–99	City of Liverpool Museum
1999–2007	Museum of Science and Industry in Manchester
2007–Present day	Museum of Liverpool

Summary Details

	As Built (*per* Wishaw – 1840)	As Preserved
Track gauge:	4ft 8½in (1435mm)	4ft 8½in (1435mm)
Driving wheel diameter:	5ft (1524mm)	5ft (1524mm)
Cylinder diameter:	11in (279mm)	14in (355mm)
Piston stroke:	20in (507mm)	18in (457mm)
Boiler length:	7ft 5in (2260mm)	8ft 8½in (2654mm)
Boiler diameter:		
vertical:	3ft 6in (1067mm)	3ft 9in (1143mm)
horizontal:	3ft 3in (991mm)	3ft 9in (1143mm)
Tubes:	126 x 1⅝in (41mm)	98 x 2in (51mm)
Total heating surface:	470.32ft^2 (43.7m^2)	c. 515ft^2(48m^2)
Grate area:	8.1ft^2 (0.75m^2)	c. 12.7ft^2(1.2m^2)
Working pressure:	50lbf/in^2 (3.4bar)	50lbf/in^2 (3.4bar)
Valve gear:	Gab gear	'Opposing' gab gear
Weight in working order:	c. 14 tons 9cwt (14.7 tonnes)	18 tons 17cwt (19.15 tonnes)

Right: Detailed view of firebox back plate of *LION*. (Author)

Far right: Right-side detailed view of *LION*, showing frame, horn and spring arrangements. (Author)

crosshead water feed pumps, is supported by three brackets each side on the outside sandwich frame.

The wrought-iron plated, oak sandwich frame, with front and back transverse oak beams, is probably original. The replacement driving axle springs are mounted above the frame, the carrying axle spring being below. The horn plates are bolted to the inner and outer faces of the frame, but the carrying axle plates were renewed in 1929, the original ones having been cut to accommodate the dock pumping machinery. The bottoms of the horn plates are tied to each other, and to the frame, by wrought-iron bars. The driving wheels are unmatched as the crank axle wheels have eighteen rectangular wrought-iron spokes whilst the leading wheels have sixteen. They are apparently in-service replacements, being inscribed 'Rothwell and Company Bolton', the locomotive manufacturer of that Lancashire town.

Wrought-iron inner frames, bracketed to the smokebox back plate and firebox front plate, carry the crank axle inner bearings and springs. In contrast to the Stephenson practice of bolting the slide bars to the inner frames, the two pairs of slide bars for each cylinder are secured at the front by tapered studs into the cylinder covers, and at the rear by transverse 'spectacle' frames, bolted under the boiler support brackets, through which pass the connecting rods. LION's cylinders and valve chests, in the bottom of the smokebox, are inclined upwards at 4½ degrees, the connecting rods passing under the leading axle.

LION's gab gear is of Buddicom's arrangement which was probably fitted when it was rebuilt in around 1841, as delay beyond that time may well have resulted in the fitting of link motion with its cost-saving advantages of variable steam cut-off (Chapter 13). It increased lap and lead, whilst providing a fixed cut-off of 81 per cent, and was operated by a reversing lever on the right side of the firebox.

Underside forward-facing view of LION, showing Buddicom's gab gear arrangement, with the forward gabs engaged with the valve drive rocker pins. (Author)

LION has been used on three occasions in feature films, the most notable being in 1952, when it took the leading role in the comedy film *Titfield Thunderbolt*. In the 1980s, a Westinghouse air brake system was fitted to allow passenger train operations. Air reservoirs were fitted to the tender, charged from a portable trackside compressor. LION is now displayed as a static exhibit at the Museum of Liverpool.

DE AREND (THE EAGLE) 2-2-2
OPERABLE REPLICA AND TENDER

This broad gauge replica was made in 1938 to commemorate the following year's centenary of the Netherlands railway system. The original *DE AREND* was one of four locomotives, ordered by the Hollandsche IJzeren Spoorweg-Maatschappij (HIJSM – Holland Iron Railway), to operate the country's first 16km (10 miles) line between Amsterdam and Haarlem. *DE AREND* was a standard *Patentee*, built to a track gauge of 1945mm (6ft 4⅜in), with 1828mm (6ft) diameter driving wheels. It was built in the summer of 1839 by R.B. Longridge & Company of Bedlington, Northumberland (Works No. 119), which had only commenced locomotive production in the latter part of 1837. It was similar to *BAYARD* (p.124), also built at Bedlington.

The manager of the Longridge Company (named after his son, Robert Bewick Longridge (1821–1914)) was Michael Longridge (1785–1858), who had been one of the founding partners of Robert Stephenson & Co. in 1823. He thus had a good knowledge of the *Patentees*, most of his first production series being of this type. The HIJSM order was placed through Longridge's agent, Edward Starbuck (died *c*.1855), who specialised in representing British companies in the growing European railway markets. In 1840, he broke his association with Longridge and for many years successfully represented Robert Stephenson & Co. in the continental market.

DE AREND was shipped in parts to the Netherlands, and erected under the supervision of Longridge's foreman, James Smith, in time for the September opening of the railway. It operated on the line for 18 years before being scrapped in 1857.

Anticipating the railway centenary, the NV Nederlandse Spoorwegen (Dutch Railways), which had been formed in January 1938, saw good opportunity for a commemorative event, which would also serve to focus attention on its new status. Design and construction work on the replica was undertaken by the Dutch Railways' Centrale Werkplaats (Central Workshop) in Zwolle.

Operable replica of *DE AREND* on temporary display at the Verkehrshaus der Schweiz, Luzern, in 1997. (Author)

Forward-facing footplate view of *DE AREND*, showing reversing lever on the right side. (Author)

DE AREND 2-2-2 Operable replica

Built

1938	NV Nederlandse Spoorweg, Centrale Werkplaats, Zwolle

Ownership

1938–53	NV Nederlandse Spoorweg (Dutch Railways)
1953–Present day	Het Nederlands Spoorwegmuseum (Dutch Railway Museum)

Display

1939	'De Trein 1839–1939' event in Amsterdam
1939–48	Zwolle workshops (in store)
1948–53	Hoorn shed – occasional operations around the Netherlands
1953–Present day	Het Nederlands Spoorwegmuseum, Utrecht

Summary Details

Track gauge:	1945mm (6ft 4⅜in)
Driving wheel diameter:	1828mm (6ft 0in)
Cylinder diameter:	356mm (14in)
Piston stroke:	450mm (17¾in)
Boiler length:	2730mm (8ft 11½in)
Boiler diameter:	1143mm (3ft 9in)
Tubes:	98 x 44mm (1¾in)
Total heating surface:	48m² (516.5ft²)
Grate area:	1.13m² (12.2ft²)
Working pressure:	4bar (56.9lbf/in²)
Valve gear:	Gab gear
Weight in working order:	19.3 tonnes (19 tons)

Rear-facing view of the right side of *DE AREND*, showing reversing rod and valve motion links. (Author)

General arrangement drawings of the sister locomotive *DE LEEUW* (*THE LION*) had largely survived, and formed the basis for preparation of working drawings. It was built using the materials and construction methods of the 1930s, resulting in an increase in weight of about 7 tonnes. Additions included an injector and boiler pressure gauge. Its four fixed-eccentric valve gear has a reversing lever on the locomotive's right side which raised and lowered the upward-facing gabs.

The centenary event, 'De Trein 1839–1939' was held in Amsterdam between September and October 1939. In spite of the fast approaching war, *DE AREND* and its three replica coaches conveyed 160,000 visitors over some 3,000km (1,850 miles).

DE AREND was stored in the Zwolle workshops during the war and suffered some damage, eventually being restored there in 1948. It was then based in Hoorn motive power depot and occasionally used for public demonstrations until 1953, when it was transferred to the newly established Spoorwegmuseum in Utrecht. It has since remained on permanent display there, being steamed on special occasions and operated along a circular broad gauge track. Between 1987 and 1989, it was completely overhauled in the Dutch Railways workshops in Tilburg. In that latter year it was a major feature at the '150 jaar Spoorwegen in Nederland' commemorative event.

BAYARD 2-2-2
OPERABLE REPLICA AND TENDER

(See p.105 for colour image.) *BAYARD* is a replica of the first locomotive to operate in the nation states that amalgamated in 1861 to form Italy. The Royal Neapolitan Railway was established as a concessionary railway to provide services between Naples and Nocera in what was then the 'Dual Kingdom of the Two Sicilies'. The concession was granted in 1839 to the French engineer, Armand Bayard de la Vingtrie, who was quick to organise the construction of the initial 5-mile stretch of line between Naples and Portici and to order the first locomotives and rolling stock.

Two locomotives were built in Bedlington in 1839 by R.B. Longridge & Co. The first of them, *BAYARD*, named after the railway's concessionaire, began services on the line in October 1839. Built about the same time as

Arrangement drawings of the *BAYARD* replica, prepared prior to manufacture by the Florence workshops of Ferrovie dello Stato. (Museo Nazionale Ferroviario)

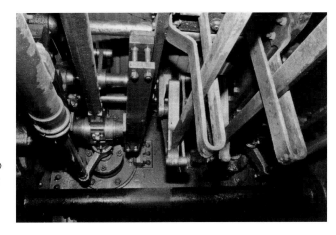

Underside forward-facing view of *BAYARD* replica, showing driving and valve motions. (Author)

DE AREND, the locomotive was similar in arrangement and shared many design characteristics, although built to the standard gauge (1435mm (4ft 8½in)). It had smaller driving wheels (1676mm (5ft 6in) diameter) but cylinder bore and piston were the same. Its gab gear was similar to that for *DE AREND*, with upward-facing eccentric rod gabs.

The centenary of the opening of the Naples–Portici line was marked in 1939 by the construction of a replica locomotive and train of carriages. *BAYARD* was designed and built by the Ferrovie dello Stato (State Railways) at its workshops in Firenze (Florence). It operated at the centenary celebrations, but was afterwards placed in the National Museum of Italian Railways in Rome, where it remained until 1964 before the contents of that museum were transferred to the Science Museum in Milan.

In 1989, *BAYARD* was restored to operable condition at the State Railways' workshops in Cremona to enable it to take part in the 150th anniversary celebrations that year. The date coincided with the opening of the National Railway Museum in Pietrarsa near Naples, in which it is now displayed.

BAYARD 2-2-2 Operable replica

Built

1939	Ferrovie dello Stato (State Railways) workshops in Firenze

Ownership

1940–64	Museo Nazionale delle Ferrovie Italiane (Italian National Railway Museum)
1964–82	Museo della Scienza e della Tecnica (Museum of Science and Technology)
1982–Present day	Ferrovie dello Stato (State Railways)

Display

1940–64	Museo Nazionale delle Ferrovie Italiane, Termini Station, Rome
1964–82	Leonardo da Vinci Museo Nazionale della Scienza e della Tecnica, Milan
1982–89	Pietrarsa workshops, Napoli (Naples) (in store)
1989–Present day	Museo Nazionale Ferroviario, Pietrarsa, Napoli (Naples)

Summary Details

Track gauge:	1435mm (4ft 8½in)
Driving wheel diameter:	1676mm (5ft 6in)
Cylinder diameter:	355mm (14in)
Piston stroke:	457mm (18in)
Boiler length:	2500mm (8ft 2½in)
Boiler diameter:	1067mm (3ft 6in)
Tubes:	80 x 52mm (2in)
Grate area:	*c.* 0.8m² (8.5ft²)
Working pressure:	3.4bar (50 lbf/in²)
Valve gear:	Gab gear
Weight in working order:	*c.* 13 tonnes

FIRE FLY 2-2-2
OPERABLE REPLICA AND TENDER

(See p.106 for colour images.) The GWR gained operating experience with several different locomotive types, including *NORTH STAR*, on the first stretches of its line in 1838–39. Daniel Gooch (p.118) learned that maintaining a fleet of non-standard locomotives was both time consuming and expensive. He therefore resolved that the fleet required for the commencement of through services between London and Bristol in 1841 would be to standard designs.

Gooch's standardisation policy was an important step in locomotive design evolution, whereby a railway specified its design requirements to manufacturers rather than accepted those of the manufacturers themselves. The specification was accompanied by drawings and templates to ensure inter-changeable components between locomotives built by different companies. Although he introduced several design changes, the design was derived from the *Patentee* type, notably the successful *NORTH STAR*.

The first locomotive to be delivered was *FIRE FLY* which gave its name to a class of sixty-two locomotives built by seven manufacturers between 1840 and 1842. *FIRE FLY* itself was built by Jones, Turner & Evans of the Viaduct Foundry, Newton-le-Willows.

The *Fire Flies* performed well, whilst improved maintenance and economy confirmed Gooch's standardisation policy. On *FIRE FLY*'s first recorded run, in March 1840, a maximum speed of 58mph (93kph) was attained when hauling three vehicles. The class was noted for free running, but those built by Fenton, Murray & Jackson of Leeds, with a wheelbase increased by 2in (51mm) to 13ft 4in (4067mm), were particularly successful.

The *Fire Flies* had an operating life of 25–30 years, albeit with mid-life modification and rebuilding, and some accumulated 500,000 miles in service. The last example was withdrawn in 1879.

Right-side driving wheel of the *FIRE FLY* replica. (Author)

With no surviving example of such an important locomotive class, the Fire Fly Trust was established in 1982 to design and build a working replica. The availability of a short stretch of 7ft (2140mm) gauge track at the Great Western Society's Didcot site was to make it possible to operate the locomotive. Construction was undertaken by a volunteer team, including experienced engineers and locomotive fitters. After initial work in Bristol, the fabrication and erection work was largely carried out at Didcot, being completed in 2004.

To accommodate large driving wheels, the outside sandwich frames were arched over the driving axle boxes, with the springs beneath the frame within slotted horn assemblies. Four inside frame bars, between the smokebox back plate and the firebox front plate, supported the crank axle bearings, two of which were sprung, as well as the slide bars, boiler feed pumps and valve motion. The 7ft (2133mm) diameter driving wheels had rectangular-section wrought-iron spokes offset from a radial line following the Stephenson 'gas pipe' arrangement. The ends of each spoke were forged into a segment of the rim, the whole being hammer welded to shape and turned, before a tyre was shrunk on. Such a wheel was thus built up from 140 sections.

FIRE FLY 2-2-2   Operable replica

Built

2004	The Fire Fly Trust, Bristol and Didcot

Ownership

2004–13	The Fire Fly Trust
2013–Present day	Great Western Preservations Ltd

Display

2004–Present day	Great Western Society, Didcot

Summary Details

	Original	Replica
Track gauge:	7ft¼in (2140mm)	7ft¼in (2140mm)
Driving wheel diameter:	7ft (2133mm)	7ft (2133mm)
Cylinder diameter:	15in (381mm)	15in (381mm)
Piston stroke:	18in (457mm)	18in (457mm)
Boiler length:	8ft 6in (2591mm)	8ft 6in (2591 mm)
Boiler diameter:	4ft (1219mm)	4ft (1219mm)
Tubes:	131 x 2in (51mm)	Not available
Total heating surface:	699ft^2 (65m^2)	Not available
Grate area:	13.5ft^2 (1.25m^2)	Not available
Working Pressure:	50lbf/in^2 (3.4bar)	Not available
Valve gear:	Gab gear	Gab gear
Weight in working order:	c. 24 tons	Not available

Downward view on the right side of the *FIRE FLY* replica, showing the upward-facing gabs and operating gear. (Author)

The *Fire Flies* had a domed or 'Gothic' firebox, which was later employed by several manufacturers, including the Stephenson Company with later examples of the *Star* class. As with *NORTH STAR*, the class took advantage of the broad gauge by having a large fire grate (13.5ft^2 (1.26m^2)) providing a 1:52 ratio with total heating surface, compared to the 1:57/58 ratio of contemporary standard gauge locomotives.

Gooch's specification to manufacturers was detailed, including material requirements. The contact faces of the four eccentrics were to be well steeled, for example, with the gab jaws required to be of steel and hardened. The gab gear was reversed by a lever on the right side of the firebox, its long reversing rod lifting the upward-facing gabs of the eccentric rods located just inside the outer frames.

To enable the replica to operate passenger services at Didcot, it was built to modern safety and legislative standards, using welded steel construction, whilst following the design of the original locomotives as closely as possible. Air brakes have been fitted to operate with replica passenger vehicles.

AJAX 0-4-2
STATIC ORIGINAL AND CONTEMPORARY
TENDER

The first railway in Austria, from 1837, was the Kaiser Ferdinands-Nordbahn (KFNB). By 1842, it was operating a 150 mile (240km) route from Wien (Vienna) north-eastwards to Brünn (Brno) and Olmutz in Moravia (present-day Czech Republic). In that year, the KFNB had a fleet of forty-three locomotives, all but seven being of British manufacture. The largest supplier was Jones, Turner & Evans at the Viaduct Foundry which had also made *FIRE FLY*.

Each locomotive imported into Austria was subjected to rigorous testing, under which a 'learned professor' carried out trials, including an hydraulic boiler test at 150lbf/in^2 (10.3bar), or more than double its working pressure. Some fireboxes were pressed in by that loading, but the 'strong stays' of the first locomotive from the Viaduct Foundry found favour with the railway.

The KFNB ordered two, more powerful, 0-4-2s from Jones, Turner & Evans with outside sandwich frames and inside plate frames. The first was *AJAX*, delivered in 1841, which was given the railway's No. 23, although this was never carried. It operated until 1874, and then, being the oldest locomotive, was passed to the newly formed Austrian State Railway Museum. The running number had been changed several times, concluding with No. 37.

AJAX was retained in store in Wien, initially at the KFNB's workshops, until the city's new Technical Museum, which absorbed the railway collection in 1914, opened at the end of the Great War. From this time *AJAX*, together with *STEINBRÜCK* (Chapter 12) became prominent exhibits in the museum's large middle hall.

It is not known with certainty which components date from 1841, although the wheels, which perpetuate the Stephenson-form offset tapered spoke arrangement, remain. It is known that the boiler was replaced in 1857 during a major overhaul. Its pressure of 6.8bar (98lbf/in^2) and its fittings, such as the smokebox door with a centre lever catch and tall dome, reflect this period of construction. A blower is fitted, and a blast pipe exit that could be varied by a turn handle to allow for the burning of different fuels. There is a remarkably small steam space due to the low height of the firebox crown, with the gauge glass being almost at the top of the boiler.

Although comparable with *LION*, *AJAX* also incorporates a number of design amendments. The two mirrored cylinder and steam chest castings, which are vertically bolted to each other, are mounted to the frames rather

The preserved *AJAX* locomotive and contemporary tender, displayed at the Technisches Museum in Vienna. (Author)

Firebox back plate view of *AJAX*, showing the reversing lever on the right side. (Author)

THE NORRIS TYPE – LATE 1830s TO 1850

The Norris Locomotive Works, in Philadelphia, Pennsylvania, begun in 1833 by William Norris (1802–67), became a prominent locomotive builder. In 1844 the firm was reconstituted as Norris Bothers, when Richard Norris became the dominant partner. The Norris types were derivatives of Edward Bury's locomotives including the 'D'-plan, round-topped firebox and bar frame (Chapter 11). Whilst the early English imports had been largely ill-suited to American track, the company's adoption of the four-wheel swivel truck improved stability, and the longer wheelbase placed a higher proportion of the locomotive weight onto the driving wheels to aid adhesion.

The Norris Works came to prominence in July 1836 when an early 4-2-0, *GEORGE WASHINGTON*, demonstrated impressive load hauling capabilities up the 7 per cent grade of the Schuylkill (Belmont) incline of the Philadelphia & Columbia Railroad in Philadelphia, normally worked by cable. With a trailing load of almost 16 tons, the locomotive went up the ½-mile incline in less than 2½ minutes, although a steam pressure of nearly 100lbf/in^2 (6.9bar) would have been necessary. Some 8,700lb (3950kg) of its total weight of 14,930lb (6780kg) was on the driving wheelset.

In the 1830s and 40s, American manufacturers sought to develop valve gears with early cut-off capabilities that would be operationally beneficial as speeds increased, and provide significant savings in fuel and water usage (White, 1979). Different forms of early cut-off valves, separate from the main slide valves, were developed by different manufacturers. In 1844, Norris introduced a 'riding' cut-off valve fitted directly above the main slide valve. This was driven at first by a separate rod attached to the forward eccentric rod, but later versions adopted a third eccentric. Norris abandoned the 'riding' valve in the mid-1850s in favour of the British-developed link motion with its variable cut-off capabilities (Chapter 13).

The reputation of Norris' early designs became widespread in the USA and, in 1837, exports commenced to Europe. The Norris influence on European locomotive designs was profound, with several manufacturers adopting its design features. The type may now be seen through two surviving locomotives and three replicas in America and Europe.

LAFAYETTE 4-2-0
OPERABLE REPLICA AND TENDER

This replica, completed in 1927 at the Baltimore & Ohio (B&O) Railroad's shops in Baltimore, is a representation of the railroad's first horizontal-boilered locomotive, built in 1837. *LAFAYETTE* followed shortly after the last of the vertical boilered 'grasshoppers' (Chapter 9). Named after the French Marquis and military leader in the War of Independence, it was the first of eight locomotives delivered to the B&O by Norris, and was numbered 13.

New features were incorporated, including connecting rods driving outside crank pins, instead of inside half-cranks used on *GEORGE WASHINGTON*. It had outside cylinders, sloping at 10 degrees, bolted to the smokebox sides. Although *LAFAYETTE* initially had Winans' cam valve gear, as fitted to the 'grasshoppers', the remainder had the Norris fixed eccentric and 'drop-hook' gear described below. As Norris expanded construction, such locomotives became known as type 'B'. The crews nicknamed them '*One-Armed Billies*', suggested by the connecting rod motion and their builder's first name.

4-4-0 locomotives were introduced from 1839, three months before the last of the '*Billies*' was delivered, which were thus soon relegated to secondary duties. *LAFAYETTE* was in service until the early 1860s, although the name had been removed a decade earlier.

The replica, first named *WILLIAM GALLOWAY* to honour the railroad's early locomotive engineer, was built to help illustrate the B&O's early motive-power development. It featured at the 'Fair of the Iron Horse' centennial pageant in 1927 alongside the 'grasshoppers'. Prior to the opening of the Baltimore & Ohio Museum in 1949, however, it was renamed *LAFAYETTE*.

The replica is a robust and coarse interpretation of the original *LAFAYETTE*. The B&O, although using contemporary drawings and lithographs, had insufficient time, and perhaps budget, to provide the detailed finish of an accurate replica. There are also a few deliberate changes, including 3ft 6in (1067mm) diameter driving wheels, reduced from 4ft (1219mm), and 9in x 18in (228mm x 457mm) cylinders, reduced from *c.* 10in x 20in (253mm x 508mm).

LAFAYETTE has a 3½in x 1¾in (89mm x 44mm) bar frame, strengthened to an overall 4½in (114mm) depth between the footplate and the motion plates. The frame is braced by round bars sloping down to the bottom of the driving axle horns and behind the horns up to the footplate. The frame is united by the front beam and stretchers under the boiler, and also a stretcher under the footplate to which the draw pin is fixed. The front of the boiler is supported on the frame by brackets, and at the rear by firebox expansion brackets.

The outer firebox is made of steel plate, butt-jointed with a strap and two rows of rivets, whilst the round top has six lap-riveted plates turned up at the crown to receive the dome plate. A steel dome cover, accommodating a spring balance safety valve, is substituted for the original's ornate brass dome cover. Prominent and crude manifolds are fitted on either side of the dome,

employing fountain feeds to a safety valve and whistle on the right, and safety valve and injector on the left. The firebox has a latter-day rocking grate.

There are two fixed-eccentrics per cylinder, driving drop-hook eccentric rods which are engaged or disengaged by pivoted lifting rollers worked by a quadrant lever on the right side of the footplate. The hooks engage pins on cast iron rocking levers, fitted to transverse shafts which reciprocate, providing motion to the outside valve spindles. The spindles are extended back to a transverse footplate rocking shaft, at the right end of which are two stub lever ends, over which socket-ended levers are placed to enable the crew to reverse the valves. Removal of these levers whilst in motion avoided the hazardous reciprocating lever-action characteristic of manual valve change locomotives.

The replica has remained with the B&O's historic collection, appearing at world and railroad fairs on several occasions, and has been used several times for motion pictures. It is now exhibited at the Baltimore & Ohio Railroad Museum in Baltimore.

Far left: Replica of *LAFAYETTE* now displayed at the Baltimore & Ohio Railroad Museum, Baltimore. (Hays T. Watkins Research Library, Baltimore & Ohio Railroad Museum)

Left: Footplate view of *LAFAYETTE*, showing firebox (with dome plate removed), regulator handle, transverse valve rocking shaft and eccentric rod lifting quadrant lever. (Author)

Underside forward-facing view of *LAFAYETTE*, showing right-side eccentric rods and pivoted lifting rollers. (Author)

LAFAYETTE 4-2-0 Operable replica and tender

Built

1927	B&O shops, Mount Clare, Baltimore

Ownership

1927–72	B&O Railroad
1972–80	C&O–B&O Railroads
1980–87	CSX Corporation
1988–Present day	B&O Railroad Museum Inc.

Display

1927–35	Halethorpe, Maryland (in store)
1935–49	Bailey's Roundhouse, Baltimore (in store)
1949–Present day	B&O Museum, Baltimore

Summary Details

	Original	Replica
Track gauge:	4ft 6in (1372mm)	4ft 8½in (1435mm)
Wheel diameter:	4ft (1219mm)	3ft 6in (1067mm)
Cylinder diameter:	10in (or 10½in) (254–267mm)	9in (228mm)
Piston stroke:	20in (508mm)	18in (457mm)
Boiler length:	*c.* 7ft 10in (2387mm)	8ft (2438mm)
Boiler diameter:	2ft 9in (838mm)	2ft 9in (838mm)
Tubes:	Not known	52 x 2¼in (57mm)
Total heating surface:	Not known	*c.* 273ft² (25.4m²)
Grate area:	Not known	*c.* 4.8ft² (0.45m²)
Working pressure:	Not known	90lbf/in² (6.2bar)
Valve gear:	Winans' Cam gear	drop-hook gear
Weight in working order:	*c.* 10.3 tons	*c.* 18 tons

BEUTH 2-2-2
STATIC REPLICA WITHOUT TENDER

This replica was built by the firm of Borsig-werke at its works in Tegel, Berlin. It was completed in 1912 and exhibited at the 75th anniversary celebrations of the founding of the firm by J.F. August Borsig (1804–54) in 1837. The company began locomotive construction in 1841 at its original site in Berlin's Chaussestrasse. Seven of its earliest examples were adaptations of Norris designs (but with a 4-2-2 wheel arrangement), otherwise similar to the several 4-2-0 locomotives imported from Philadelphia between 1839 and 1841 for use on the Berlin–Potsdam and Berlin–Frankfurt railways.

Borsig then set out to improve upon the Norris arrangement and achieve an advanced design that would allow him to offer locomotives to the rapidly expanding market in the German states, in competition with English and American imports.

The original *BEUTH* (works No. 24) was completed in 1844 and was a major success at the Berlin Industrial Exhibition that year before being delivered to the Berlin Anhaltische Eisenbahn. It is likely that *BEUTH* had been commenced in 1842, as the Borsig papers suggest that it was subjected to trials and modifications in the works for several months before the exhibition. This evidence prompted the fitting of an 1842 builder's plate to the replica in 1912. The success of its design led to a class of seventy-one locomotives that were widely employed on railways throughout northern Germany.

BEUTH was chosen for replication both because of its prestige from the Berlin Exhibition, and because of the availability of a fine set of arrangement drawings published in the *Proceedings of the Association for the Advancement of*

Prussian Industry in 1846. It was named after the prominent Prussian trade director, Christian Peter Wilhelm Beuth (1781–1853), who founded the association in 1821. *BEUTH* was withdrawn from service in 1864.

The replica followed the original design closely, although materials and construction practices of 1912 were employed. Contrary to some accounts, no components from the original locomotive were employed.

BEUTH has a prominent Norris type round-topped firebox surmounted by a large dome. Instead of bar frames however, wrought-iron plate frames were adopted which ran the length of the locomotive, joined by the front buffer beam and stretchers behind the leading axle and to the rear of the firebox. To accommodate the firebox, the frames were widened slightly round its circumference.

The boiler is fixed by brackets to the frame with no allowance for expansion. Drawbar loading is taken by the boiler and the frame together, the draw pin brackets being riveted to the rear of the firebox as well as being bolted to the rear transverse frame-member. The unlagged outside cylinders are angled at 12 degrees and bolted to the smokebox side plates.

A particular feature was the adoption of Borsig's patented valve gear. The trial and modification of this gear was undertaken at the works between 1842 and 1844, and was developed in time for the Berlin Exhibition. It sought to improve upon the Norris 'riding' cut-off gear, whilst also adopting, for ease of reversal only, Stephenson's link motion introduced in 1842 (Chapter 13). Separate upper and lower slide valves were adopted above the outside cylinders, each controlled by quadrant levers on the footplate.

The lower valves were set for either forward or reverse direction without cut-off variation. They were driven by eccentric pairs via curved slotted links, similar to the Stephenson motion. Easy reversal was achieved controlled by the inner, three-position (forward, neutral, reverse) quadrant lever, the

Above: Replica of *BEUTH* locomotive on display at Museum Für Verkehr Und Technik in Berlin. (Author)

Left: Footplate view of *BEUTH* showing its 'D'-form round top firebox. (Author)

Right: Forward-facing right-side view of *BEUTH*, showing the variable cut-off valves (upper) and main steam valves (lower). (Author)

Far right: Right-side view of the footplate on *BEUTH*, showing the valve control quadrant levers. (Author)

BEUTH 2-2-2 Static replica without tender

Built

1912	Borsig Lokomotiv-Werken GMBH

Ownership

1912–24	Borsig Lokomotiv-Werken GMBH
1924–Present day	Deutsches Museum, Munich

Display

1912–24	Borsig Lokomotiv-Werken GMBH (in store)
1924–83	Deutsches Museum, Munich
1983–Present day	Museum Für Verkehr und Technik, Berlin

Summary Details

Track gauge:	1435mm (4ft 8 ½in)
Driving wheel diameter:	1524mm (5ft)
Cylinder diameter:	330mm (13in)
Piston stroke:	558mm (22in)
Boiler length:	3.1m (10ft)
Boiler diameter:	1.02m (3ft 4in)
Tubes:	111 x 50mm (1$^{15}/_{16}$ in)
Total heating surface:	46.5m^2 (500ft^2)
Grate area:	0.83m^2 (8.9ft^2)
Working pressure:	5.6bar (81lbf/in^2)
Valve gear:	Borsig patent gear
Weight in working order:	18.15 tonnes

Underside rear-facing view of *BEUTH*, showing the left-side eccentrics and sloping variable cut-off drive rod on the outside eccentric. (Author)

Underside forward-facing view of *BEUTH*, showing the left-side slotted link for the three-position (forward/neutral/reverse) operation of the main steam valve. (Author)

reversing rod adjusting the die block position. The upper valves provided variable cut-off, the extent of their travel being governed by straight slotted links, bracketed to the boiler sides, whose reciprocating action was driven by sloping rods from the outer-eccentrics only. They were adjusted by the outer quadrant lever, whose control rod altered the die block position.

The prominent water pumps, on either side of the footplate, were operated by levers from rear wheel crank pins, driven by coupling rods from the connecting rod big ends. Although potentially an operable locomotive, the pedantic accuracy of its design omitted the left-side water pump, because it had not been shown on the 1846 drawings. It has never been steamed and latter-day safety regulations would now make it impossible to operate under steam without modification.

The replica remained at the Tegel works after the 1912 celebrations, but was not on regular public display. In the summer of 1924, *BEUTH* was donated

and transported to the Deutsches Museum in Munich, where it remained on display for the next 59 years. With the opening of the Museum Für Verkehr Und Technik (Transport and Technical Museum) in Berlin in 1983, it was returned to Berlin on long-term loan and is appropriately housed in the city's Anhalter goods and locomotive sheds. It is the centrepiece of the 'German Railways to 1848' Exhibition Hall.

NO. 1 *LIMMAT* 4-2-0
OPERABLE REPLICA AND TENDER (WITH CONTEMPORARY COMPONENTS)

(See p.108 for colour image.) The Norris influence on central European locomotive design was consolidated when Emil Kessler (1813–67) completed his first locomotive of the type in 1841. He had started up his workshops in Karlsruhe in the German state of Baden 4 years earlier. In the early 1840s, a major railway commission, from the neighbouring state of Württemberg, undertook an extensive enquiry into railway and locomotive construction and operation in France, Belgium, England and the United States. It reported in favour of Norris type locomotives and, in 1844, invited tenders for 4-2-0s and 4-4-0s for the Königlich Württembergischen Staats-Eisenbahnen (KWStE – Royal Württemberg State Railways). Whilst a few were built in Philadelphia by Norris, the bulk of the order was awarded to Kessler. In 1846, he opened a second factory, the Maschinenfabrik Esslingen, in Württemberg, to cope with the orders.

As with Borsig, whilst generally adopting the Norris wheel arrangement, Kessler introduced several features of his own, most notably using plate iron rather than bars for the inside frames, and horizontal rather than sloping outside cylinders. He also favoured the Stephenson-style rectangular firebox and Gothic dome, rather than the Bury type round firebox. Stephenson link motion was fitted, and, at more than 3.7m (12ft) long, the boilers were of the Stephenson 'long-boiler' pattern (Chapter 13).

In 1844 the opening of the Strasburg to Basel railway emphasised the commercial and travel opportunities railways would bring to Switzerland. This led to routes between its cantons, then moving towards Confederation, achieved in 1848. The first concession, to the Schweizerischen Nord-Bahn (SNB – Swiss North Railway), was for a route linking Zürich and Basel. Its initial 25km (15.5-mile) length between Zürich and Baden along the Limmat river valley opened in 1847. It earned the name 'Spanischebrötli-Bahn' (Spanish Biscuit line) because it conveyed to Zürich a much sought-after confection made in Baden.

Right-side view of *LIMMAT*, showing detail of its cruciform pattern wheel spokes and crosshead-driven boiler feed pump. (Author)

Kessler received an order for four 4-2-0 locomotives for the SNB in 1846, their design being very similar to the Württemberg fleet. The first was named *LIMMAT*. The SNB became part of the Schweizerische Nordostbahn (Swiss North-East Railway) in 1853. *LIMMAT* was rebuilt as a four-coupled tank locomotive in 1866 and, renumbered 201, was scrapped in 1882.

Anticipating the centenary of the SNB in 1947, the Schweizerischen Eisenbahnmuseums (SEM – Swiss Railway Museum) in Zürich initiated the project to build an operable replica of *LIMMAT* in its original form. The museum's director, Ingenieur Eugène Fontanellaz, visited several German towns and workshops to obtain information about Kessler's early locomotive practices. Twenty original arrangement drawings of similar locomotives provided the basis for the design work, which was carried out by the Schweizerische Bundesbahnen (Swiss Federal Railways) under the direction of Ing. Dr Konrad Witzig. Construction was undertaken by the SLM Company of Winterthur and completed in 1947.

The SEM had inherited an 1857-built locomotive, *SPEISER*, also built at Maschinenfabrik Esslingen for the Schweizerischen Centralbahn (Swiss Central Railway), and withdrawn in 1902. Although part of the Swiss National Collection and occasionally exhibited, it was in poor condition and was dismantled to provide several components for the replica. The components, similar to those of the original locomotive, were the complete wheelsets, springs, eccentrics, pistons, cylinders and control handles, and the copper casing for the Gothic firebox. Otherwise adopting 1947 materials, construction methods and safety requirements, the replica is a good representation of an early Kessler locomotive and of the original *LIMMAT*.

The original locomotive had a long oval boiler, *c.* 900mm (3ft) in diameter, fitted to the frame with fixed brackets, but the replica boiler is cylindrical

Replica of *LIMMAT*, displayed at the Verkehrshaus der Schweiz in Luzern. (Verkehrshaus der Schweiz)

LIMMAT 4-2-0 Operable replica and tender

Built

1947	Schweizerischen Lokomotiv und Maschinenfabrik (SLM), Winterthur (Works No. 3937)

Ownership

1947–59	Schweizerischen Eisenbahnmuseums
1959–Present day	Verkehrshaus der Schweiz

Display

1947–59	Schweizerischen Eisenbahnmuseums, Zürich
1959–Present day	Verkehrshaus der Schweiz, Luzern

Summary Details

	Original	Replica
Track gauge:	1435mm (4ft 8½in)	1435mm (4ft 8½in)
Driving wheel diameter:	1530mm (5ft ¼in)	1530mm (5ft ¼in)
Cylinder diameter:	362mm (14¼in)	360mm (14⅛in)
Piston stroke:	560mm (22in)	560mm (22in)
Boiler length:	3735mm (12ft 3in)	3691mm (12ft 1¼in)
Boiler diameter:	c. 900mm (2ft 11½in)	c. 900mm (2ft 11½in)
Tubes:	Not known	93 x 41mm (1⅝in)
Total heating surface:	57.35m² (617ft²)	50.3m² (541ft²)
Grate area:	0.86m² (9.25ft²)	0.87m² (9.36ft²)
Working pressure:	c. 4.9bar (70lbf/in²)	6.1bar (88lbf/in²)
Valve gear:	Stephenson link	Stephenson link
Weight in working order:	19 tonnes	20.9 tonnes

and the firebox fitted with slide expansion brackets. The regulator valve was placed in the base of the smokebox above the steam chests. The quadrant regulator handle and control rod were fitted to the right side of the locomotive, the latter turning in a gland in the smokebox side plate. The blast pipe was fitted with a flap to vary its cross-sectional area to control the draught, the control rod for which was on the left side of the boiler. A large chimney, fitted with a latter-day spark arresting arrangement, permits the burning of wood. A blower has been added for the replica, and an injector supplements the feed-water pumps.

The outside cylinders, with large vertical steam chests and valves, were bolted to the leading end of the frames. The slide bars were bolted to the rear cylinder covers, and supported at the rear by frame brackets, through which passed the connecting rods and crosshead driven boiler feed pumps.

The leading bogie, set behind the smokebox and steam chests, was a substantial truck which bridged the two wheelsets. The upper edges of the bridge plates, which were double-plated, were linked by a cross-bracing incorporating the pivot bearing. A subframe, bolted between the rear of the smokebox and the leading frame stretcher, incorporated the bogie pivot.

The wheels had wrought-iron 'T'-form segmental spokes fitted back to back in a cruciform pattern and secured by a wrought-iron rim. Stephenson link motion was fitted, with short eccentric rods and long valve spindles. The short wheelbase of 2.79m (9ft 2in) and outside cylinders made the locomotive unstable, and speed was generally kept to within 30kph (19mph).

The replica *LIMMAT* and its train of carriages were used on special trains around Switzerland for the centenary celebrations in 1947. Operation confirmed the unstable riding of the original, and small balance weights were inserted between two driving wheel spokes. After initial display in Zürich, the replica was transferred to the Verkehrshaus der Schweiz (Swiss Transport Museum) in Luzern in 1959, where it is occasionally steamed.

STEINBRÜCK 4-4-0
STATIC ORIGINAL AND TENDER

STEINBRÜCK was one of a class of twenty-two locomotives built between 1848 and 1850 and known as the 'Kleine (Small) Gloggnitzer' type. They had smaller cylinders, but larger driving wheels, than their contemporary stablemates of the 'Grosser (Large) Gloggnitzer' type.

Both types were constructed at the Vienna workshops of the Wien Gloggnitzer Eisenbahn (Vienna–Gloggnitz Railway). The workshops were established in 1840 by John Haswell (1812–97), a 28-year-old Scot, who was formerly engaged with William Fairbairn in Manchester. Haswell was a talented manager and resourceful engineer, who developed the Vienna works into a major locomotive building establishment. He had many successful designs to his name before his retirement in 1882, and his work was acknowledged by a knighthood from the Austrian Emperor.

His first locomotives, completed in 1841, were developments of the Norris types, several early examples of which had been imported into Austria from Philadelphia. As with Borsig and Kessler, Haswell introduced several design and construction improvements from the Norris practice. The first 4-4-0 'Gloggnitzer' locomotives were completed in 1844.

The kaiserlich-königliche Südliche Staatsbahn (k.k.SStB – Imperial-Royal Southern State Railway) was Austria's first state railway which commenced

Preserved Haswell locomotive, *STEINBRÜCK*, displayed in the Technisches Museum, Vienna. (Author)

operations from Murzzuschlag to Graz in 1844. Following the opening of the line through the Semmering Pass, it was extended throughout between Gloggnitz and (from 1857) Trieste in present-day Slovenia. In 1859 the railway was amalgamated with two other railways, and passed to an independent company, the kaiserlich-königliche privilegierte Südbahngesellschaft (k.k.Priv.SB – Imperial-Royal Privileged Southern Railway).

On delivery from the Vienna–Gloggnitz Railway's workshops, the 'Kleine Gloggnitzer' locomotives achieved 50–55kph (32–35mph) on passenger services. On level track they were recorded as hauling 235 tonnes at 30kph (19mph). On the stretch between Murzzuschlag and Laibach they were said to have hauled passenger trains of 122–134 tonnes and goods trains of 155–290 tonnes. *STEINBRÜCK*, named after the junction town for the Trieste and Zagreb lines (Zidani Most in present-day Slovenia) was allocated running number 827 by the Südbahn in 1859.

The following year, after 12 years' service, it was hired out by the Südbahn to the railway and mining company, the Graz-Koflacher Eisenbahn und Bergbaugesellschaft. After some time this arrangement was made permanent with the outright purchase of the locomotive by the Graz-Koflacher company which renamed it *SÖDING*. After a further 18 years of service, it was withdrawn in 1878, and left at the back of the shed at Voitsberg, about 10km (6 miles) east of Koflach. This would seem to be as much due to indecision as sentiment or historic interest. In the words of one observer, it lay there concealed and dusty with a 'sleeping beauty' existence.

In 1908 the technical press drew attention to its existence, as the result of which *SÖDING* was donated by the Graz-Koflacher company to the Historisches Museum der Österreichischen Eisenbahnen (Museum of Austrian Railways) in 1910. The following year it was sent to the workshops of the kaiserlich-königliche Österreichischen Staatsbahnen (kkStB –Austrian State Railways) at Knittelfeld, not just for restoration, but to return it to its 'original appearance' of 1848 with the name *STEINBRÜCK*.

After restoration it was taken for safe keeping to an old coach house of the former Kaiser Ferdinands Nordbahn in Vienna to await completion of the new Technical Museum. It was placed, with *AJAX* (Chapter 10), in the museum's new premises in 1914 which, because of the First World War, did not open for another 4 years.

No report about *STEINBRÜCK* was prepared in 1911 and no detailed survey has since been carried out. It is believed that it is relatively unmodified and would therefore provide much knowledge about Haswell's construction methods.

STEINBRÜCK is fitted with plate frames, being one of the more notable departures from the Norris practice that Haswell developed. Its 1422mm (4ft 8in) diameter wheels are formed with rectangular cross-section wrought-iron spokes, and are fitted with counterweights. The leading two-axle truck is of the Norris type, pre-dating Haswell's later radial truck development.

The two outside cylinders are angled down at 12 degrees. The two valve chests, located under the smokebox, were cast integrally with the cylinders. Large crossheads, guided by round-iron slide bars, also drove boiler feed pumps fitted to the outside of the cylinders. The round-section iron connecting rods have broad big end bearing housings. Inside Stephenson link valve gear is worked off two pairs of eccentrics on the leading driving axle.

Underside rear-facing view of the leading bogie truck on *STEINBRÜCK*. (Author)

STEINBRÜCK 4-4-0 Static original and tender

Built

| 1848 | Wien workshops of the Wien Gloggnitzer Eisenbahn (Works No. 87) |

Ownership

1848–59	k.k.SStB – Imperial-Royal Southern State Railway
1859–60	k.k.Priv.SB – Imperial-Royal Privileged Southern Railway
1860–c. 1865	Graz-Koflacher Eisenbahn und Bergbaugesellschaft (on hire)
c. 1865–1910	Graz-Koflacher Eisenbahn und Bergbaugesellschaft
1910–18	Historischen Museum der Österreichischen Eisenbahnen (Museum of Austrian Railways)
1918–80	Österreichisches Eisenbahnmuseum (Austrian Railway Museum)
1980–Present day	Technisches Museum, Wien (Vienna Museum of Technology)

Display

1878–1910	Voitsberg shed (in store)
1910–14	KFNB coach-house in Wien (in store)
1914–18	Historischen Museum der Österreichischen Eisenbahnen (in store)
1918–92	Technisches Museum, Wien
1992–2006	Eisenbahnmuseum Strasshof (Das Heizhaus)
2006–08	Wien Nordbahnhof (for restoration)
2008–Present day	Technisches Museum, Wien

Summary Details

Track gauge:	1435mm (4ft 8½in)
Driving wheel diameter:	1422mm (4ft 8in)
Cylinder diameter:	369mm (14½in)
Piston stroke:	579mm (22¾in)
Boiler length:	3740mm (12ft 3¼in)
Boiler diameter:	1142mm (3ft 9in)
Tubes:	103 x 52.8mm (2⅛in)
Total heating surface:	69.6m² (749ft²)
Grate area:	1m² (10.75ft²)
Working pressure:	6.4bar (93lbf/in²)
Valve gear:	Stephenson link
Weight in working order:	25.1 tonnes

STEINBRÜCK's boiler appears to be original, and is a combination of the original Bury type round firebox, but, needing a large volume for wood burning, it had a rectangular forward extension. It had a spark arresting chimney.

The 'restoration' in 1911 introduced several replacement components to return the locomotive to an 1848 appearance. Comparison with a pre-restoration photograph of the *SÖDING* shows that the ornate brass dome cover replaced its iron 'pepper pot' dome cover. Although sheet metal boiler cladding remains, a large sandbox was removed, as was a footplate canopy and weatherboard.

Other additions are wooden imitations of the nameplates, steam whistle and clack valves. An interesting component, albeit replicated in wood, is the cylinder indicator, a precursor to steam gauges. An important component that was not replicated was an auxiliary steam pump and attendant flywheel and pipework.

The two-axle tender is high-sided for wood carrying, and dates from *STEINBRÜCK*'s operating career. The Museum of Technology undertook cosmetic restoration of the locomotive and tender in the 2 years prior to their return to its restored gallery in 2008.

Underside forward-facing view of *STEINBRÜCK*, showing left-side eccentrics and eccentric rods to Stephenson link valve motion. (Author)

Forward view of *STEINBRÜCK*'s footplate, showing round top firebox back plate and Stephenson link quadrant lever. (Author)

COPIAPÓ 4-4-0
STATIC ORIGINAL WITHOUT TENDER

(See p.109 for colour image.) *COPIAPÓ* is the oldest surviving locomotive built by Norris Brothers. It has been little altered in service or in preservation, and therefore illustrates well the standard design characteristics, materials and construction methods of America's then biggest locomotive builder.

It was built for the Copiapó Railroad, which served a barren, rocky region in north-central Chile, about 500 miles north of Santiago. The region held large deposits of silver and copper ore, the mining concession being obtained by the prominent mid-nineteenth century entrepreneur William Wheelwright (1798–1873). In 1838, he had initiated South America's first Pacific coast steamship service, serving the small Chilean port of Caldera. The 50-mile (80km) standard gauge railroad, from the Copiapó mines to Caldera, constructed between 1850 and 1852, had a maximum gradient of 1 in 88, and rose to 1327ft (405m) above sea level.

COPIAPÓ was built in 1850, probably for the line's contractors, Allan and Alexander Campbell of Albany, New York. The locomotive worked on the line until 1891, accumulating about 190,000 miles. In that year, the Chilean revolution brought about the shelling of Caldera and closure of the railroad. The line was subsequently altered to metre gauge.

COPIAPÓ was preserved, and in 1894 exhibited at the Santiago Exposition of Mines. In 1901 it was sent to Buffalo, New York, as part of the Chilean exhibit at the Pan-American Exposition. In 1929, it was returned to working order to pull a special train for delegates attending the South American Railway Congress in Santiago.

The locomotive was exhibited for many years at the School of Arts and Crafts in Santiago but, in 1945, it was returned to Copiapó and placed on a length of track in an open courtyard of the State School of Mines, now part of the Universidad de Atacama, where it remains on display. *COPIAPÓ* was surveyed in 1965 by John H. White Jr, then curator of transportation at the Smithsonian Institution in Washington DC. The author is indebted to him for his published description (White, 1968/1979/1997, pp.311–319).

The boiler has an extended 'D'-plan, oval top firebox, giving over 10ft^2 (0.9m^2) of grate area. The railroad's water supply was treated to overcome its high lime content, and the plates of the 38in (965mm) diameter barrel remain in good condition. The unclad outer firebox plates reveal double-lap riveting for the side plates, the earliest surviving example of this practice, and single-lap riveting for the six shoulder plates.

The firebox dome cover is cast brass and was fitted with a spring balance safety valve, although this was missing at the time of White's survey. An early diaphragm steam gauge is present inside the cab. The smokebox front is a cast-iron plate with raised letters announcing 'NORRIS BROTHERS PHILADELPHIA 1850'.

The 4in (102mm) wide by 2in (51mm) deep rectangular bar frame runs the full length of the locomotive. Rising stays support the leading end of the frame from the leading horn faces, whilst similar short rising stays support the rear of the frame from the rear horn faces. The two horn sets form pedestals, the bottoms of which are secured to each other by a lower frame. The rear frame stretcher is a heavy iron casting that serves also as the footplate. The frame arrangement is thus a substantial upgrading of that adopted for *LAFAYETTE*.

A single spring set serves each driving wheelset, hung beneath a large equalising beam to which the hangers are bolted. The assembly pivoted on the underside of the frame bar using a ball-and-socket bearing on the top of the spring strap. This arrangement was abandoned by Norris in favour of independent spring sets in the early 1850s.

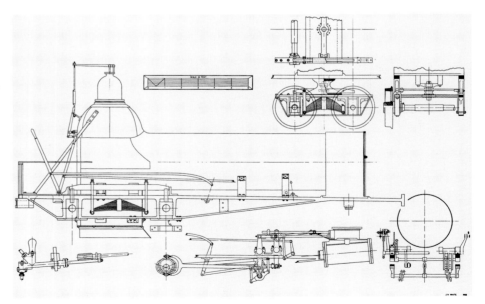

Right: Arrangement drawings of *COPIAPÓ*, showing frame arrangement and other component detail. (John H. White Jr)

The leading bogie truck is formed of boiler plate mounted above cast-iron pedestals, with a similar springing arrangement to the driving wheels. The weight of the locomotive at the front end is taken by two cast-iron side bearings that rub on the underside of the main frame, thereby restricting the truck's turning ability. The equalising beams pass through hollows in these bearings.

The cylinder castings, including smokebox mounting-brackets and steam and exhaust pipes, slope down at 5 degrees. Separate horizontal valve chests were provided. The piston rod driven boiler feed pumps are remarkably long to accommodate the unusual 26in (660mm) piston stroke.

The valve gear on *COPIAPÓ* is the only surviving example of the Norris 'riding' cut-off valve gear, and it is remarkable that it survived without being replaced by link motion. The gear is a later version of the original type, driven by a third eccentric rod for each valve, to allow its use for forward or reverse movement, rather than by the forward eccentric rod only. This may therefore have provided a cut-off of about 50 per cent in either direction. The two-position 'engaged' or 'disengaged' option was provided through the use of a linked upper and lower gab at the end of the valve spindle, positioned by a control lever on the footplate, and an intermediate bell crank. When

COPIAPÓ 4-4-0 Static original without tender

Built

1850	Norris Brothers, Philadelphia, Pennsylvania

Ownership

1850–51	Allan and Alexander Campbell
1851–94	Copiapó Railroad
1894–1945	Escuela de Artes y Oficios (School of Arts & Crafts), Santiago
1945–81	Escuela de Minas (State School of Mines), Copiapó
1981–Present day	Universidad de Atacama, Copiapó

Display

1891–94	Copiapó (in store)
1894–1945	Escuela de Artes y Oficios (School of Arts & Crafts), Santiago
1945–81	Escuela de Minas (State School of Mines), Copiapó
1981–Present day	Universidad de Atacama (North Campus), Copiapó

Summary Details

Track gauge:	4ft 8½in (1435mm)
Driving wheel diameter:	5ft (1524mm)
Cylinder diameter:	13in (330mm)
Piston stroke:	26in (661mm)
Boiler length:	c. 11ft (3350mm)
Boiler diameter:	3ft 2in (965mm)
Tubes:	113
Total heating surface:	c. 645ft² (60m²)
Grate area:	c. 10.8ft² (1m²)
Working Pressure:	Not known
Valve gear:	Norris 'riding' cut-off
Weight in working order:	c. 19 tons

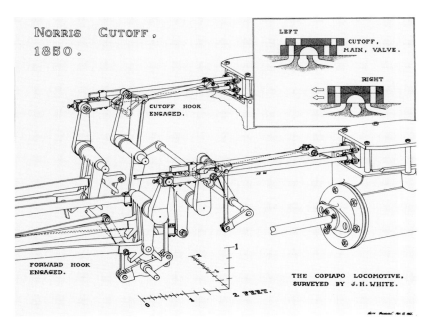

Valve gear arrangement drawings of *COPIAPÓ*, showing the 'riding' cut-off arrangement. (John H. White Jr)

disengaged, the cut-off valve travelled with the main valve without effect. The main valve motion was a common gab gear using 'V'-form gabs, the jaws of which, lowered and raised by links, engaged with a common rocking lever pin.

COPIAPÓ's cast-iron wheels have robust 'T'-form spokes, double crank pin bosses and counterweights. The leading truck has 28in (711mm) diameter wheels, also with 'T'-form spokes, and a 42in (1067mm) wheelbase. The sandbox is original, but the stack, bell and whistle are replacements. An iron cab and headlight have been fitted during preservation. Regrettably, the tender was separated from the locomotive in 1945 and it is not known if it has survived.

13

THE LONG-BOILER TYPE 1840s

The long-boiler type was patented and introduced by Robert Stephenson & Co. in 1841. It became a standard type on railways in Britain and several countries in Continental Europe. The type was characterised by the firebox positioned behind the rear axle, allowing a lengthening of the boiler, whilst maintaining a short wheelbase of around 12ft (3.7m). This answered the need to continue using the many short turntables that had been installed on early railways.

The longer boilers increased the heating surface of the tubes, giving improved heat transfer, thus raising efficiency through reduction in waste heat. It allowed a reduction in firebox size to provide a more balanced proportion of firebox to tube heating surface. Although cylinder sizes and wheel diameters were comparable with the *Patentees* (Chapter 10), the reduction in boiler diameter and numbers of tubes meant that the smaller grates were harder worked. The resulting hotter flue gases used the longer tubes to transfer the majority of the heat, providing higher efficiencies. Further, it reduced excessive smokebox temperatures which had been experienced with later *Patentees*.

The type embodied further significant changes from the Stephenson Company's previous designs, not least the adoption of inside plate frames. These replaced the outside sandwich frame and inside frames for slide bars and inner cranked axle bearings that had been used on their *Planet* and *Patentee* types (Chapters 7 and 10). Plate frames were significantly cheaper to construct than sandwich frames, as the company responded to increased competition in the locomotive-building industry. The horn plates were bolted to either side of the main frame plates, the extra width of the horns in turn providing increased width for the axle bearings. The upper frame stretchers also acted as the boiler support brackets, whilst round bar stays between the lower horn assemblies maintained the frame's lower rigidity.

The Stephenson Company had adopted better quality iron for crank axle manufacture, endeavouring to overcome frequent failures in the late 1830s, which then encouraged it to adopt plate frames with four crank axle bearings. However, crank axle failures persisted in European countries where the iron quality remained poorer than in Britain. To overcome this problem, from 1843 the Stephenson Company took full advantage of the inside plate frame arrangement to introduce outside cylinder designs, avoiding crank axles altogether. Both survivors of the 'long-boiler' type are examples of this arrangement.

In contrast to American endeavours through the 1830s and 1840s to develop a steam cut-off capability through the use of separate valves to the main steam valves (Chapter 12), efforts were made in Britain and Europe to develop a variable cut-off capability for the steam valves through ingenious valve gear geometry. The first successful gear, introduced on 'long-boiler' locomotives in 1842 by Robert Stephenson & Co., was the 'Stephenson link' motion. Replacing its previous gab gear (Chapter 10), the company's slotted link arrangement, with a die block sliding within a curved eccentric-driven link, could vary the extent of reciprocating action to allow variable valve setting for steam cut-off. This provided significant economies through lower steam, and hence fuel, usage. The valve cut-offs were adjusted by a quadrant lever on the footplate and the settings were balanced by a weight on a linked weigh bar. The unpatented link motion was a significant advance in locomotive economy, and was adopted by many manufacturers.

Boiler feed pumps, operated by eccentric rods from the rear axle, were also introduced at this time.

The type was notable for its low centre of gravity, and successfully performed at 25–35mph (40–60kph) operation. However, the greater expectations of Britain's railways, stimulated by the 'Gauge Wars' of 1845–46, led to higher train speeds making the 'long-boilers' unsuitable as they oscillated badly. Indeed, the inherent oscillation problem of long-stroke, outside cylinder engines with a short wheelbase limited their use to lower speed services. For their many years of operation in Europe, where speeds remained generally lower than in Britain, oscillation was not so much of a problem.

The 'long-boiler' type was popular in France because of economy in the use of expensively imported coke. Many 2-2-2, 2-4-0 and 0-6-0 examples were used. In addition to locomotives imported from Britain, several French manufacturers were licensed by Robert Stephenson to manufacture them, for which a royalty fee was payable.

Some locomotives continued operating well into the twentieth century, and the only two surviving pre-1850 locomotives of the type are both preserved in the Cité du Train Museum (French National Railway Museum) in Mulhouse.

NO. 6 *L'AIGLE (THE EAGLE)* 2-2-2
STATIC ORIGINAL WITHOUT TENDER

(See p.109 for colour image.) *L'AIGLE* is a splendid example of an outside cylinder 'long-boiler' locomotive, built by Robert Stephenson & Co. for the Chemin de fer d'Avignon à Marseille (Avignon–Marseille Railway) in 1846. The company's agent, Edward Starbuck (Chapter 10), obtained many orders for the Newcastle-Upon-Tyne factory, including one for thirty 2-2-2 passenger and 0-6-0 goods locomotives from the railway. This had been arranged through

Underside forward-facing view of *L'AIGLE*, showing right-side vertical valve chest. (Author)

Underside rear-facing view of *L'AIGLE*, showing left-side eccentric-driven water pump, plate frame and round bar horn stay. (Author)

Underside rear-facing view of *L'AIGLE*, showing right-side slotted link motion, plate frame and round bar horn stay. (Author)

the French engineer, Paulin Talabot, with whom Robert Stephenson was well acquainted. Under the terms of the contract, half the order was subcontracted to L. Bennet & Cie., of La Ciotat, just down the coast from Marseille.

The passenger locomotives, named after birds, included *L'AIGLE* which was sent from Newcastle to Marseille in May 1846, and given the running No. 6. The 120km (75-mile) line between Marseille and Avignon was opened in sections between 1847 and 1849. The passenger locomotives hauled trains of 150 tonnes at 45kph (28mph) on level track but, because of oscillation problems, their maximum speed was limited to 60kph (37mph).

On the formation of the Chemin de fer de Paris–Lyon–Mediterranée (PLM – Paris,–Lyon–Mediterranean Railway) in 1857, absorbing the Avignon–Marseille Railway, *L'AIGLE* was renumbered 206. It was withdrawn from service in 1865 and laid aside, but from the beginning of 1871 it was used as a mobile boiler at Valence. In 1880, it was again transferred, this time to the Oullins workshops in Lyon, where it supplied steam for the machinery in the foundry for the next 34 years.

No. 6 *L'AIGLE* (*THE EAGLE*) 2-2-2 Static original without tender

Built

1846	Robert Stephenson & Co. (Works No. 408)

Ownership

1846–57	Chemin de fer d'Avignon à Marseille
1857–1937	Chemin de fer de Paris–Lyon–Méditerranée
1938–69	Société Nationale des Chemins de fer Français
1969–Present day	Association du Musée Français du Chemin de fer (French National Railway Museum)

Display

1914–71	Oullins workshops, Lyon, and Chalon-sur-Saône (in store)
1971–76	Mulhouse Nord depot, Musée Français du Chemin de fer
1976–2005	Mulhouse Dornach, Musée Français du Chemin de fer
2005–Present day	Cité du Train Museum, Mulhouse Dornach

Summary Details

Track gauge:	4ft 8½in (1435mm)
Driving wheel diameter:	5ft 7½in (1700mm)
Cylinder diameter:	13in (330mm)
Piston stroke:	24in (610mm)
Boiler length:	12ft 6in (3800mm)
Boiler diameter:	3ft 1in (940mm)
Total heating surface:	620ft^2 (57.64m^2)
Grate area:	8.6ft^2 (0.83m^2)
Working pressure:	85lbf/in^2 (5.9bar)
Valve gear:	Stephenson link
Weight in working order:	22.1 tonnes

In 1914, *L'AIGLE* was sent as an exhibit by the PLM to the Exposition Internationale in Lyon. It was subsequently exhibited by the railway at the Exposition Houille Blanche & Tourisme at Grenoble in 1925, masquerading as No. 1 of the Avignon–Marseilles Railway, with the name *LE PIERROT* (*THE SPARROW*), but this substitution was later reversed.

In 1968, *L'AIGLE* was taken into the SNCF workshops at Sotteville and restored to its 'original' 1846 condition for eventual display at the new Musée Français du Chemin de fer (French National Railway Museum) in Mulhouse.

L'AIGLE's boiler has 3.8m (12ft 6in) long tubes which, with its tall 'haycock' firebox, provided a total heating surface of 58m^2 (620ft^2). The firebox has 0.8m^2 (8.6ft^2) of grate area. Twin safety valves, served by Salter spring balances, are set into the top of the firebox. The regulator is fitted into the steam riser in the firebox crown.

The locomotive retains its original Stephenson link valve gear, operated by pairs of eccentrics on the driving axle, which worked vertical slide valves between the cylinders.

The wheels are of the contemporary Stephenson practice, with spokes and rims formed of 'T'-form angle-iron set into cast-iron hubs. The locomotive has eccentric-driven boiler feed pumps mounted ahead of the firebox.

No detailed survey of *L'AIGLE* has been written up from which to ascertain which components are original and which are replacements. It is evident, however, that a number of external fittings were added during the locomotive's 'restoration', prior to museum display. The tender has not survived.

NO. 5 *SÉZANNE* 2-2-2
STATIC ORIGINAL WITHOUT TENDER

SÉZANNE, a French-built 'long-boiler' locomotive, is also displayed at the Mulhouse railway museum. It was manufactured by Alfred Hallette et Cie., a small, short-lived company from Arras. Alfred was the son of Alexis Hallette (1788–1846), the noted engineer and inventor who, in 1828, had acquired one of the earliest Stephenson locomotives and subjected it to trials. In 1847, following the manufacture of just twenty-four locomotives and components, the company ceased trading.

In 1845, the company had received an order for sixteen 2-2-2 long-boiler locomotives from the Chemin de fer de Montereau à Troyes in the Champagne region, construction of which was about to commence. This 100km (62-mile) long railway was built along the valley of the River Seine, and opened in sections during 1848. It was absorbed into the Chemin de fer Paris à Strasbourg in 1853, before it too became a constituent of the Chemins de Fer de l'Est (East Railway) on its formation in January 1854.

One of the locomotives, *SÉZANNE*, named after the town just north of the railway route, was delivered to the line in 1847. It was given the running No. 5, but in 1853 the Strasbourg company renumbered it 291, which it retained on the formation of the East Railway shortly afterwards.

In July 1868, *SÉZANNE* was used as a test bed for a series of experiments into the burning of viscous mineral oil which was little, if at all, refined. These were conducted under the direction of the East Railway's engineer, and in conjunction with the well-known chemist, M. Henri-Étienne Sainte-Claire Deville (1818–81).

The modification to the firebox was relatively simple, the oil being piped from a converted tender, and distributed through a 'vertical grill' in the firebox onto bars at each side of the grate, which served to vaporize and ignite the oil as well as draw the heat to the centre. The bottom of the firebox was built up as a brick arch and faced over with refractory brick.

Ignition of the oil was difficult at first, and steam took more than 2½ hours to raise, although this was reduced to 75 minutes when a blower from another machine was used. The oil flow was controlled by a simple graduated cock and adjusted in accordance with the density of the exhaust. During the trials, *SÉZANNE* was said to have developed approximately 250hp (186kW) with a 90-tonne train, whilst maintaining 60kph (37mph). Although the trials went well, the cost of the fuel was even more expensive than coke, and the equipment was removed.

SÉZANNE was withdrawn from service in May 1871, but retained as a mobile boiler for several years, before being taken to the East Railway's Epernay workshops to be used as a stationary boiler, where it was jacked up off the rails on axle-carriers.

In 1926, the East railway thought to place it on display at its new station in Paris, in preparation for which *SÉZANNE* was given an overhaul and 'restored' to its 1847 appearance. Following a change of mind, however, it remained stored at Epernay workshops for many years before being transferred to Saint Dizier depot, and then, in more recent years, becoming part of the SNCF collection at Chalon-sur-Saône. In 1971 it was transferred

Underside forward-facing view of *SÉZANNE*, showing left-side cut-off valve connecting rod and slotted link (nearer), with eccentric rod and forward/reverse gab gear (behind). Also showing the plate frame, boiler bracket stretcher and 'T'-form wheel spokes. (Author)

to the Mulhouse railway museum, where it remains on permanent display. Its tender has not survived.

The outside cylindered *SÉZANNE* closely follows the Stephenson Company's 1843 long-boiler layout. This suggests that, not only did Stephenson license Alfred Hallette et Cie., but he may also have provided working drawings. These could have been made available provided that the locomotives 'may be in all respects equal to those which come from his works in Newcastle', such being the condition placed upon the La Ciotat company (p.153).

The layout of the locomotive is thus similar to *L'AIGLE*, with the major exception of the valve gear. In place of the Stephenson link valve motion, it adopts the American practice of separate cut-off slide valves for each cylinder (Chapter 12), although the valves are vertical rather than horizontal.

The cut-off valves were activated in motion by partial rotation of a slotted link on the driving axle, repositioning the die block and longitudinal alignment of its connecting rod. The connecting rod shifted the valve between neutral and a partial cut-off position. The rear ends of the connecting rod are forked and located in a bush on the driving axle. The slotted link was rotated by a quadrant lever on the right side of the footplate.

Preserved *SÉZANNE* displayed at the Cité du Train Museum, Mulhouse. (Cité du Train Museum)

The main steam valves were driven by gab-ended rods driven by eccentrics on the driving axle, and engaged with forward or reverse pins, through a control rod and weigh bar linkage, by a lever on the right side of the footplate.

The boiler has been replaced at least once during the life of the engine. In contrast to the eccentric-driven pumps on *L'AIGLE*, there is a single crosshead-driven water feed pump on the left side, feeding the boiler through

Underside rear-facing view of *SÉZANNE*, showing driving axle with cut-off connecting rod, and bush and slotted link (inner) and eccentrics and eccentric rods (outer). Also showing boiler bracket stretcher and firebox front plate. (Author)

Underside forward-facing view of *SÉZANNE*, showing left-side cut-off connecting rod and cut-off valve (nearer), and forward/reverse gab gear (behind). Also showing plate frame/ horn/bearing arrangement and horn stay. (Author)

SÉZANNE 2-2-2 Static original without tender

Built

1847	Alfred Hallette & Cie., Arras

Ownership

1847–53	Chemin de fer de Montereau à Troye
1853–54	Chemin de fer de Paris à Strasbourg
1854–1937	Chemin de fer de l'Est
1938–71	Société Nationale des Chemins de fer Français
1971–Present day	Association du Musée Français du Chemin de fer (French Railway Museum)

Display

1926–71	Epernay, Saint Dizier and Chalon-sur-Saône (in store)
1971–76	Mulhouse Nord depot, Musée Français du Chemin de fer
1976–2005	Mulhouse Dornach, Musée Français du Chemin de fer
2005–Present day	Cité du Train Museum, Mulhouse Dornach

Summary Details

Track gauge:	1435mm (4ft 8½in)
Driving wheel diameter:	1690mm (5ft 6½in)
Cylinder diameter:	340mm (13¼in)
Piston stroke:	550mm (21½in)
Boiler length:	c. 3600mm (11ft 10in)
Boiler diameter:	c. 1000mm (3ft 3in)
Total heating surface:	62.9m^2 (676.8ft^2)
Grate area:	0.86m^2 (9.25ft^2)
Working pressure:	5.9bar (88lbf/in^2)
Valve gear:	Gab gear with separate cut-off valves
Weight in working order:	20.1 tonnes (19.78 tons)

a clack valve fitted towards the top of the barrel. The top of the 'haycock' firebox houses twin safety valves with Salter spring balances. The wheels are similar to those on *L'AIGLE*, with cast-iron hubs and 'T'-form wrought-iron spokes and rims.

No detailed survey has been carried out to ascertain which components date from 1847, and which are in-service replacements or date from the 1926 'restoration'.

14

THE CREWE TYPE 1840s

From its opening in 1837, the Grand Junction Railway (GJR) in Britain operated *Patentee* type locomotives (Chapter 10), but their loads and speeds led to several crank axle failures. Whilst manufacturers strove to improve wrought-iron quality, the line's engineer-in-chief, Joseph Locke (1806–60), appointed one of his assistants, William Barber Buddicom (1816–87), as locomotive superintendent from January 1840, with the remit to reduce the failure rate of the fleet. Also in this endeavour, Alexander Allan (1809–91) was recruited from George Forrester & Co. to be foreman of the GJR's workshops in Edge Hill, Liverpool.

Whilst Robert Stephenson & Co.'s development work of plate frames for the 'long-boiler' type during 1840 continued the use of inside cylinders and crank axles (Chapter 13), Buddicom and Allan pursued outside cylinder designs from the outset. By February 1841, they developed a scheme for rebuilding the *Patentees* with outside cylinders, adopting some features of 2-2-2 locomotives that had been constructed by Forresters. They rebuilt three *Patentees*, the first of which, *AEOLUS*, was completed about August 1841. It was the prototype of what became the 'Crewe' type, or 'Allan' type as it is sometimes known. As with the 'long-boiler' locomotives, these first locomotives of the type had a similar short wheelbase of up to 12ft (3660mm).

Directly after this development work, Buddicom left for France to set up, with William Allcard (1809–61), a company to make locomotives for Locke's new railways in Normandy. Anticipating the opening of the Chemin de fer de Paris à Rouen, Allcard, Buddicom & Cie. established its Les Chartreux workshops at Petit-Quevilly, near Rouen. The works were quickly established, and the first locomotive, completed at the end of 1842, was for the Paris–Rouen line which opened the following May. Its design followed Buddicom and Allan's work on the *AEOLUS*, and the type (known as the 'Buddicom' type in France) operated successfully on the new lines. Many locomotives of the type were subsequently built by Allcard and Buddicom, latterly at a new factory at Sotteville, south of Rouen, for several railways around France.

With Buddicom's move to France, the GJR appointed Francis Trevithick (1812–77) as locomotive superintendent, assisted by Allan. Based on the *AEOLUS*, four outside cylinder 2-2-2s were built for the railway by Jones & Potts of the Viaduct Foundry, Newton-le-Willows in Lancashire. Under its previous partnership, Jones, Turner & Evans, the foundry had manufactured *AJAX* in 1841 (Chapter 10). Jones & Potts went on to build many Crewe type locomotives for use in Britain and France.

To accommodate outside cylinders whilst retaining the benefits of the outside sandwich frame, separate inside main frame plates and robust outside frame plates were adopted, these forming the basic features of the Crewe type. Both were supplemented with auxiliary frames, with a 4in (102mm) separation, which preserved the sandwich frame strength and stiffness characteristics. The driving axle horn plates were attached to the main inside frames and its auxiliary frames, whilst the carrying axle horn plates were attached to the outside frames and its auxiliary frames. All were located and stiffened by transverse stretchers.

The cylinders were attached between the main and outside frames, with the slide bars attached to the outer and auxiliary frames. The original inside frame plates of the early locomotives were 'crooked', being cranked outwards slightly between the front buffer beam and the motion plate, and similarly to the rear of the throat plate, whilst reducing in thickness to both front and rear. The arrangement was progressively simplified thereafter.

Their much improved reliability convinced Joseph Locke, as well as Trevithick and Allan, of the benefits of full-length inside and outside iron plate frames, inside driving axle bearings, and outside carrying axle bearings, together with sloping outside cylinders and slide bars. Trevithick's attention was diverted between 1841 and 1843 as he established the railway's new workshops at Crewe, and locomotive production did not commence there until May 1843. Thus the term 'Crewe' type is derived from all the development work undertaken there after 1843, rather than being the site of its introduction.

NO. 33 *ST PIERRE* 2-2-2
STATIC ORIGINAL WITH REPLICA TENDER

(See p.110 for colour image.) *ST PIERRE* is the earliest surviving example of a Crewe type locomotive. It was one of the original class of forty, named after saints, and built at Les Chartreux workshops in 1843–45 for the Paris–Rouen line. Notwithstanding a marked tendency to a 'galloping' movement, particularly at their upper speed of 60kph (37mph), the class distinguished itself for longevity of service. Several locomotives continued in service until the twentieth century, and one was said to have achieved 1.31 million km (810,000 miles) by 1900.

The Paris–Rouen railway was absorbed into the Chemin de fer de l'Ouest (Western Railway) in 1856, which, in the 1860s, rebuilt twenty-six of the class as 2-2-2 well tanks, by which time they had lost their names. No. 33, which continued to operate trains between Dieppe and Paris for much of its career, was renumbered 131, and subsequently 0131. The Western railway was absorbed into the Réseau de l'État in 1908 and, in the following year, the locomotive was allocated the number 12-010, until its retirement from service in 1916.

It was preserved in Sotteville's Quatre-Mares workshops until 1946, when the Société Nationale des Chemins de fer Français (SNCF) restored it for its slightly delayed centenary. This restoration removed the well tank and, in an endeavour to return it to an early working condition, a replica tender was also constructed. For an unknown reason it was allocated the number 3, but remained nameless. It appeared, in steam, at a number of celebrations including, in 1951, the Festival of Britain in London, making part of the journey under its own steam. Research in that year, however, revealed that the locomotive's correct identity was No. 33 and its original name had been *ST PIERRE*.

In 1967, the Sotteville workshops undertook a further restoration, to return the locomotive to 'original' condition and bestow its correct number and name. Pending establishment of the French Railway Museum, it was stored for a time at the SNCF's Chalon-sur-Saône depot.

No surveys or reports of the 1946 or 1967 restorations have been published, from which to learn how many components can be traced back

No. 33 *ST PIERRE* 2-2-2 Static original and replica tender

Built

1844–45	Allcard, Buddicom & Cie., Les Chartreux, Rouen

Ownership

1845–1856	Chemin de fer de Paris à Rouen
1856–1908	Chemin de fer de l'Ouest
1908–38	Chemins de fer de l'État (Réseau de l'État)
1938–69	Société Nationale des Chemins de fer Français
1969–Present day	Association du Musée Français du Chemin de fer

Display

1916–67	Quatre-Mares workshops, Sotteville (in store)
1967–71	Chalon-sur-Saône (in store)
1971–76	Musée Français du Chemin de fer (French National Railway Museum), Mulhouse Nord depot
1976–2005	Musée Français du Chemin de fer, Mulhouse (Dornach)
2005–Present day	Cité du Train Museum, Mulhouse (Dornach)

Summary Details

Track gauge:	1435mm (4ft 8½in)
Driving wheel diameter:	1720mm (5ft 7½in)
Cylinder diameter:	355mm (14in)
Piston stroke:	535mm (21in)
Tubes:	145
Boiler length:	2600mm (8ft 6½in)
Boiler diameter:	1296mm (4ft 3in)
Total heating surface:	57.64m² (620ft²)
Grate area:	0.90m² (9.684ft²)
Working pressure:	5.9bar (85lbf/in²)
Valve gear:	Gab gear
Weight in working order:	17 tonnes

to 1844, and in what years modifications or replacements may have been carried out. *ST PIERRE* is, nevertheless, a fine survivor of an early Crewe type locomotive.

Its cylinders slope down at 10 degrees. The valve chests are above the cylinders, and were fed by steam pipes through the sides of the smokebox. The use of outside horizontal slide valves was an arrangement perpetuated by Buddicom long after the Crewe-built examples had moved to inside vertical slide valves activated by link motion.

Underside rear-facing view of *ST PIERRE*, showing left-side gab (pied de biche) valve gear. (Author)

View of the firebox-mounted steam dome on *ST PIERRE*, showing spring balance safety valve, and gab gear three-position quadrant lever. (Author)

fireboxes, with larger grate areas, better suited to French-sourced fuel. The original grate area was 0.79m^2 (8.48ft^2), but a replacement firebox has been fitted, increasing the grate area to 0.90m^2 (9.7ft^2).

The four-wheel replica tender is fitted with a single screw-operated parking brake on its right side.

NO. 1868 *COLUMBINE* 2-2-2
STATIC ORIGINAL AND TENDER

No. 1868, the twentieth locomotive completed at the GJR's Crewe workshops in July 1845, is the oldest surviving locomotive built there. It was the first of the GJR's 'standard' singles, incorporating Stephenson link motion with inside vertical-faced slide valves. Previous locomotives were fitted with gab valve gear, linked to horizontal slide valves above the outside cylinders, as fitted to *ST PIERRE*, although link motion had previously been tried experimentally. It was subsequently classified as the SFB (small firebox) type to distinguish it from the later large firebox locomotives.

It was given the running number 49 and named after the comic theatrical character 'Columbine'. Its name was retained by the successor London & North Western Railway (LNWR), although it was probably removed in

ST PIERRE retains its gab valve gear operated by a simple three-notch quadrant lever on the right side of the footplate. There are two boiler feed pumps driven by the crossheads on the outside of the frame. A small injector has, however, been added at some stage in the locomotive's career, as has a boiler pressure gauge dial.

The boiler and cylinders are covered by teak cladding, secured by brass banding. A tall steam dome is mounted on a plinth directly above the firebox, into which is fitted a 'butterfly' regulator valve. One of the two Salter spring balance safety valves is fitted into the top of the steam dome; the other is fitted into a column on the leading boiler ring. A whistle is fitted to the side of the steam dome.

The original design incorporated a coke burning firebox, requiring imports of English coke. Subsequent designs built at Sotteville had bigger

1868 'Columbine' displayed in the London Science Museum. (Author)

1871. Nevertheless, the name has been perpetuated through common usage since that time.

Columbine operated express passenger services over the LNWR's Northern Division to North Wales, Carlisle, Liverpool and Manchester. Joseph Locke stated in evidence to the Gauge Commissioners in 1847, that, with its 6ft (1830mm) driving wheels and 14½in (368mm) cylinders, it had achieved speeds of up to 57mph (92kph). Columbine was rebuilt or modified in 1856, 1871 and 1875. It briefly ran as 'duplicate' No. 1198 in 1871, after which it was numbered 1868. In 1877, it was retired from revenue service to become a departmental locomotive, named Engineer Bangor, hauling a district engineer's saloon, in which service it continued until withdrawn in 1902.

The locomotive was then stored in Crewe works paint shop, with only occasional outings for exhibitions, including the British Empire Exhibition in 1925 and the Liverpool & Manchester Centenary celebrations in 1930,

for which events the name Columbine was revived but not carried on the engine. In 1934, by agreement with the London & North Eastern Railway, it was sent to the York Railway Museum for exhibition. It was transferred to the National Railway Museum in 1975, and remained there on display until 1999. The locomotive, without its tender, was then transferred to the London Science Museum as an artefact in the 'Making of the Modern World' gallery. The tender was placed in store at Wroughton, the Science Museum Group's large reserve artefact facility in Wiltshire.

A number of its components date from the 1870s, changes being made under the auspices of the LNWR's chief mechanical engineer, Francis Webb (1836–1906). The boiler dates from 1871 or 1875 as, whilst the original working pressure had been 75lbf/in^2 (5.2bar), that of the surviving boiler is 120lbf/in^2 (8.3bar). The original small coke burning firebox has been replaced by a coal burning box, whilst the chimney also dates from this time. During one of the rebuildings, Columbine's original 'crooked' inside frames were replaced by 'straight' plates.

During its departmental service, and much of the time in preservation, the locomotive was fitted with a large cab, the front plate of which was in advance of the dome cover on top of the firebox. In 1980, the National Railway Museum removed the cab (and a weatherboard fitted to the tender) to allow restoration to its pre-1877 condition. It is now displayed in LNWR 'blackberry black' livery, as 1868.

The cylinders, sloping down at 5 degrees, were originally 14½in (368mm) diameter, but they are now bored to the later Crewe standard of 15¼in (387mm).

Stephenson link motion (Chapter 13) was fitted to Columbine, but the use of double cranks with lateral distance between them was necessary to get

Rear view of 'Columbine', showing inner and outer frame and wheel bearing arrangement. (Author)

Right-side forward-facing view of 'Columbine', showing the outer frame and cylinder, and slide bar arrangement. (Author)

Downward view of 'Columbine's mid-section, showing inner frame and the rear of the right-side steam chest, valve rod and guide. (Author)

Underside rear-facing view of 'Columbine', showing the left-side eccentrics and rods, together with boiler feed pump drive with sickle-type connecting rod. (Author)

No. 1868 *Columbine* 2-2-2 Static original with tender

Built

1845	Crewe Works, Grand Junction Railway

Ownership

1845–46	Grand Junction Railway
1846–1923	London & North Western Railway
1923–34	London, Midland & Scottish Railway
1934–47	London, Midland & Scottish Railway (on loan to the London & North Eastern Railway)
1948–62	British Transport Commission
1963–75	British Railways Board
1975–2012	National Museum of Science and Industry (Accession No. 1975–7016)
2012–Present day	Science Museum Group

Display

1902–34	Crewe Works Paint Shop (in store)
1934–41	York Railway Museum
1941–47	Reedsmouth (in store – war safety measures)
1947–74	York Railway Museum
1975–2000	National Railway Museum, York
2000–Present day	London Science Museum (locomotive only – tender in Wroughton)

Summary Details

	Originally	As Preserved
Track gauge:	4ft 8½in (1435mm)	4ft 8½in (1435mm)
Driving wheel diameter:	6ft (1830mm)	6ft 3in (1905mm)
Cylinder diameter:	14½in (368mm)	15¼in (387mm)
Piston stroke:	20in (508mm)	20in (508mm)
Boiler length:	9ft 9in (2972mm)	9ft 9in (2972mm)
Boiler diameter:	3ft 6in (1067mm)	3ft 6in (1067mm)
Total heating surface:	775ft² (72m²)	709ft² (66m²)
Grate area:	10.5ft² (1m²)	10.5ft² (1m²)
Working pressure:	75lbf/in² (5.2bar)	120lbf/in² (8.3bar)
Valve gear:	Indirect Stephenson link	Indirect Stephenson link
Weight in working order:	*c.* 16 tons	20.4 tons

the valve gear action to the steam chests. In this arrangement the eccentric rods were inclined downwards to the expansion links, below the motion plate. The die block motion was communicated to the valves by levers and rocking shafts providing lateral and vertical offset. The link was suspended from one side only by a cranked arm, and was balanced by a short torsion coil-spring, whilst the valve rods themselves had external guides. This so-called asymmetric 'indirect action' type was employed at Crewe between 1845 and 1851.

The short-stroke boiler feed pumps are in their original position, fixed to the frame near the throat plate, but were driven by subsequently fitted sickle-type rods, instead of short rods, from the eccentric straps. In addition an early 'White' injector has been added to the right side of the firebox at a late stage in the locomotive's service life.

Two Salter spring balance safety valves are fitted, one in the top of the steam dome, the other in the inspection hole cover plate over the boiler's middle ring. The wooden frame tender is an early LNWR type, which although paired with the locomotive in later service, could well have been contemporary with it.

MATARÓ 2-2-2
OPERABLE REPLICA AND TENDER

(See p.111 for colour image.) The original *MATARÓ* was the first locomotive to operate in Spain, along the 29km (18-mile) Mediterranean coastal railway between Barcelona and Mataró. The line was built by the Sociedad del Camino de Hierroe de Barcelona a Mataró (Barcelona–Mataró Iron Road Company), which was granted a concession in 1845. A driving force in the company was José Maria Roca, a London-based Catalan businessman, who was familiar with British railway developments.

To engineer the line, Roca sought the services of Joseph Locke, who in turn engaged his nephew, William, as resident engineer and the contractors William Mackenzie and Thomas Brassey to build the line. It was opened in 1848 to a track gauge of 6 Castilian feet (1672mm/5ft 5⅝in). Locke specified Crewe type locomotives for the line.

Four 2-2-2s, costing £2,000 each, were built by Jones & Potts of the Viaduct Foundry. The first of the fleet, *MATARÓ*, left the factory in May 1847. More than a year before the opening of the line, it is likely that it was employed in its construction. After the opening, the four locomotives were mostly used on passenger services. These expanded rapidly, and gave rise to the need for further locomotives, of generally similar design, which were erected in the railway's own workshops in Mataró.

Following its withdrawal in 1877, *MATARÓ* was preserved in Barcelona. In that year, the city hosted a trade exhibition at the university, in preparation for which the locomotive (without a tender) was lifted to the top of an 8m-high ceremonial gateway into the campus. The idea of using it at the exhibition (for comparison with a modern locomotive) may have been initiated by an engineering student, Manuel Moreno, who had prepared measured drawings of the locomotive and tender in 1875/76.

MATARÓ remained at the university for many years, but in 1929, during the Barcelona International Exhibition, it fell off its stand, and suffered so much damage that it had to be scrapped.

In 1947, Spain was keen to commemorate the centenary of the opening of its first railway, and Red Nacional de los Ferrocarriles Españoles (RENFE – Spanish National Railways), ordered a replica of *MATARÓ* to be built using Moreno's drawings. The large Barcelona engineering company, La Maquinista Terrestre y Maritima, constructed the replica locomotive and tender in accordance with manufacturing practices and materials of the day. No original components were thought to have been incorporated in the replica.

MATARÓ 2-2-2 Operable Replica and Tender

Built

1948	La Maquinista Terrestre y Maritima (Land & Maritime Machinist), Barcelona (Works No. 649)

Ownership

1948–85	Red Nacional de los Ferrocarriles Españoles (RENFE)
1985–99	La Fundación de los Ferrocarriles Españoles (FFE – Spanish Railways Foundation)
1999–Present day	Museu de la Ciència i de la Tècnica de Catalunya (mNACTEC – Museum of Science & Technology of Catalonia)

Display

1948–72	Historic Collection, Cuenca (in store)
1972–90	Depot in Vilanova i la Geltrú (in store)
1990–Present day	Museu del Ferrocarril de Vilanova i la Geltrú (Vilanova Railway Museum), Catalonia

Summary Details

Track gauge:	
Original:	1,672mm (5ft 5⅝in–6 Castilian feet)
Replica:	1,668mm (5ft 5⅔in)
Driving wheel diameter:	1754mm (5ft 9in)
Cylinder diameter:	356mm (14in)
Piston stroke:	508mm (20in)
Boiler length:	3410mm (11ft 2¼in)
Boiler diameter:	1150mm (3ft 9¼in)
Tubes:	144 x 51mm (2in)
Total heating surface:	70.95m² (763.4ft²)
Grate area:	1.0m² (10.76ft²)
Working pressure:	9.6bar (140lbf/in²)
Valve gear:	Stephenson link
Weight in working order:	*c.* 26 tonnes

MATARÓ and its train of replica carriages hauled a commemorative train between Barcelona and Mataró on 25 October 1948, a century after the initial service, which began a week-long programme of festivities. The replica has been occasionally used for commemorative events elsewhere in Spain, but was otherwise stored for many years out of service.

The replica represents *MATARÓ* at the end of its service life and, although it had probably been reboilered, it appears to have remained largely as built and is a typical Crewe type locomotive of the 1840s. The 'paddlebox' splashers, outside cylinders and slide bars sloping at 5 degrees, and the sloping valance covers over the steam chest and cylinders, retain a very British appearance. Stephenson link motion is fitted, driving vertical-faced slide valves.

The replica has a boiler pressure of just over 9.6bar (140lbf/in^2), nearly double the original pressure of 5.2bar (75lbf/in^2). The firebox is surmounted by a large steam dome, the design of which is not typically British, and presumably matches that fitted to the original locomotive when it was reboilered. A Salter spring balance safety valve is set into the dome. The original MATARÓ had a second Salter valve set into the mid-boiler inspection hatch cover, but this has not been replicated. The boiler is served by an injector.

A four-wheeled steel-framed tender, fitted with a 'U'-tank and screw down brake, closely follows the appearance of the original tender.

In 2006, MATARÓ was fully restored and brought up to modern operating standards by the Associació per a la Reconstrucció i Posta en Servei de Material Ferroviari Històric (ARMF – Association for Rebuilding and Operating Historic Railway Rolling Stock). It now operates in steam monthly at the Vilanova Railway Museum in Catalonia.

3020 CORNWALL 2-2-2
STATIC ORIGINAL AND LATER TENDER

(See pp.111–2 for colour images.) CORNWALL, built in 1847 at Crewe workshops, was an experimental locomotive designed under Francis Trevithick's supervision. It probably owes its name to the county from which he originated. It was rebuilt on several occasions and only a few components can be traced back to 1847, but it nevertheless retains the distinctive characteristics of a Crewe type locomotive. Its 8ft 6in (2591mm) diameter driving wheels were the largest ever used on the standard gauge, being thought essential to demonstrate that high speed was safe during the comparative trials with the broad gauge locomotives of the Great Western Railway.

It was first fitted with an unconventional boiler, slung under the driving axle, in the manner of the patents of Thomas Crampton (1816–88), but which had to be cut into above the tubes to accommodate the axle. This arrangement was to overcome the supposed difficulties of getting a reasonable size boiler, in conjunction with a low centre of gravity. The centre line of the 4ft (1219mm) diameter boiler was just above the carrying axles, requiring a reduced diameter front-ring to clear the front axle, whilst the firebox was fitted with a transverse tube through which passed the rear axle, requiring in situ wheel-fixing.

The large driving wheel diameter meant that the horizontal cylinders were necessarily high, with inclined steam chests above them. The Stephenson valve gear was located outside the frames, using Crampton's large eccentrics.

With the running number 173, CORNWALL got off to an inauspicious start in November 1847. After suffering a minor collision, its initial trials showed it to be overweight and damaging to the track. To spread the weight, an additional carrying axle was added under the smokebox, and the axle weights adjusted. Its subsequent trials were cautious and restricted to goods trains.

The locomotive was later reported to have run well and to have achieved high speeds on passenger services, but the reality was probably quite different. It is unlikely that it was much used, but further research would be needed to determine its true capabilities. CORNWALL was exhibited at the Great Exhibition in London in 1851. Somewhat questionably, it was awarded a medal, but Trevithick later wrote that this was not presented because the LNWR secretary's name, rather than the designer's, was 'officially attached'.

As well as having a long rigid wheelbase to spread the weight, the boiler was a maintenance nightmare, and several extraordinary schemes for replacement boilers were devised in the 1850s. On Trevithick's retirement in 1857, John Ramsbottom (1814–97) became locomotive superintendent and inherited the CORNWALL 'problem'. He placed the young Francis Webb (1836–1906), who had just concluded his apprenticeship, in charge of redesigning the locomotive along conventional lines.

In 1858, CORNWALL duly underwent a major rebuilding to make it a more conventional Crewe type locomotive. It was given a high-pitched

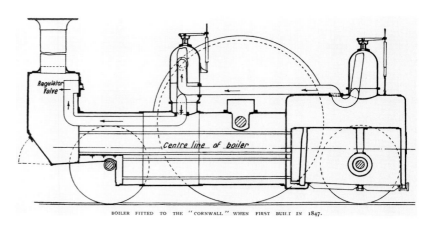

Outline drawing of CORNWALL as originally built at Crewe in 1847. (*The Railway Magazine*, Vol. 43, 1918, p.147)

boiler, with a back sloping grate and throat plate air holes, mounted over the driving axle. The reduced weight allowed it to be returned to a 2-2-2 wheel arrangement. New horizontal cylinders were fitted, together with vertical steam chests set inside the frames, with new inside valve gear operated, through rocking shafts, by Stephenson link motion. The locomotive became a reliable addition to the fleet and operated for several years based at Crewe.

No. 3020 *CORNWALL* 2-2-2 Static original and later tender

Built

| 1847 | Crewe Works, London & North Western Railway (Works No. 75) |

Ownership

1847–1922	London & North Western Railway
1923–47	London, Midland & Scottish Railway
1948–62	British Transport Commission
1963–75	British Railways Board
1975–2012	National Museum of Science and Industry (Accession No. 1975-7026)
2012–Present day	Science Museum Group

Display

1933–62	Crewe Works paint shop (in store)
1962–74	Museum of British Transport, Clapham
1974–79	Crewe Works (in store)
1979–84	Severn Valley Railway
1984–Present day	National Railway Museum, York and Shildon

Summary Details (As preserved)

Track gauge:	4ft 8½in (1435mm)
Driving wheel diameter:	8ft 6in (2591mm)
Cylinder diameter:	17¼in (437mm)
Piston stroke:	24in (609mm)
Boiler Length:	14ft (4266mm)
Boiler diameter:	3ft 11in (1194mm)
Total heating surface:	1068.3ft² (99.3m²)
Grate area:	15ft² (1.4m²)
Working pressure:	140lbf/in² (9.6bar)
Valve gear:	Stephenson link
Weight in working order:	29 tons 18cwt (30.4 tonnes)

CORNWALL was again modified in 1871, with a new cab, chimney and Webb's encased safety valves. In 1886, it was renumbered 3020 in the LNWR's duplicate series, and in 1887 it was further reboiled. This boiler and its 8ft 6in (2591mm) diameter driving wheels have remained with the locomotive to the present day. The firebox was located behind rather than over the main axle.

From 1890, *CORNWALL* was based at Edge Hill, Liverpool and regularly employed on the 40/45 minute expresses to Manchester. Further modifications were made between 1895 and 1900, including the fitting of oil instead of grease axle boxes, displacement cylinder lubricators and vacuum brake pipes for passenger train use. These were operated by a crosshead pump on the right side, but in 1915 a vacuum ejector was installed, and brakes fitted to the locomotive's driving wheels.

It was withdrawn from service in 1907, and stored pending a decision on its outcome. In 1911, it was restored to revenue earning service but, in 1913, it was transferred to service stock and semi-permanently coupled to the chief mechanical engineer's six-wheeled coupé inspection saloon, which doubled up as a tender.

In 1917, it was fitted with a shorter chimney, polished brass dome cover and rear driving wheel sandboxes, these being the final modifications to the form now seen in preservation. In 1920, a tender replaced the coupé, but this was removed during the Second World War. A replacement tender, dating from 1897, is now preserved with the locomotive. *CORNWALL* ceased work in 1922, but remained on the active list until withdrawn by the London Midland & Scottish Railway in 1933.

It was stored in the Crewe works paint shop until being transferred to the new British Transport Commission's Museum at Clapham in south London in 1962. On the closure of that museum in 1974, no room was found at the new National Railway Museum in York, and it was again returned to Crewe Works for storage.

In 1979, *CORNWALL* was taken to the Severn Valley Railway preservation workshops at Bewdley, Worcestershire, with a view to being returned to working order in time for the 'Rocket 150' celebrations in 1980. This was not achieved however and it remained at Bewdley as an exhibit until 1984. It was then delivered to the National Railway Museum, who undertook a repaint prior to its dispatch, in early 1985, to Japan, to take part in a year-long tour of the country as part of the World's Great Railway Exhibition. It has thereafter been displayed at the National Railway Museum sites at York and Shildon.

OTHER SINGLE DRIVER LOCOMOTIVES, 1840s

In addition to the Bury type (Chapter 11), Stephenson 'long-boiler'-type (Chapter 13) and the Crewe type (Chapter 14), a number of other 'single-driver' design schools were also developed during the 1840s. The variety of types, each adopting variations of valve gear, frame configuration and weight distribution, reflected the different operating conditions on railways in Britain, Continental Europe and North America, and the several development programmes of locomotive manufacturing firms in each region.

Passenger operations in Britain and Europe were mainly undertaken using locomotives with a single driving wheelset. Their designs benefited from knowledge built up through experience of operating and maintaining the earlier 2-2-2 types. Whilst adhesion was limited, the 'singles' offered greater speed opportunities over the coupled locomotives used for goods trains. In North America, whilst many railroads pursued four-coupled designs from the early 1840s (Chapter 16), the use of 'singles' persisted for a number of years on other lines with restrictive track capabilities.

This chapter brings together descriptions of the surviving examples of these other designs, together with working replicas. Described in the order in which they were built allows opportunity for comparison and greater understanding of the design variations which were taking place to satisfy the requirements of the world's evolving railway system.

PAYS DE WAES 2-2-2ST
STATIC ORIGINAL TANK LOCOMOTIVE

Pays de Waes (*Waasland* in Flemish) was the second of a class of nine locomotives built in 1842 for the Chemin de fer d'Anvers à Gand (Antwerp–Ghent Railway). The 49km (30-mile) line was the first independently financed 'concessionary' railway in Belgium. Its engineer, Gustave De Ridder

(1795–1862), had gained much experience with his brother-in-law, Pierre Simons (1797–1843), as joint chief engineer of Belgium's state railway system. The nature of the terrain between Antwerp and Ghent led De Ridder to adopt the unusual narrow gauge of 1140mm (3ft 9in), the first example of a reduced gauge main-line railway.

The railway was an important link between the two cities, both already served by the State railway network. The line passed through the area of East Flanders known as the Pays de Waes (Waes Country named after Saint-Nicolas-Waes), after which the locomotive was named, although the nameplates are no longer carried on the locomotive.

Pays de Waes was built in Brussels by the Société du Renard, which had commenced building locomotives in 1839. It was later reconstituted as the Société de Bruxelles pour la Fabrication de Machines et Méchaniques (Brussels Machine and Mechanical Manufacturing Company), and continued to build locomotives until 1860.

Designed under De Ridder's supervision, the locomotive was unconventional in several respects, incorporating innovative features. It was an early example of a tank engine, its large saddle tank fitted to the full length of the boiler barrel and smokebox, combining boiler insulation and preheating. Contrasting with conventional design practice, its rear-facing cylinders were located adjacent to the firebox.

It has a substantial 35mm (1⅜in) thick plate frame running the full 7.9m (26ft) length of the locomotive. Its 180mm (7in) depth is increased to 510mm (20in) around the driving axle box and 448mm (17.5in) around the cylinders, but with openings for weight reduction. It has a rigid wheelbase and the driving wheels are flanged.

The boiler is rigidly supported by saddles bolted to three frame stretchers and by angled support brackets on the outer firebox plates to a fourth rear stretcher. The frame plates also have light-duty end plates at front and rear.

Above: Preserved *Pays de Waes*, displayed at Musée des Chemins de fer Belges, Gare de Bruxelles-Nord. (Author)

Right: Firebox of *Pays de Waes*, showing 'Hackworth' type and spring balance safety valves, and valve gear control levers. (Author)

Far right: Right-side, rearward-facing cylinder of *Pays de Waes*, showing auxiliary (upper) and main (lower) steam chests for cut-off and regular steam admission respectively. (Author)

A single crosshead driven boiler feed pump is fitted on the left side. Water was pumped from the underside of the saddle tank to an inlet clack valve at the rear of the firebox just below the footplate.

Whilst retaining several original features, *Pays de Waes* was rebuilt on more than one occasion before the 1880s. The boiler appears to date from the 1850s/1860s, being single lap-riveted with machine-fitted rivets. The firebox is basically a Bury type, 'D'-plan, domed top design (Chapter 11), providing a large steam space over the firebox crown. It is surmounted by both a spring balance safety valve and a 'Hackworth' type plate spring safety valve (Chapter 6), which are surrounded by a tall open housing.

The regulator valve, operated by a handle on the back face of the firebox, fed left and right-side steam pipes which pass down below the waterline between the inner firebox and its outer casing. Although the cylinders are bolted to the frames, the valve chests, above the cylinder assemblies, are bolted to the side faces of the firebox housing.

Separate valves providing early cut-off were located in auxiliary valve chests located above and inboard of the main valve chests. They either copied early imports from the American Norris company or the Borsig patented form, such as may be seen on *BEUTH* (Chapter 12). It is likely that they were fitted as a modification later in the 1840s.

These valves could either be disengaged, to give late cut-off when starting, or engaged when in motion to provide early cut-off, being independently operated by quadrant levers on either side of the firebox. The levers lowered and raised the gabbed ends of eccentric rods to engage or disengage pins

Right: Downward view of the right side of *Pays de Waes*, showing rearward-facing auxiliary (inner) and main (outer) steam chests for cut-off and regular steam admission respectively. (Author)

Below: Underside forward-facing view of *Pays de Waes*, showing right-side gab-ended eccentric rod for cut-off control (nearer) and combined 'X'-form double gab for forward or reverse valve selection (behind). (Author)

gear, derived from Charles Carmichael's arrangement, had been adopted briefly in 1835 by Robert Stephenson & Co. (Chapter 10), including their initial *Patentee* locomotives for the Belgian State Railway. The valve and driving motion are today both fitted with 'marine' bearings and forked rods, probably dating from the latter part of the century.

The driving and trailing wheels are formed of cast-iron naves and wrought-iron 'T'-section spokes riveted back to back and to the wrought-iron rim. The leading wheels are similarly formed, but have channel-section spokes riveted back to back.

The locomotive is fitted with 'sled' brakes which acted on the rails just behind the driving wheels. Linked by a square section transverse bar, they were lowered by an operating arm, controlled by a screw handle mounted on the left side of the coke bunker.

Pays de Waes 2-2-2ST Static original

Built

1842	Postula de Bruxelles (Atelier du Renard)

Ownership

1842–90	Chemin de fer d'Anvers à Gand
1890–96	Chemin de fer d'Anvers à Gand (In preservation)
1896–1926	Chemins de fer de l'État
1926–Present day	Société Nationale des Chemins de fer Belges (SNCB)

Display

1896–1951	Malines (Mechelen) central workshops (in store)
1951–58	Musée des Chemins de fer Belges, old Gare de Bruxelles-Nord
1958–Present day	Musée des Chemins de fer Belges, new Gare de Bruxelles-Nord

Summary Details

Track gauge:	1140mm (3ft 9in)
Driving wheel diameter:	1500mm (4ft 11in)
Cylinder diameter:	280mm (11in)
Piston stroke:	460mm (18in)
Boiler length:	4300mm (14ft 1¼in)
Boiler diameter:	700mm (2ft 3½in)
Total heating surface:	44.67m² (480.65ft²)
Grate area:	0.53m² (5.70ft²)
Working pressure:	6.1bar (88.5lbf/in²)
Valve gear:	Gab gear with separate cut-off valves
Weight in working order:	17.55 tonnes

---

which drove, through intermediate rocking shafts, the cut-off valve motion. They also controlled push rods to move these auxiliary valves to a fully open position when cut-off was disengaged.

The regular valves were driven, via intermediate rocking shafts, by separate pairs of fixed-eccentrics. These eccentric rods are attached to combined 'X'-form double gabs engaging with either of two vertically separated pins on a rocking lever, for forward or reverse movement. Selection was by a long valve lever, the handle for which is on the right side of the footplate. This

Pays de Waes was converted to burn fuel oil as early as 1853 and continued in this form until at least 1862. It was withdrawn from service in 1890, and placed in store for many years at the Central Workshops in Malines (Mechelen). In 1925, it was sent to Darlington for the Stockton & Darlington Railway centenary exhibition. It was damaged by bombing in 1944, but repaired and restored in 1950–51 to become the centrepiece of the new SNCB Museum in the old Brussels Gare du Nord Station. It was moved in 1958 to the Museum Hall in the rebuilt Gare du Nord, where it remains on display.

NO. 7 *PIONEER* 4-2-0
STATIC ORIGINAL WITHOUT TENDER

Pioneer is the only survivor of the once ubiquitous iron bar framed American 4-2-0 locomotive. It is the oldest surviving locomotive built at the Philadelphia works of Matthias Baldwin (1795–1866), which became the largest of the American locomotive manufacturers. It is an important artefact because it remains largely as built, and thus exhibits many characteristics of American locomotive design, materials and construction methods of the late 1830s and 1840s.

There is no consensus over the origin of this locomotive. *Pioneer* is displayed as having been built in 1837 for the Utica & Schenectady Railroad in New York State, and originally named *ALERT*. However, the railroad historian, John H. White Jr, has written an authoritative history (White, 1976) that concludes that it may well have been built in 1843 for the 43-mile (69km) Tonawanda Railroad, linking Rochester and Batavia in New York State. In contrast to its earlier wooden-framed locomotives, the railroad received an iron-framed 4-2-0 in 1843, named *BATAVIA*. The earliest known illustration of a Baldwin locomotive fitted with an iron bar frame dates from 1839, the company developing the Bury practice, as taken up by Norris (Chapter 12).

In October 1848, the locomotive was sold and shipped to the then small town of Chicago, Illinois. Its apparently original iron frame suggests that it is the former *BATAVIA*. Later named *PIONEER*, it was the first to operate out of the town, helping to build its first railroad, the Galena and Chicago Union (GCUR), a 'strap-rail' line built westwards towards Galena on the Mississippi. The railroad's first driver, and later its master mechanic, John Ebbert (1813–99), later recalled its Tonawanda Railroad origins.

For a short time in 1850, it was leased to the connecting Aurora branch line, before returning to haul regular trains on the GCUR. By 1858 it was relegated to light duties, but was involved in a collision 2 years later.

About 1874, it was withdrawn by the Chicago & North Western Railroad (CNWR), which had merged with the GCUR some 10 years earlier. At a time of low scrap prices the now unnamed *Pioneer* was dumped at Turner Junction yard, west of Chicago. In 1880, a resident of the city, John West, campaigned successfully to prevent it from being scrapped.

Pioneer was first exhibited in 1883 by the CNWR at Chicago's National Exposition of Railway Appliances. For this event it was 'restored', some later features being removed. It was again exhibited in the city in 1893 at the World's Columbian Exposition, after which, along with other locomotives, it became part of the Transportation Exhibition in the city's Field Museum.

In 1904, all the museum's transport exhibits were removed by the Baltimore & Ohio Railroad (B&O), including *Pioneer*. First exhibited at the Louisiana Purchase Exposition in St Louis, Missouri, the B&O later stored the collection at Martinsburg, West Virginia. By 1927, *Pioneer* had been returned for display in the CNWR's Chicago Station, and from 1934 it was exhibited in the city's Museum of Science and Industry.

In 1947 however it was 'restored' to working order by the CNWR as a touring exhibit for its 1948 centennial celebrations, and was afterwards kept in the railroad's workshops until a 'permanent' home could be found. In 1972 it was donated to the Chicago Historical Society and placed in a new wing of its museum, where it remains today without a tender.

Preserved *Pioneer* displayed at the Chicago Historical Museum. (Author)

Rear-facing right-side view of *Pioneer*, showing the compound bar frame and outside gab-ended eccentric rods and valve rocking shaft. (Peter Davidson)

Pioneer's three-ring boiler and wood burning, 'D'-plan, round top firebox is probably original. The 27in (686mm) wide barrel plates are rolled and cut, typically to a length of 44in (1118mm), and single lap-riveted by hand, at three plates per ring. However, the front plate of the firebox and the underplate of the rear boiler ring are replacements. The drawbar bracket is riveted to the back plate of the firebox. The boiler is bolted to the frame by firebox and mid-barrel support brackets and, indirectly via the cylinders at the smokebox. The boiler lagging and large dome-topped whistle were removed in the 1883 'restoration'.

Pioneer has a compound iron bar frame built up from three main components on each side, all of 4in x 1½in (102mm x 37mm) section. It has upper and lower sloping bars to the rear, and a single horizontal bar to the fore, the union of which incorporates the mid-boiler brackets and stretcher bar, which seem to be as built. The rear sloping members from above and below the driving axle horns have twin cast-iron pedestals providing load bearing support under the firebox brackets. The horizontal bars are cantilevered forward to the cylinder assemblies, which are bolted to the smokebox sides.

The driving wheels are conventional uncushioned 'T'-spoked cast wheels, to the rear of the firebox. The cast-iron driving axle is of Baldwin's 'half-crank' design, with crank pins fitted off-centre to the wheel-bosses, and connecting rods working just inside the wheel faces. This efficient use of space maximised the width available for the firebox. The fulcrum for the four-wheel, short wheelbase, iron-frame truck is a load bearing bracket and pivot on the underside of the smokebox, the underplate of which has

been replaced. Its solid cast-iron wheels are post-1862 replacements for the original wheels.

Pioneer was originally fitted with Baldwin's single-eccentric gab valve gear, some witness of which remains, which provided steam admission for the full stroke. The replacement valve gear has two fixed-eccentrics at each end of the driving axle, outside the horns, providing the opportunity for a fixed cut-off. The eccentric rods have 'V'-form forward and reverse gabs to

No. 7 *Pioneer* 4-2-0 Static original without tender

Built

c. 1843	Baldwin & Whitney, Philadelphia (Works No. 184)

Ownership

c. 1843–48	Tonawanda Railroad, New York state (probably)
1848–64	Galena & Chicago Union Railroad Company
1864–74	Chicago & North Western Railroad (in operation)
1874–1972	Chicago & North Western Railroad (in preservation)
1972–Present day	Chicago Historical Society

Display

1874–93	Chicago (in store)
1894–1904	Field Museum, Chicago
1904–27	Martinsburg, West Virginia (in store)
1927–33	CNWR's Terminal Station, Chicago
1934–47	Chicago Museum of Science and Industry
1948–72	CNWR's 40th Street shops, Chicago (in store)
1972–Present day	Chicago Historical Museum

Summary Details

Track gauge:	4ft 8½in (1435mm)
Driving wheel diameter:	4ft 6in (1372mm)
Cylinder diameter:	
Originally:	10in (249mm)
Latterly:	11in (279mm)
Piston stroke:	18in (457mm)
Boiler length:	6ft 11in (2108mm)
Boiler diameter:	3ft 4in (1016mm)
Total heating surface:	c. 435.6ft² (40.5m²)
Grate area:	c. 7.5ft² (0.7m²)
Working pressure:	100lbf/in² (6.9bar)
Valve gear:	Gab gear with outside eccentrics
Weight in working order:	c.12 tons

Underside view of the left-side driving wheel of *Pioneer*, showing cast wheel and driving axle incorporating Baldwin's 'half-crank' arrangement. (Peter Davidson)

Rear-facing left-side view of *Pioneer*, showing detail of the outside valve gear and the substantial valve rocking shaft. (Author)

drive the substantial valve rocking shaft. A reversing rod, on the right side of the boiler, exchanged the gabs on the drive pins, and was connected to the left side by an under boiler transverse shaft. This form of gab gear had been first tried out at the Michigan Central Railroad's (MCR) shops in Detroit, where John Ebbert had previously been an engineer. He may, therefore, have undertaken this modification himself.

The unmatched cylinders slope down at 8 degrees, the piston rods being guided by combination crosshead guides and feed-water pump rods. A number of *Pioneer*'s features, added during its service career, remain. These include a large wooden cab, boiler top bell, cow-catcher and squat 'bonnet' smoke stack.

In addition, the 1947 'restoration' saw the addition of several fittings, including an injector, spring balance safety valve, additional 'pop'-type safety valve, steam gauge and back plate fittings which, together with a re-tube, enabled *Pioneer* to be steamed. Unfortunately this work resulted in some damage and alterations to the original fabric. A replica four-wheel tender was also built, but this is now separately displayed at Villa Park in Chicago.

NO. 1 *LA JUNTA* (*THE BOARD*) 4-2-2
STATIC ORIGINAL AND TENDER

LA JUNTA is the oldest surviving locomotive built by Rogers, Ketchum & Grosvenor of Paterson, New Jersey, and retains the initials, 'R.K. & G. N J', on its driving wheel splashers. It is the least modified of all preserved early American-built locomotives. Founded in 1832 by Thomas Rogers (1792–1856), with Jasper Grosvenor and Morris Ketchum, the works built its first locomotive in 1837. By 1850 it had become one of the big four American locomotive companies, with Baldwins, Norris and Hinkley.

The locomotive was one of several 4-2-2s, possibly speculatively built at a time of slow demand. Originally named *LA JUNTA DE FOMENTO* (*The Board of Public Works*), in recognition of the 'great work' of the Conde de Villanueva, it was purchased by the British-owned Matanzas Railway in Cuba. In November 1843 it opened the 22-mile (35km) line, linking Matanzas, on Cuba's north coast, with La Unión. The line eventually crossed the Matanzas region to Cumanayagua.

LA JUNTA was withdrawn about 1900 and placed on display at Matanzas' Estación matancera de Sabanilla (Sabanilla Station). Following the railway's acquisition by the 'United Railways of the Havana and Regla Warehouses Ltd', the locomotive was moved to the capital and placed on display in the

Preserved *LA JUNTA* displayed in the Museo del Ferrocarril Cubano, Havana, Cuba. (Herb MacDonald)

new Estación Central de La Habana (Havana Central Station) for many years. In 1979 it was moved to an open-sided shelter in Havana's Lenin Park. More recently, the Estación Cristina (Cristina Station) in Havana has become the site of the Museo del Ferrocarril Cubano (Cuban Railway Museum). *LA JUNTA* was declared a National Monument and placed in the museum's main hall.

The locomotive was surveyed in 1983 by John H. White Jr, curator of transportation at the Smithsonian Institution in Washington DC (White, 1984). Four years later it was given a thorough overhaul for the 150th anniversary of the first Cuban railroad, and was exhibited at the conclusion of the XVII Pan-American Railway Congress.

LA JUNTA retains its Bury type boiler with 'D'-plan round top firebox. The outer firebox plates are single lap-riveted, but the boiler barrel remains unseen under wooden lagging and Russia iron cover sheets. The latter's glossy surface has, regrettably, been overpainted several times, and is creased from incorrect slinging during lifting. A splendid brass dome is mounted on the firebox, on top of which the single safety valve is served by a Salter spring balance.

A large ornate sandbox sits over the rear boiler ring, its side sporting a cast image of Diana, the Roman hunter goddess, suggesting a novel subtlety with the locomotive's Spanish name. The bell and its ornate frame appear to be

original, but the stack, smokebox door and cab are in-service replacements, and the whistle is refitted high above the cab roof.

The inside frame is of compound construction, the main lengths being of common bar but forged flat and deep in the centre to accommodate the crosshead pumps and valve rocking shaft bearings. The leading ends have been strengthened, being a sandwich of two 4in (102mm) wide bars, with iron spools bolted through as spacers. Round and square bar stays link the driving axle and trailing axle horns. The frames are cross-braced by a leading oak beam and rear iron beam, whilst two intermediate stretcher bars are forged with boiler support brackets.

Footboards, which run the length of the locomotive, are formed of 3½in (89mm) deep wooden rails, to which are bolted wrought-iron plates. These also help to secure the slide bar yokes. The cylinders, inclined at 10 degrees, have cast brass covers and brass jacketing. Each piston rod's four slide bars and twelve-sided crossheads are typical of early American locomotive practice. They are secured at their trailing ends to yokes which are mainly secured by brackets to the boiler shoulder plates.

Right-side mid-section view of *LA JUNTA*, showing inner and outer frame members, and boiler bracket, together with valve rod, crosshead, connecting rod and boiler feed pump. (Herb MacDonald)

Right-side forward view of *LA JUNTA*, showing sloping cylinder, slide bars and boiler-bracketed yoke, together with steam chest and valve rod. (Herb MacDonald)

The driving axle has conventional leaf-springs, but the trailing wheels are served by a heavy forged equalising beam and leaf-springs set transverse to the main frame. A large screw, passing through the footplate, could be turned to bear down on one end of the beam as a primitive form of traction enhancement. The footplate is a substantial casting, albeit now cracked and repaired, below which is secured a 'V'-shaped bracket with a hole to receive the draw pin.

The driving wheels are cast iron with hollow oval spokes and large bosses for the crank pins. The rear wheels are in-service replacements, being solid castings with strengthening ribs.

LA JUNTA's leading truck is another survivor of the early American short wheelbase design. The weight of the locomotive's front end bears down on the truck through inverted leaf-springs at each side (one now broken and crudely repaired), which are held securely in brackets bolted to the truck frame. Rectangular rubbing plates are sandwiched between the locomotive frame and the springs. The truck's frame is a four-sided, one-piece forging, to which are bolted the four horn assemblies, stiffened by round bar rails between them. The pivot is a forging with three feet, bolted upside down to the bottom of the smokebox.

The truck has 30in (762mm) diameter cast-iron spoked leading wheels, possibly original, the hubs of which are split into three segments and closed with lead or zinc. However, the rear 29in (737mm) wheels are in-service

No. 1 *LA JUNTA* 4-2-2 Static original and tender

Built

1843	Rogers, Ketchum & Grosvenor, Paterson, New Jersey (works no. 42).

Ownership

1843–c. 1900	Matanzas Railway
c. 1900–12	Matanzas Railway (in preservation)
1912–53	United Railways of the Havana & Regla Warehouses Ltd
1953–60	Ferrocarril Occidentales de Cuba S.A.
1960–2000	Ferrocarriles Nacionales de Cuba
2000–Present day	Museo del Ferrocarril Cubano (Cuba Railway Museum)

Display

c. 1900–12	Matanzas, Estación matancera de Sabanilla (Sabanilla Station)
1912–79	Estación Central de La Habana (Havana Central Station)
1979–87	Parque Lenin (Lenin Park)
1987–2002	Estación Central de La Habana (Havana Central Station)
2002–Present day	Museo del Ferrocarril Cubano (Cuba Railway Museum)

Summary Details

Track gauge:	4ft 8½in (1435mm)
Driving wheel diameter:	4ft 6in (1372mm)
Cylinder diameter:	11in (279mm)
Piston stroke:	18in (457mm)
Boiler length:	c. 7ft 6in (2286mm)
Boiler diameter:	c. 3ft (914mm)
Total heating surface:	Not known
Grate area:	c. 8ft² (0.74m²)
Working pressure:	Not known
Valve gear:	Gab gear
Weight in working order:	c. 13 tons

Underside mid-section view of the right side of *LA JUNTA*, showing the gab-ended eccentric rods and lifting arm, together with detail of the leading truck. (Herb MacDonald)

replacements with European style, star-form, segmental flat spokes, marked as 'Krupp 1879'.

The original 'V'-hook gab valve gear, with two pairs of fixed-eccentrics, remains. Each pair of eccentric rods were raised or lowered for the required rod to engage with its drive pin, by lifting arms dropped down from the reversing shaft. The inner bearings of the cast-iron rocking shafts are bolted to the underside of the boiler. The complex castings include arms cranked over the frame to connect with the valve spindles. Reversing was undertaken with a large quadrant lever on the right side of the footplate.

The four-wheeled tender is probably the original, having a substantial wooden frame reinforced with tie rods, and a horseshoe shaped tank. The wheelsets have been replaced by solid cast sets, the front pair being 33in (838mm) diameter and the rear pair only 30in (762mm). The horn castings are ornately panelled. A drawbar runs the length of the tender, bolted to the underside of the centre sill. Tender brakes act on both pairs of wheels, with timber shoes, operated by a turn handle and chain.

ODIN 2-2-2
OPERABLE REPLICA AND TENDER (UNDER CONSTRUCTION)

(See p.113 for colour image.) The first stretch of railway to be built in Denmark was opened in June 1847 between København (Copenhagen) and Roskilde by the Sjællandske Jernbaneselskab (Zealand Railway). Four locomotives and tenders were built by Sharp Brothers & Co. of Manchester

for operating on the line. The first of them, *ODIN*, named after the principal God of the 'áss pantheon' in Norse paganism, was delivered in August 1846. None of the locomotives has survived, and conscious of the omission in its collection of historic locomotives, the Danmarks Jernbanemuseum (Danish Railway Museum) and its volunteer assistants have been constructing an operable replica at the former steam locomotive depot in Roskilde.

Detail of the front of the *ODIN* replica, showing its ornate and characteristic dome cover and chimney. (Poul Thestrup, Danmarks Jernbanemuseum, Odense)

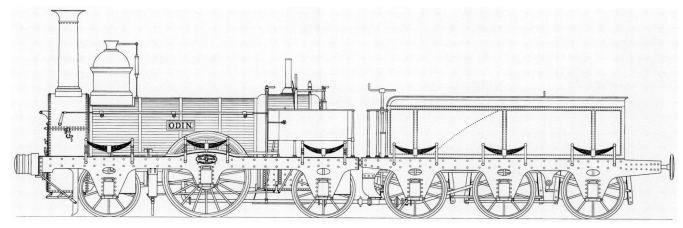

General arrangement drawing of *ODIN*, prepared for the Danmarks Jernbanemuseum, Odense, Denmark, prior to construction of the operable replica. (John Glithero)

Although some contemporary arrangement drawings of other Sharp Brothers' locomotives have been preserved, none related to *ODIN*. A major study was therefore carried out in 2004 by the author of this volume and John Glithero, into the specific component designs and arrangement of the original locomotive and tender.

The arrangement was typical of Sharp Brothers' designs of the era, often known as 'Sharpies', examples of which were built for several railways in Britain and Continental Europe. They were outside frame, inside cylinder types, with the rear carrying axle located behind the firebox. They were also characterised by a large, plinth-mounted brass dome cover over a dome which incorporated the regulator valve and leading spring balance safety valve. A second spring balance valve was fitted above the firebox.

The outside sandwich frames, accommodating the bearings for the three wheelsets, were made of ash timber flanked on either side by wrought-iron plates. Additional inside frames were fitted between the rear of the smokebox and the front of the firebox, and accommodated inside bearings for the cranked driving axle.

ODIN 2-2-2 Operable replica and tender (under construction)

Built

Current	Danmarks Jernbanemuseum (Danish Railway Museum) and volunteers

Ownership

Current	Danmarks Jernbanemuseum

Display

On completion	Danmarks Jernbanemuseum, Odense

Summary Details

Track gauge:	4ft 8½in (1435mm)
Driving wheel diameter:	5ft (1524mm)
Cylinder diameter:	15in (381mm)
Piston stroke:	20in (508mm)
Boiler length:	10ft (3048mm)
Boiler diameter:	3ft 6in (1067mm)
Total heating surface:	831ft^2 (77.3m^2)
Grate area:	10.6ft^2 (0.98m^2)
Working pressure:	80lbf/in^2 (5.5bar)
Valve gear:	Stephenson link motion
Weight in working order:	Not yet known

The vertical steam valves were served by a common steam chest between the cylinders. The valve motion had variable cut-off using a Stephenson link motion arrangement controlled by a quadrant lever on the left side of the footplate.

ODIN was accompanied by a six-wheeled, 1,000 gallon capacity tender. Its sandwich frame was similar to that of the locomotive. A transverse draw spring was fitted, through which the train load was transmitted.

The Danish Railway Museum plans to complete the locomotive and tender and transfer them to its main site in Odense in 2014, where it will provide visitors with the experience of an early train journey along its reserved track.

IRON DUKE (2+2)-2-2
OPERABLE REPLICA AND TENDER

The British 'gauge wars' of the mid-1840s, which compared the Great Western Railway's (GWR) broad gauge (7ft ¼in/2140mm) locomotives with standard gauge examples, stimulated progress in locomotive design. In 1846, Sir Daniel Gooch, the GWR's locomotive superintendent, constructed a much enlarged version of the *Fire Fly* type (Chapter 10), with 8ft (2438mm) diameter driving wheels, in the railway's Swindon workshops. Successful trials with this locomotive, *GREAT WESTERN*, were carried out, encouraging Gooch to introduce further improvements.

A larger locomotive, *IRON DUKE*, was completed at Swindon in April 1847. Named after the military hero and former Prime Minister, the Duke of Wellington, on whose birthday the locomotive was first tried out, it became the first of a class of twenty-nine built over the following 8 years. They operated, with varying modifications, until the 1870s–80s, each averaging some 600,000 miles in service, although, after rebuilding, three of them achieved a million miles each.

Gooch took advantage of the wider gauge by fitting *IRON DUKE* with a much larger boiler. Instead of a Gothic firebox, the boiler was domeless with a raised firebox casing, and incorporating the recently patented perforated steam pipe feeding to a 'grid-iron' slide valve regulator in the smokebox. The large firebox had a deep transverse water partition to increase the direct heating surface.

With pressure increased to 100 and later 115lbf/in^2 (6.9–7.9bar), the locomotive's nominal tractive effort rose to nearly 8000lbf (3629kgf). This was five times that of the prototype *Patentee* completed some 14 years earlier, and thus represented the ultimate form of that type.

The leading axle on *GREAT WESTERN* originally carried too much weight, requiring the locomotive to be rebuilt with an additional leading axle. *IRON DUKE* was therefore built with two independent leading axles, giving an overall wheelbase of 18ft 6in (5650mm), made possible by flangeless driving wheels.

The locomotive's sandwich frame was arched over the crank axle bearings to accommodate the large driving wheels. The driving axle springs were fitted beneath the axle boxes within the slotted horn assembly, whilst the trailing axle spring was above the frame. The two leading axles were fitted with a common inverted spring reminiscent of North American equalising beams. Two wrought-iron inside plate frames, together with a centre stay, were fitted between the back of the cylinders and the firebox front plate. The crank axle thus ran in five bearings fitted to these and the outside frames.

IRON DUKE was fitted with Gooch's stationary link valve motion, which he introduced in 1847 as a variation of Stephenson's link motion (Chapter 13). The only surviving pre-1850 example of the Gooch stationary link valve gear is fitted to *MEMNON* of 1848 (Chapter 17).

The '*Iron Duke*' class undertook trials in 1847/48, both as part of the gauge trials and to obtain train resistance data. *IRON DUKE* itself achieved an average 53.4mph (85.9kph) for an average gross load of 105 tons, including locomotive and tender. The highest recorded speed during the trials was 78.2mph (126kph) down a 1 in 100 gradient.

Replica of *IRON DUKE* operating at the National Railway Museum, York. (The late Harold Bowtell)

IRON DUKE (2+2)-2-2 Operable replica and tender

Built

1985	Resco (Railways) Ltd, Aylesford, Kent (locomotive assembly) and British Railways Cathays workshops, Cardiff (tender fabrication)

Ownership

1985–2012	National Museum of Science and Industry (Accession No. 1985-1989)
2012–Present day	Science Museum Group

Display

1985–2012	National Railway Museum, York
2012–Present day	Great Western Society, Didcot (planned)

Summary Details:

	Original	Replica
Track gauge:	7ft ¼in (2140mm)	7ft ¼in (2140mm)
Driving wheel diameter:	8ft (2438mm)	8ft (2438mm)
Cylinder diameter:	18in (457mm)	18in (457mm)
Piston stroke:	24in (609mm)	26in (660mm)
Boiler length:	11ft (3353mm)	10ft 2in (3099mm)
Boiler diameter:	4ft 9¾in (1467mm)	4ft 3in (1295mm)
Tubes:	303 x 2in (51mm)	181
Total heating surface:	1944.99ft² (181m²)	961ft² (89.3m²)
Grate area:	21.66ft² (2m²)	16.8ft² (1.6m²)
Working pressure:		
Original:	100lbf/in² (6.9bar)	170lbf/in² (11.7bar)
Later:	115lbf/in² (7.9bar)	
Valve gear:	Gooch stationary link	Gooch stationary link
Weight in working order:	35.5 tons	36 tons

One member of the class, *LORD OF THE ISLES*, was preserved at Swindon, from 1884, and occasionally exhibited. The subject of some controversy, however, the locomotive was scrapped in 1906, together with *NORTH STAR* (Chapter 10).

Anticipating the GWR's 150th anniversary in 1985, the London Science Museum supervised the design and construction of an operable replica of *IRON DUKE*, with assistance from the Friends of the National Railway Museum. It was designed to incorporate the boiler, cylinders, valves and valve gear, crank axle and inside frames of a 1940s-built 'J94'-class tank locomotive. Several dimensional and design compromises were made, the replica thus being a good representation of *IRON DUKE*, rather than an accurate reproduction.

At 4ft 3in (1295mm), the boiler barrel diameter is just over 6in (152mm) less than the original, but its centre line was raised to allow the barrel top to be at the correct height above rail level. The raised boiler made room for the larger than original crank webs. A new smokebox, chimney, saddle and boiler support brackets were fabricated. Modification to the front tube plate and work on the firebox and cylinders was carried out. The modern back head has a manifold serving the whistle, blower, vacuum brake ejector and two boiler-feed injectors, but the plain back head appearance has been preserved by the cladding, only the operating handles being visible.

The sandwich frames were built up from flame-cut steel plates and plywood, and a new drag-box fabricated. Separate steam chests were retained but connected by two 4in (102mm) diameter pipes. The crank axle was cut and

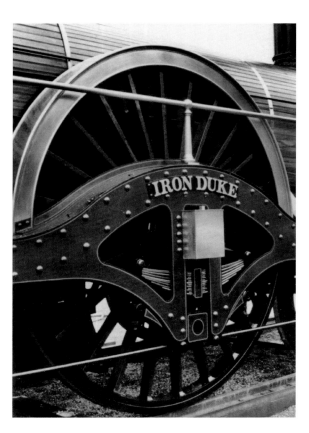

Right-side view of the *IRON DUKE* replica, showing the sandwich frame and springing arrangement for the driving wheel. (Author)

lengthened for the wider gauge. The 8ft (2438mm) diameter driving wheels, with twenty-four rectangular steel spokes, are of new, welded construction. The carrying wheels were adapted from a withdrawn diesel locomotive. Some modification was necessary to reverse the Stephenson valve gear links to the Gooch configuration, which was achieved with little difficulty.

The replica was erected by Resco (Railways) Ltd at its Aylesford, Kent, workshops, whilst the tender was built at the British Railways Cathays workshops in Cardiff. *IRON DUKE* was first publicly steamed in the summer of 1985, on a length of broad gauge track in Hyde Park, London, near the Science Museum. Plans are in hand to base the replica at the Great Western Society's site at Didcot.

JOHN MOLSON 2-2-2
OPERABLE REPLICA AND TENDER

(See p.114 for colour image.) The original *JOHN MOLSON* was constructed in 1849 for the Champlain & Saint Lawrence Rail Road (CSLR) by Kinmond, Hutton & Steel (KHS), probably at its Wallace Works in Dundee, Scotland. Two further locomotives of its type had already been delivered to the Montreal and Lachine Rail Road, and all three came together in 1857 when both companies merged into the Montreal and Champlain Rail Road. *JOHN MOLSON* was named after the influential Montreal brewer (1763–1836), whose son was president of the CSLR. The engine apparently worked until 1874, latterly on the Lachine Division of the Grand Trunk Railway.

Following the establishment of the Canadian Railway Museum by the Canadian Railroad Historical Association (CRHA) in 1961, consideration was given to designing and building an operable replica of an early Canadian locomotive of the pre-1870 era. After due consideration, the *JOHN MOLSON* was favoured for replication, the cost of which was met by Molson's Brewery Ltd of Montreal. It was built adopting modern materials and construction and safety practices, but would be as close a replication of the original as limited information would allow.

With no surviving drawings of the locomotive, considerable research was required to understand the arrangement and component practices of KHS. The CRHA benefited hugely in the 1960s from the assistance provided by William Gordon Small, a talented draughtsman instructor at Alloa Academy in Scotland. He undertook a programme, with assistance from museum personnel in Dundee and Glasgow, to develop a design of the *JOHN MOLSON* that accorded as far as possible with the known facts.

JOHN MOLSON 2-2-2 Operable replica and tender

Built

| 1970 | Kawasaki Heavy Industries Ltd, Kobe (Works No. 3240) and Kyosan Kogyo Co. Ltd, Fukushima (Works No. 291) |

Ownership

| 1971–Present day | The Canadian Railroad Historical Association |

Display

| 1971–Present day | Exporail, The Canadian Railway Museum, Delson, Montreal |

Summary Details

	Original	Replica
Track gauge:	4ft 8½in (1435mm)	4ft 8½in (1435mm)
Driving wheel diameter:	5ft 6in (1676mm)	5ft 6in (1676mm)
Cylinder diameter:	14in (355mm)	13in (330mm)
Piston stroke:	20in (508mm)	18⅞in (480mm)
Boiler length:	10ft 6in (3200mm)	c. 8ft 6in (2591mm)
Boiler diameter:	4ft (1219mm)	4ft (1219mm)
Total heating surface:	c. 650ft² (60.45m²)	570.5ft² (53m²)
Valve gear:	Gooch stationary link	
Weight in working order:	c. 23 tonnes	

The debate during the design stage was whether the locomotive had been built as a 2-2-2 or a 4-2-2. It was concluded that it was built as the former, but may have been subsequently modified with the longer wheelbase due to difficulties on the CSLR's early track.

Gordon Small prepared working and arrangement drawings for the project, and these were finalised following discussions with Kawasaki Heavy Industries Ltd, of Kobe, which had been selected to construct the locomotive and tender.

JOHN MOLSON is an outside cylinder locomotive with an inside frame and bearings, and the trailing axle behind the firebox. A welded steel boiler and firebox was fabricated and steel tubes adopted. Although made to the original 4ft (1219mm) diameter, the boiler's length was reduced by about 2ft (609mm). The reduction in length may have been attributed to the selection of the three-axle design. The cylinder bore and stroke were both reduced as the design sought to compensate for the shorter boiler.

Two steam injectors were adopted instead of feed pumps, and a dial pressure gauge was fitted to the back head. It has a large dome over the centre of the boiler flanked fore and aft by brass funnels housing two modern safety valves. Steel wheels were fabricated by hammer welding. As with IRON DUKE, the original Gooch stationary link valve gear was replicated.

JOHN MOLSON usually operates during the summer months at the Delson museum site in Montreal.

THE AMERICAN 4-4-0 TYPE 1840s

The varying standards of early American railroad track led to locomotive development that was quite different from those employed on the more expensive and robust track of the European railways. The need for increased power during the 1840s, with larger boilers and fireboxes, in turn gave need for the growing weight of locomotives to be spread over four axles. The 'single driver' designs (Chapter 15) gave way to two coupled driving wheelsets with 'equalising' spring beams that maintained 'three-point contact' to deal with the often undulating track. The beams were a patented innovation of Eastwick & Harrison, the manufacturing company of Philadelphia, Pennsylvania, that made a small number of locomotives in the late 1830s/early 1840s. It later turned its attention to the manufacture of locomotives in Russia.

The American 4-4-0 became a standard type adopted for many years by manufacturers and railroads throughout North America, before the type was considered for European railways. Fortunately, two most interesting early examples of the type have survived, allowing opportunity for a good understanding of component development in this important era in American locomotive manufacturing.

NO. 3 *SHAMOKIN* 4-4-0
STATIC ORIGINAL AND TENDER

The history of No. 3, the earliest surviving 4-4-0, is little known. Its design was derived from an 1839-built locomotive, named *GOWAN AND MARX*, constructed for the Philadelphia & Reading Rail Road Co. (PRR) by Eastwick & Harrison. In a trial run in 1840, this locomotive hauled a 101-car train of 423 tons on the 50-mile (80km) route between Reading and Philadelphia.

Encouraged by this success, the railroad ordered more than a dozen similar locomotives, albeit with a wheelbase increased from 10ft (3000mm) to 14ft 10in

(4500mm). At least two were built by Eastwick & Harrison and delivered in the autumn of 1842. The remainder were built both by the 'Proprietors of Locks and Canals on Merrimack River', of Lowell, Massachusetts, and by the New Castle Manufacturing Company of New Castle, Delaware.

No. 3 is thought to be one of these locomotives, built in 1843. It may, however, have been one of the Eastwick & Harrison pair, but evidence is lacking. It is also thought that it may have been the locomotive known as *SHAMOKIN*, after the Pennsylvania town of that name. However the paperwork in the archives of the Franklin Institute, Philadelphia, where the locomotive is now exhibited, suggest that other names may have been applied to the locomotive at other times, namely *ROTATION*, *CONESTOGA* and *WHIPPERWILL*.

It is likely that the locomotive was sold by the PRR to an industrial concern in the mid-century. In 1873 it was purchased by the Peoples' Railway of Pottsville, Pennsylvania, that operated a 4½-mile (7.2km) route between Pottsville and Minersville. It operated as the railway's No. 3, and,

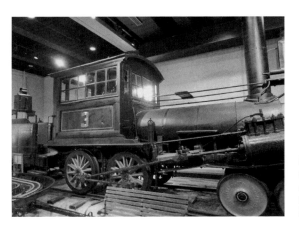

Preserved No. 3 (*Shamokin*) displayed at the Franklin Institute, Philadelphia. (Daderot, licensed via Wikimedia)

Footplate view of No. 3 (*Shamokin*), showing the extended rectangular firebox base and original firebox crown. (John Glithero)

beams, the fulcra of which bear onto leaf-spring sets slung beneath the frame. The lever pins on the beams bear directly onto the axle boxes.

The leading truck has been replaced, probably in the late 1840s or 1850s. Its solid cast-iron replacement wheels, 30in (762mm) in diameter, were cast by A. Whitney & Sons of Philadelphia, whose foundry was established in 1846.

The outside cylinders, sloping down at 9 degrees, are bolted to the frames and smokebox sides using brackets. The drive to the rear axle is achieved with long piston and connecting rods. The six-sided slide bars are hollow, and also serve as boiler feed pumps driven at the rear by the crossheads.

The locomotive was originally fitted with separate cut-off valves above the main valves similar to the Norris Company's 'riding' valves (Chapter 12). The original deep steam chests survive, with the upper stuffing box openings being plugged.

The surviving valve gear is in the form of two-position (forward and reverse) linked gabs, giving a fixed cut-off. The gabs are under the footplate, the motion being driven by short backward facing eccentric rods from two pairs of fixed-eccentrics on the rear axle. The valve spindles reaching to the rear of the locomotive are remarkable in being more than 12ft (3660mm) long.

although it was seldom used in later years, it was retained until 1923 when the PRR reacquired it with some of the line's other rolling stock. In October 1933, the PRR made No. 3 available for display at the Franklin Institute in Philadelphia, together with its earlier locomotive, *ROCKET* (Chapter 11).

The locomotive is a fine example of 1840s design and construction practice, representing the transition between the small-grate Bury firebox types of the late 1830s (Chapter 11), and the large firebox, longer wheelbase types of the late 1840s.

The firebox is a main feature of the locomotive. Whereas the Bury firebox provided a small grate area, suitable for wood, soft coal or coke, No. 3 and its sister locomotives were originally fitted with a firebox which was oval in plan to provide for an increase in grate area to about 11ft^2 (1m^2). Of particular interest, however, is the modification made to the firebox at a later stage to enable it to burn high-calorific anthracite.

The lower part of the original firebox has been replaced by a rectangular box, whose interior length is no less than 4ft 8½in (1435mm) between the tube plate and back plate. The rear wrapper plates of the original firebox have been 'opened out' to form the two side wrapper plates, with a new back plate being fitted. The area of this replacement grate is just under 14ft^2 (1.3m^2).

No. 3 has a frame made from lengths of 3¾in (95mm) wide timber, the 9¾in (247mm) height of which is increased by ½in (12mm) deep wrought-iron straps above and below. The driving wheels are fitted with cast-iron equalising

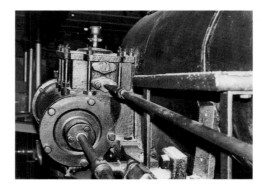

Left-side forward-facing view of No. 3 (*Shamokin*), showing cylinder and steam chest with main valve rod and plugged upper stuffing box. (Peter Davidson)

Underside forward-facing view under the footplate of No. 3 (*Shamokin*), showing backwards-facing eccentric rods from fixed-eccentrics on the rear axle, and two-position linked gabs. (Author)

In 1893, accompanied by *ALBION*, the mine's 1854-built locomotive, *Samson* returned to Chicago for exhibition at the World's Columbian Exposition. At the close of the exposition they remained in the city with other historic locomotives on exhibition in the Field Museum. In 1904 *Samson* and *ALBION* joined the Baltimore & Ohio Railroad's (B&O) collection which was exhibited at the Louisiana Purchase Exposition in St Louis, Missouri, before being moved into long-term storage in Martinsburg, West Virginia.

In 1927 both locomotives were again exhibited, at the B&O's 'Fair of the Iron Horse' centennial celebrations. Through the lobbying of Stewart Gibson, an engineer of Halifax, Nova Scotia, with the assistance of the Province's Prime Minister, the B&O agreed to return the locomotives. They were formally handed over to the province in 1928 and put on open display outside the Canadian National Railway Station in Halifax where *Samson*'s condition deteriorated. *Samson* was later moved to a less conspicuous part of the station, but by 1950 it was returned to Stellarton to undergo restoration. It was then displayed under inadequate cover in nearby New Glasgow where its condition further deteriorated.

In 1990, the setting up of the province's Museum of Industry in Stellarton saw *Samson* and *ALBION* transferred into a new museum building and in 1992 a comprehensive survey, with recommendations for conservation, was undertaken by the author and John Glithero. It revealed important detail about design and manufacturing practices, and subsequent maintenance practice during the nineteenth century. The resulting work carried out by the museum has conserved both locomotives to museum exhibition standard.

Despite its chequered career in preservation, with the loss of some components and damage to others, *Samson* has survived in remarkably good condition. Much of the original material has survived, but there have been some component modifications. Although the configuration has been altered, *Samson* reveals a remarkable conservatism on Hackworth's part, the simplicity of its design changing little since *Royal George* and *Sans Pareil*, built a decade earlier (Chapter 6). It retains vertical cylinders over the driving axle, Freemantle parallel motion and no frames. It also has six wheels with their distinctive two-piece cast design, including some locally cast replacements.

The boiler is remarkable on two counts. Firstly it retains a return flue, which tapers from 25in (635mm) diameter at the grate to 19in (483mm) at the exit. Secondly, it has an extraordinary back plate much of which is set 2ft 6in (762mm) inside the barrel. The dome, however, with its regulator valve, sits over the rear of the barrel. To accommodate this backwards extension of the pressure vessel, the specially forged upper part of the back plate was

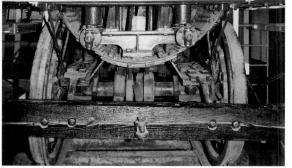

Above: Interior, rear-facing view of the boiler of *Samson*, showing the exterior of the return flue.

Left: Rear view of *Samson*, showing the 'duck's tail' pressure vessel within the boiler barrel, and the rear boiler brackets, together with the steam pipes and regulator handle, valve motion and boiler feed pumps. (Author)

cantilevered back in the form of a 'duck's tail'. Holes cut out of the barrel beyond the back plate allowed the rear axle driven eccentric rods to operate the valve gear and boiler feed pumps, and allowed the steam pipes passage to the cylinders.

At first it was thought that *Samson's* boiler may have been repositioned away from a more 'balanced' central position. However, subsequent research has revealed that it is most likely to have been built with the surviving configuration. The boiler is of 'long-plate' rather than concentric-ring construction, this practice persisting in the north-east of England until the mid-nineteenth century. The locomotive was one of the last to be built with vertical cylinders and retains its original compact 'Freemantle' type parallel motion, examples of which Hackworth had adopted on his locomotives since *Royal George*. The 'V'-hook gab gear is set up vertically above the driving axle and driven by four fixed-eccentrics on the latter, but the valve gear was unfortunately damaged during preservation, doubtless through ill-considered movement whilst the motion was engaged.

The chimney, sitting on top of a crude external 'smokebox', is a mid-life adaptation, but the boiler front plate still shows the fixing points for the original off-centre chimney. Some of the lower boiler plates and the fire tube have been replaced, but most of the boiler is original. One plate carries a 'Low Moor' stamped mark, evidence of its origin at Low Moor in Yorkshire, the iron from which was of high quality, particularly suited to boilers. A curious feature is the routing of the exhaust pipe through the inside of the boiler, emerging just behind the chimney.

The axle boxes and horns are much as made, supporting the original front and middle boiler brackets, although the springs are now in poor order. The rear, springless brackets are of a different pattern.

Front view of *Samson*, with smoke box removed, showing the fire grate within the flue tube (left), and the exit to the chimney (right) revealing stress cracks and patching above and below. (Author)

Samson 0-6-0 Static original without tenders

Built

1838	T. Hackworth, Soho Works, Shildon, Co. Durham

Ownership

1839–71	General Mining Association (GMA), London
1871–93	GMA Limited, London
1893–1900	GMA Ltd, on loan to Field Museum, Chicago, Illinois
1900–04	Nova Scotia Steel Co., on loan to Field Museum, Chicago
1904–28	*de facto* B&O Railroad
1928–90	Province of Nova Scotia
1990–96	Museum of Industry, Stellarton, Nova Scotia
1996–Present day	Province of Nova Scotia

Display

1885–93	Stellarton, Nova Scotia (in store)
1893–1904	Field Museum, Chicago, Illinois
1904–28	B&O depot, Martinsburg, West Virginia (in store)
1928–50	Plinth outside CNR Station, Halifax, Nova Scotia
1950–90	Plinth at New Glasgow, Nova Scotia
1990–95	Museum of Industry, Stellarton, Nova Scotia (in store)
1995–Present day	Museum of Industry, Stellarton, Nova Scotia

Summary Details

Track gauge:	4ft 8in (1422mm)
Driving wheel diameter:	4ft (1219mm)
Cylinder diameter:	15in (381mm)
Piston stroke:	16½in (419mm)
Boiler length:	13ft 4in (4064mm)
Boiler diameter:	4ft 4in (3121mm)
Fire tube heating surface:	*c.* 140ft² (13m²)
Grate area:	*c.* 6.75ft² (0.63m²)
Original working pressure:	*c.* 70lbf/in² (4.8bar)
Valve gear:	Gab gear
Tare weight:	18 tons

A water tender at the rear and a coal tender at the front would have been supplied in 1838, but latter-day service photographs show a replacement combined tender at the front. This no longer survives but, about 1950, a replica tender was made to represent this latter vehicle. This is no longer displayed with the locomotive.

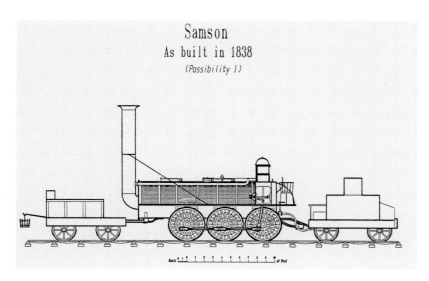

Speculative drawing of *Samson* showing its probable operating arrangement, based on the archaeological survey conducted in 1992. (John Glithero)

NELSON 0-6-0
INCOMPLETE ORIGINAL WITHOUT TENDER

(See p.116 for colour images.) *Nelson* was known for many years as 'Braddyll', but recent research concluded that the former name is more likely to have been carried. It appears to have been constructed around 1839, but the builder is unknown. It seems to have operated from East Hetton Colliery in County Durham, apparently hauling coal trains to Hartlepool over the Hartlepool Dock & Railway's line, which was taken over by the York, Newcastle & Berwick Railway in 1846. *Nelson* was then apparently moved by the East Hetton Coal Company to its sister South Hetton Colliery. Its coal was shipped out through Seaham Harbour and Sunderland, for which purpose the locomotive was probably employed in marshalling wagons for the steep 'Stony Cut' descent to Seaham Harbour.

Nelson was substantially rebuilt, including a new boiler, in about 1853–54, from which date the South Hetton coal was partially shipped to Sunderland via the new Londonderry Railway. It was probably set aside during the 1860s/early 1870s. In 1876 the South Hetton Coal Company converted it into an unpowered vehicle, to which was fitted a number of large iron sheets in the form of a snowplough. Its cylinders, motion and boiler fittings

were apparently removed at this time. It remained as a standby snowplough at South Hetton for a number of years before being abandoned in a siding there. That it was not scrapped may have been due to the interest of two generations of the Coulthard family who, as the colliery's engineers, were instrumental in the longevity of several other locomotives.

Nelson came to notice in December 1919 when *The Locomotive* magazine published a photograph of it at South Hetton. The accompanying article stated that 'the engine bore the name "Nelson" and the number 2 on the panel plate', but there is no longer any evidence of this and there are no further references to the use of the name or number.

The vehicle remained in the open at South Hetton until the coal industry was nationalised in 1947. The new National Coal Board (NCB) considered scrapping it at a time of austerity, with scrap iron at a premium price. A successful campaign to save it was conducted by members of the Stephenson Locomotive Society, and the NCB arranged, in October that year, to move it to the Philadelphia Engine Works at Lambton, County Durham. This was for 'posterity' and 'to bring to the attention of the many visitors to these shops the historical association between coal and the railways.'

The vehicle remained on display on a plinth outside the works for 25 years, labelled as 'Braddyll', but no explanation was provided for the name. In 1973, the NCB closed the works and the vehicle was acquired by Shildon Rural District Council (Sedgefield District Council from 1975), and moved to the town where it was stored in a council yard.

The Timothy Hackworth Victorian and Railway Museum was established in Shildon in 1975, in buildings associated with Hackworth. In 1978 *Nelson* was moved to a length of track outside the museum's newly restored 'Soho Shed'. It was moved inside the shed in 1994, the first time for at least 120 years that it had been under cover.

In 1996 a thorough conservation programme was carried out on *Nelson* by the author and John Glithero. It was slurry-blast cleaned to remove years of accumulated tar which had been used to preserve it, together with dirt and rust. Taken down to bare metal, the ironwork was then chemically conserved to protect it from further deterioration and afterwards painted with under and top coats. Although the lower boiler barrel plates had become badly corroded, the locomotive otherwise remains in remarkably good condition, in spite of its long exposure to the elements. The adopted livery was pale green, with orange detailing, which matched that of paintwork uncovered during the conservation programme.

A survey of *Nelson*'s remains, undertaken prior to conservation, was supplemented by further discoveries revealed during the work. It was thus

Interior rear-facing view of *Nelson*'s boiler before restoration, showing the semi-cylindrical firebox with its elliptical crown. (Author)

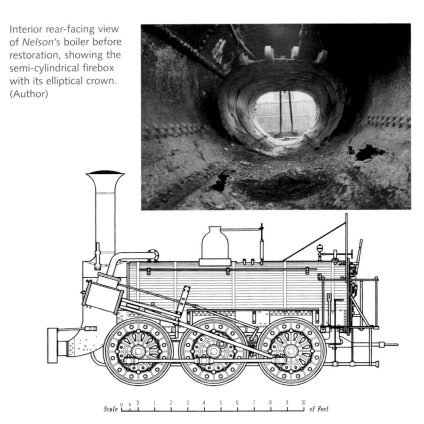

Speculative drawing of *Nelson* showing its probable operating arrangement, based on the archaeological survey conducted during its restoration programme. (John Glithero)

Nelson 0-6-0 Incomplete original without tender

Built

Late 1830s/1853–4	Possibly built/rebuilt by Fossick & Hackworth, Stockton-on-Tees

Ownership

Late 1830s/1840s–1947	South Hetton Coal Co.
1947–73	National Coal Board
1973–75	Shildon Rural District Council
1975–2008	Sedgefield District Council
2008–12	National Museum of Science and Industry (Accession No. 2008-7058)
2012–Present day	Science Museum Group

Display

1948–73	NCB Engine Works, Philadelphia, Co. Durham (on plinth)
1973–78	Shildon Rural District Council (in store)
1978–2005	Timothy Hackworth Victorian & Railway Museum, Shildon
2005–Present day	Locomotion Museum, Shildon, Co. Durham

Summary Details

Track gauge:	4ft 8½in (1435mm)
Driving wheel diameter:	4ft (1219mm)
Piston stroke:	20in (508mm)
Boiler length:	13ft 6in (4115mm)
Boiler diameter:	4ft 2in (1270mm)

possible to develop an understanding of its likely appearance in its last years as a working locomotive. The conservation revealed remarkable patching work on both the boiler barrel and firebox which allowed the locomotive to continue operation beyond its normal working life, but no doubt restricted to reduced pressure.

Like *Samson*, *Nelson* has no frame, the boiler brackets being fitted to the tops of the axle boxes, albeit in a different form from that used on the former. The leading brackets protrude beyond the front of the boiler, indicating that it is a shorter replacement for the original. The boiler is a survivor of an unusual design patented in 1847, its firebox being semi-cylindrical with an elliptical crown. The patent was taken out by George Fossick, Thomas Hackworth and Thomas Elliot of Stockton-on-Tees. Thomas Hackworth,

brother of Timothy, had formed a partnership with Fossick to start up an engineering works in the town in 1840.

The boiler barrel, like *Samson*'s, is of 'long-plate' construction, two of the plates running the full length of the boiler. These are 13ft 3in (403mm) long and 3ft 4in (1016mm) wide, rolling-mills for which did not become available until the mid-late 1840s. The firebox plates are seam-riveted with the seam protruding into the water space. This so-called 'anti-collapsive seam' was patented by Daniel Adamson (1820–90) in 1852, an indication of *Nelson*'s rebuilding after that year. The assembly was closed at the bottom by a longitudinal plate under the fire grate.

Nelson remains on display in the Soho Shed at Shildon, ownership having been transferred from the local authority to the National Collection in 2008.

ETHERLEY
WATER TENDER ONLY FROM 'TORY' CLASS 0-6-0

This wooden-framed vehicle first came to notice in 1923 when it was owned by the Forcett Limestone Company of County Durham. Prompted by Mr R. Miller, the newly formed London & North Eastern Railway negotiated to acquire the tender for inclusion in its museum planned for establishment at York when anticipating the centenary of the Stockton & Darlington Railway (SDR).

The museum committee recorded that the tender had been made for the SDR's No. 17, *WHIG*. However, the museum subsequently believed that it had been attached to No. 18 in the SDR fleet, named *ETHERLEY* after the colliery at that location which was served by the railway. It had been made at William Lister's works in Darlington in 1840. Neither claim could be substantiated but, in any case, tenders were readily exchanged between locomotives.

The tender was exhibited at the Queen Street Museum in York, from its opening in 1925 until its closure 50 years later. It was then transferred to the North of England Open Air Museum in Beamish, County Durham, before being sent to the Timothy Hackworth Victorian and Railway Museum at Shildon.

In 1994, the author of this volume and John Glithero undertook a survey of the tender, which was written up in a report to the museum. The tender is of similar size, layout and construction as that coupled to *DERWENT* (p.190). The rectangular water tank is made of lap-riveted wrought-iron plate. It is surmounted by a cube-shaped filling box. Although it is now kept under

Underside forward-facing view of the *Etherley* tender, showing the wooden frame and un-sprung drawbar. (Author)

cover in the Soho Shed at Shildon, it had been left outside for long periods and some parts of its wooden frame have deteriorated badly in consequence.

Other parts of the substantial frame, through which passes the unsprung drawbar, have been largely protected by the tank. The tender is placed on four 2ft 6in (762mm) diameter cast-iron wheels fitted to wrought-iron axles.

Preserved tender from *Etherley* displayed at the Locomotion Museum, Shildon, County Durham. The pre-restored *Nelson* can be seen in the background. (Author)

Etherley Water tender only from *Tory* class 0-6-0

Built

1840	William Lister, Darlington

Ownership

1840–?	Stockton & Darlington Railway
?–1925	Forcett Limestone Company
1925–48	London & North Eastern Railway
1948–62	British Transport Commission
1963–81	British Railways Board
1981–2012	National Museum of Science and Industry (Accession No. 1981–426)
2012–Present day	Science Museum Group

Display

1925–75	Queen Street Museum, York
1975–81	North of England Open Air Museum, Beamish, Co. Durham
1981–2005	Timothy Hackworth Victorian and Railway Museum, Shildon
2005–Present day	Locomotion Museum, Shildon, Co. Durham

HACKWORTH TYPE LOCOMOTIVE
SURVIVING 'HACKWORTH' SAFETY VALVE

In addition to the safety valve attributed to the 1828-built 'Royal George' (Chapter 6), a second 'Hackworth' type safety valve survives in the British National Collection. Its provenance is unknown, but it is likely to date from the late 1830s. Both valves were loaned to the Timothy Hackworth Museum in Shildon from 1994, returning to the NRM stewardship on the opening of the town's Locomotion Museum in 2004. This later valve is now the token for the annual 'John Coiley' award for locomotive preservation administered by the UK's Heritage Railway Association.

Surviving example of a Hackworth safety valve in the collection of the National Railway Museum, York. (Science and Society Picture Library)

Hackworth type safety valve	Late 1830s
Built	
Late 1830s	Not known
Ownership	
1830s–1863	Probably Stockton & Darlington Railway
1863–1923	North Eastern Railway
1923–47	London & North Eastern Railway
1948–62	British Transport Commission
1962–75	British Railways Board
1975–2012	National Museum of Science and Industry (Accession No. 1978-7348)
2012–Present day	Science Museum Group
Display	
1928–75	York Railway Museum
1975–94	National Railway Museum, York
1994–2003	Timothy Hackworth Victorian and Railway Museum, Shildon
2004–Present day	Locomotion Museum, Shildon

DERWENT 0-6-0
STATIC ORIGINAL WITH WATER AND COAL TENDERS

DERWENT, the best preserved example of a locomotive of the Hackworth 'school', was built in 1845 by Alfred Kitching (1808–82) of Hopetown Foundry in Darlington. Established in 1790, the foundry was taken over by the brothers William and Alfred Kitching, who expanded the site for locomotive building, commencing in 1835. William Kitching had withdrawn from the partnership by the time of *DERWENT*'s construction.

It was delivered to the Stockton & Darlington Railway (SDR), who gave it the running number 25. Like *ETHERLEY*, it was one of the *Tory* class built between 1838 and 1845, to Timothy Hackworth's arrangement. The locomotive was probably named after the River Derwent, or the nearby Derwent Colliery, or even the Derwent Iron Company, forerunner of the large Consett Ironworks. *DERWENT* worked on the SDR line until 1868 (North Eastern Railway from 1863) when it was sold to the Pease family business, who employed it at the Pease's West Colliery in Crook, part of their extensive colliery activities in County Durham.

Preserved *DERWENT* and tenders displayed at Head of Steam, the Darlington Railway Museum. (Author)

Interior rearward-facing view inside *DERWENT*'s flue tube, showing the fire grate and the 'anti-collapsive' seams. (Author)

Interior view of the trailing end of *DERWENT*'s flue tube, showing the dished-end combustion chamber where the gases were returned through a flue tube cluster, saddle-backed over the fire tube to the leading end. (John Glithero)

In 1925, it was taken into the North Road, Darlington, workshops of the London & North Eastern Railway (successor to the NER) and prepared for operation, in steam, at the SDR centenary celebrations in the town. Under subsequent test between Stockton and Darlington, *DERWENT* was stated to have achieved 12mph (19.3kph), but no performance data is known to have been written up from these test runs.

It was returned to the Bank Top plinth and remained there for the next 50 years, save for several weeks in the North Road workshops for restoration in the spring of 1961. In 1975, *DERWENT* and *LOCOMOTION* were transferred into the newly opened Darlington Railway Museum in the historic North Road Station, where they remain on display.

DERWENT appears to be largely unmodified, and is a splendid example of SDR motive power between the 1830s and 1870s. No comprehensive survey of the locomotive has been carried out, although a measured drawing was prepared some years ago by Alan Prior and, in 1994, the author of this volume and John Glithero surveyed the fire tube, combustion chamber and flue tubes, to determine their method of construction and heating surface.

The lower part of the boiler is fitted with a 29½in (749mm) diameter fire tube, containing the fire grate at its leading end. A dished-end combustion chamber at the trailing end turns back into a flue tube cluster which is saddle-backed over the fire tube to return the gases to the leading end. A saddle-shaped smokebox is riveted to the front of the boiler.

The fire tube is an in-service replacement which, like that for *Nelson*, is of Daniel Adamson's 1852 'anti-collapsive seam' patent design. It is formed of four wrought-iron circumferential plates, whose riveted flanges in the water space are separated by iron rings, the whole being closed at the bottom by a longitudinal plate.

A large steam dome, lagged with wood, stands on a boiler top plinth. From its rear face is led an exposed, and peculiarly inefficient, external steam pipe serving a manifold. This incorporated a regulator valve from which two steam pipes fed the cylinders. Just forward of the dome is a manhole, in advance of which are two ornate safety valve columns and Salter spring balances. The wrought-iron chimney is a fine example of SDR practice, but it is not known if any of the boiler top features are original or have been replicated during *DERWENT*'s 'restorations'.

Like *Samson* and *Nelson*, the locomotive has no frame, the boiler being supported by six U-shaped wrought-iron brackets, riveted to the boiler waist plates and bolted to the horn assemblies. The steel leaf-springs are fitted through the brackets, the hangers also being bolted to the horn assemblies.

The locomotive was already considered a venerable survivor in 1881 when the Pease concern made it available for the George Stephenson Centenary event in Newcastle-Upon-Tyne. On its retirement in 1898, Messrs Pease & Partners donated *DERWENT* back to the North Eastern Railway (NER), who accepted it for long-term preservation and display, and placed it on a plinth at Bank Top Station, Darlington, alongside *LOCOMOTION* (Chapter 3).

EMPEROR was replaced in 1880. One of its plates was acquired privately in 1892, but later found its way back into railway ownership and subsequently into the National Collection (accession No. 1986-8234).

SULTAN was replaced in 1876. One of its nameplates, and possibly both, was obtained by Joseph Wilkinson, later general manager of the GWR. The surviving plate passed to the National Collection and is displayed at the National Railway Museum in York (accession No. 1975-7661). A surviving plaque (accession No. 1999-7525), displayed with the nameplate, suggests that the locomotive had only been reboilered in 1876 and that by the time it was withdrawn in 1892 it had operated nearly 1.49 million miles.

Seven more of the class were completed in 1848, but the whereabouts of only three of these are known about:

TARTAR was rebuilt in 1876 and at least one of the nameplates was sold privately in 1892. Its present whereabouts, and that of the second plate are unknown.

WARLOCK was also rebuilt in 1876. One of the nameplates was acquired privately in 1892, but subsequently found its way into the National Collection (accession No. 1986-8238). The other plate was also acquired privately and remained in private hands until acquired by the Stephenson Locomotive Society in 1920. It was on the wall of the Society's headquarters for some years, but its present whereabouts are unknown.

One of the nameplates of *HIRONDELLE* was apparently sold in 1892. The locomotive had been replaced in 1873 and withdrawn in 1890. It is now owned by the Somerset Archaeological and National History Society and displayed in the Museum of Somerset in Taunton.

Three more members of the class were completed in 1849, and at least two of the nameplates survive.

TORNADO was not replaced until 1888 and was the last member of the *Rover* class to be completed. One of its nameplates was acquired privately but later found its way into the National Collection (accession No. 1986-8239). As with *WARLOCK*, however, the other plate, also acquired privately, remained privately owned until acquired by the Stephenson Locomotive Society in 1920. Its present whereabouts are again unknown.

At least one of the nameplates from *SWALLOW* was acquired by Col Edgcumbe, a director of the railway. It is unknown if it survives.

A further four members of the class were built in 1850.

PROMETHEUS was again replaced as late as 1888. One nameplate, at least, was acquired privately in 1892, but again later found its way into the National Collection (accession No. 1986-8244).

PERSEUS continued in service, without replacement by a *Rover*-class locomotive, until 1891. At least one nameplate was sold privately and is now owned by the Somerset Archaeological and Natural History Society, and is displayed in the Somerset Museum in Taunton.

ROVER was the first locomotive to be replaced, in 1871, and thus gave its name to the new class. Both its nameplates were acquired in 1892 by Charles Mortimer, a GWR director. One at least of its plates remains in private ownership.

Other plates, from the post-1851 built locomotives, are retained and displayed at the National Railway Museum, York, the Steam Museum in Swindon and the Bristol Industrial Museum.

19

CONCLUSION

This book has sought to identify the surviving pre-1850 locomotives and components around the world and to discuss them through description, illustration and comparison. Considerable care has been taken to ensure the completeness of this review, but there is clearly the possibility that other components may have survived which are preserved in private or reserve collections and have escaped notice. The author would welcome knowledge of such artefacts, accompanied by provenance details and primary reference sources wherever possible. In the event that a reprint of the volume is proceeded with, they will of course be included.

Several themes are revealed by these comprehensive studies which it is hoped will be as much of interest to museum curatorial teams, who have inherited these prize artefacts, as to the wider readership. It is clear that, over many years, curatorial standards of preservation and conservation have varied enormously. Whilst some locomotives have been very well cared for, in some cases for a century and a half, others have deteriorated through lack of care, and some are lucky to have survived at all. Others, intended for long-term display were not so lucky and have been lost through neglect, indifference or wartime misfortune.

It is hoped that this book will focus attention on this international collection and provide museums with the context in which to place their locomotive collections, and their relationship to the other collections in other parts of the world. It is further hoped that this contextual aid will allow museums to encourage visitors with an interest in locomotive and engineering history. This will, in turn, encourage a greater understanding of the machines that offered such transport progress in the rapidly changing world of the first half of the nineteenth century.

The inclusion of operable replicas in these pages may be controversial to some readers, but they are justified when providing continuity to the story of locomotive design evolution by 'filling in the gaps'. Each replica is the product of a project requiring considerable research and understanding of the design philosophy, materials and construction methods of the original examples. We all stand to benefit from the fruits of this work, providing that the projects are concluded with a written record of all that has been learned. Sadly, this discipline has not always been pursued, and the knowledge is at risk of being lost to future generations.

Operable replicas have been shown to vary enormously in the accuracy of their design, and standard of manufacture and operation. This reflects changing opportunities for material selection, and strengthening attitudes by responsible public authorities towards increased safety requirements. This has arisen over the years both from greater safety awareness and the rise in litigious concerns. Comparison between the earliest replicas of the nineteenth century using materials largely similar to their original models, and the latest twenty-first century replicas reveals increasing need for compromise. Replicas may be judged as much by the standard of compromise as their portrayal of the original locomotives.

Readers will have gained an insight into the work of the men who designed, developed, manufactured, operated and maintained the earliest examples of locomotive power. Their growing skills, and the development of material and manufacturing technology, form a case study of engineering progress through the first half of the century. Other engineering sectors, including mining, marine and manufacturing technologies benefited from, and contributed to, their work. With the space available in a volume of this nature, the major improvements that were achieved could only be referred to briefly. The author is pleased to acknowledge fully the work of authors who have written comprehensively about specific locomotives, and encourages readers to take advantage of the bibliography. For those readers encouraged to learn more about engineering history, membership of Newcomen, the International Society for the History of Engineering and Technology, may well be rewarding.

There has always been a keen interest in locomotive technology, accompanied by a sentiment to preserve important examples of those early years, and to recreate examples of lost types. It is sobering to realise that the first locomotive to be preserved (*Invicta* – Chapter 5) was held back from scrapping as early as 1839, when many of the subjects in this book were yet to be built. It is also sobering to reflect that the age of recreation began as early as 1852 with the 'Hetton' locomotive (Chapter 3) built to lay retrospective claim to Nicholas Wood's role in the origins of steam railway development.

It has to be acknowledged that the story can only partially be told through these surviving and recreated examples. There are many other types which played important roles in the development strides of those first 50 years. There are gaps yet to be filled, which would add further to our understanding of component development. Operable replicas of groundbreaking locomotives such as an 1812 Blenkinsop type (Chapter 2), or an 1840s *JENNY LIND* (2-2-2) type from Britain, would fill important gaps, as would replicas fitted with currently unrepresented valve gears such as those early examples by Egide Walschaert (1820–1901) in Belgium, or David Joy (1825–1903) in Britain. There would be much to be learnt from unrepresented types from the early American manufacturers, such as Baldwins of Philadelphia, including a 'Camel' type 0-8-0 heavy haulage locomotive. The choices are many, and it is hoped that this volume will play a small part in inspiring project teams to follow up on this potential.

Appendix

MUSEUMS DISPLAYING PRE-1850 LOCOMOTIVES, COMPONENTS AND REPLICAS

Before making arrangements to visit any museum, readers are advised to determine their opening days and times. Also, visitors wishing to see specific locomotives should contact the museums concerned in advance to confirm whether they are currently on exhibition, or have been moved elsewhere on temporary loan. Contact details are correct up to March 2013.

British Isles

BEAMISH

BEAMISH, THE LIVING MUSEUM OF THE NORTH
Beamish, County Durham, DH9 0RG
Tel: (+44) (0)191 370 4000
http://www.beamish.org.uk/
Locomotives: *Puffing Billy* (replica) – (Chapter 2)
Steam Elephant (replica) – (Chapter 2)
'Hetton' locomotive (replica) – (Chapter 3)
LOCOMOTION (replica) – (Chapter 3)

BRIDGNORTH

c/o Severn Valley Railway
Hollybush Rd., Bridgnorth WV16 5DT
Tel: (+44) (0)1746 765 801
http://www.catchmewhocan.org.uk/news.html
Locomotive: *CATCH ME WHO CAN* (replica) – (Chapter 1)

CANTERBURY

CANTERBURY HERITAGE MUSEUM
Stour Street, Canterbury, CT1 2NR
Tel: (+44) (0)1227 475 202
http://www.canterbury.co.uk/thedms.
aspx?dms=13&venue=3030489
Locomotive: *Invicta* – (Chapter 5)

CORK

KENT RAILWAY STATION – plinth
Locomotive: *No. 36* – (Chapter 11)

DARLINGTON

Head of Steam, **DARLINGTON RAILWAY MUSEUM**
North Road Station, Darlington, County Durham, DL3 6ST
Tel: (+44) (0)1325 460 532
http://www.darlington.gov.uk/Leisure/headofsteam/
headofsteam.htm
Locomotives: *LOCOMOTION* – (Chapter 3)
DERWENT – (Chapter 17)

DIDCOT

DIDCOT RAILWAY CENTRE
Didcot, Oxfordshire, OX11 7NJ
Tel: (+44) (0)1235 817 200
http://www.didcotrailwaycentre.org.uk/guide/broadgauge.
html#
Locomotive: *FIRE FLY* (replica) – (Chapter 10)
IRON DUKE (replica) – (Chapter 15)

EDINBURGH

NATIONAL MUSEUM OF SCOTLAND
Chambers Street, Edinburgh, EH1 1JF
Tel: (+44) (0)300 123 6789
http://www.nms.ac.uk/our_museums/national_museum.aspx
Locomotive: *Wylam Dilly* – (Chapter 2)

IRONBRIDGE

IRONBRIDGE GORGE MUSEUMS
Blists Hill, Coach Road, Coalbrookdale, Telford, TF8 7DQ
Tel: (+44) (0)1952 433424
http://www.ironbridge.org.uk/our_attractions/blists_hill_
victorian_town/
Locomotive: The 'Coalbrookdale' Engine (replica) –
(Chapter 1)

LIVERPOOL

MUSEUM OF LIVERPOOL
Pier Head, Liverpool, L3 1DG
Tel: (+44) (0)151 478 4545
http://www.liverpoolmuseums.org.uk/mol/
Locomotive: *LION* – (Chapter 10)

LONDON **THE SCIENCE MUSEUM**
Exhibition Road, South Kensington, London, SW7 2DD
Tel: (+44) (0)027 942 4000
http://www.sciencemuseum.org.uk/
Locomotives: *Puffing Billy* – (Chapter 2)
ROCKET – (Chapter 5)
1868 '*Columbine*' – (Chapter 14)

MANCHESTER **MUSEUM OF SCIENCE AND INDUSTRY** (MOSI)
Liverpool Road, Castlefield, Manchester, M3 4FP
Tel: (+44) (0)161 832 2244
http://www.mosi.org.uk/
Locomotives: *Novelty* (non-operable replica) – (Chapter 6)
PLANET (operable replica) – (Chapter 7)

NEWCASTLE-UPON-TYNE **STEPHENSON RAILWAY MUSEUM**
Middle Engine Lane, North Shields, NE29 8DX
http://www.twmuseums.org.uk/stephenson/
Locomotive: *Billy* – (Chapter 3)

PENRHYN **PENRHYN CASTLE RAILWAY MUSEUM**
Penrhyn Castle, Bangor, Gwynedd LL57 4HN
http://www.nationaltrust.org.uk/penrhyn-castle/
Locomotive: *FIRE QUEEN* – (Chapter 17)

RAINHILL **COMMUNITY LIBRARY**
View Road, Rainhill, Merseyside, L35 0LE
Tel: +44 (0) 1744 677822
Locomotive: *Novelty* (second cylinder) – (Chapter 6)

SHILDON **LOCOMOTION MUSEUM**
Soho Street, Shildon, Co. Durham, DL4 1PQ
Tel: (+44) (0)138 877 7999
http://www.nrm.org.uk/locomotion
Locomotives: *CORNWALL* – 3020 – (Chapter 14)
ROYAL GEORGE (safety valve) – (Chapter 6)
Second Hackworth locomotive (safety valve) – (Chapter 17)
SANS PAREIL (original and replica) – (Chapter 6)
Nelson – (Chapter 17)
(*Etherley*) water tender – (Chapter 17)

SWANSEA **NATIONAL WATERFRONT MUSEUM**
Oystermouth Road, Maritime Quarter, Swansea SA1 3RD
Tel: (+44) (0)292 057 3600
http://www.museumwales.ac.uk/en/swansea/
Locomotive: The '*Penydarren*' Engine (replica) – (Chapter 1)

SWINDON **STEAM: MUSEUM OF THE GREAT WESTERN RAILWAY**
Fire Fly Avenue, Kemble Drive, Swindon, SN2 2TA
Tel: (+44) (0)179 346 6637
http://www.steam-museum.org.uk/
Locomotives: *NORTH STAR* (replica) – (Chapter 10)
GREAT WESTERN (nameplate) – (Chapter 18)
Iron Duke Class (nameplates) – (Chapter 18)

WROUGHTON **SCIENCE MUSEUM AT WROUGHTON**
Red Barn Gate, Wroughton, Swindon, Wiltshire, SN4 9LT
Tel: (+44) (0)207 942 4000
http://www.sciencemuseum.org.uk/wroughton/
Locomotive: *Columbine* (cab and tender only) – (Chapter 14)

YORK **NATIONAL RAILWAY MUSEUM**
Leeman Road, York, YO26 4XJ
Tel: (+44) (0)844 815 3139
http://www.nrm.org.uk/
Locomotives: Middleton Colliery locomotive (replica wheels) – (Chapter 2)
THE AGENORIA – (Chapter 4)
ROCKET (two replicas) – (Chapter 5)
Coppernob – (Chapter 11)
SULTAN (nameplate) – (Chapter 18)
COMET (nameplate) – (Chapter 18)

Continental Europe

BARCELONA **MUSEO DEL FERROCARRIL DE CATALUÑYA** (Catalonia Railway Museum)
Plaza Eduard Maristany, s/n 08800 Vilanova i la Geltrú, Catalonia
Tel: (+34) 938 15 84 91
http://www.museudelferrocarril.org/castellano/mus_presentacion.htm
Locomotive: *MATARÓ* (replica) – (Chapter 14)

BERLIN **DEUTSCHES TECHNIKMUSEUM** (German Technical Museum)
Trebbiner Strasse 9, D-10963, Berlin-Kreuzberg
Tel: (+49) (0)30 / 90 254-0
http://www.sdtb.de/Rail-transport.1148.0.html
Locomotive: *BEUTH* (replica) – (Chapter 12)

BRUSSELS **MUSÉE DES CHEMINS DE FER BELGES** (Museum of Belgian Railways)
Gare de Bruxelles-Nord, Rue du Progrès 76, 1030 Schaerbeek, Bruxelles
Tel: (+32) (0)2 224 62 79
Locomotive: *Pays De Waes* – (Chapter 15)

GÄVLE

SVERIGES JÄRNVÄGSMUSEUM (Swedish Railway Museum)
Rälsgatan 1 802 91 Gävle, Sweden
Tel: (+46) (0)26 14 46 15
http://www.trafikverket.se/Museer/Sveriges-Jarnvagsmuseum-
Gavle/
Locomotive: *Novelty* (operable replica) – (Chapter 6)

LUCERNE

VERKEHRSHAUS DER SCHWEIZ (Swiss Museum of Transport)
Lidostrasse 5, CH-6006, Luzern
Tel: (+41) (0)41 370 44 44
http://www.verkehrshaus.ch/de/museum/
Locomotive: *LIMMAT* (operable replica) – (Chapter 12)

MULHOUSE

CITÉ DU TRAIN, MUSÉE FRANÇAIS DU CHEMIN DE FER
(French Railway Museum)
2, rue Alfred de Glehn, 68 200 Mulhouse
Tel: (0)3 89 42 83 33
http://www.citedutrain.com/en/home
Locomotives: *L'AIGLE* – (Chapter 13)
           SÉZANNE – (Chapter 13)
           ST PIERRE – (Chapter 14)

MUNICH

DEUTSCHES MUSEUM (German Museum)
Museumsinsel 1, 80538 Munich
Tel: (+49) (0)89 / 2179-1
http://www.deutsches-museum.de/en/information/
Locomotive: *Puffing Billy* (Static replica) – (Chapter 2)

NAPLES

IL MUSEO NAZIONALE DI PIETRARSA (The National Railway
Museum of Pietrarsa)
Traversa Pietrarsa, 80146 Naples
Tel: (+39) (0)81 47 20 03
www.fsitaliane.it/cms/v/index.jsp?vgnextoid=7b4195d6f9ff321
0VgnVCM1000003f16f90aRCRD
Locomotive: *BAYARD* (replica) – (Chapter 10)

NÜRNBERG

DEUTSCHE BAHN MUSEUM, part of the
Verkehrsmuseum Nürnberg (Nuremberg Transport Museum)
Lessingstraße 6, D-90443 Nürnberg
Tel: (+49) (0)18 044 422 33
http://www.deutschebahn.com/site/dbmuseum/de/start.html
Locomotives: *ADLER* (static and operable replicas) – (Chapter 7)
           SAXONIA (replica) – (Chapter 11)

ODENSE

DANMARKS JERNBANEMUSEUM (Danish Railway Museum)
Dannebrogsgade 24, DK-5000, Odense C
Tel: (+45) 66 13 66 30
http://www.jernbanemuseet.dk/
Locomotive: *ODIN* (operable replica under construction) –
(Chapter 15)

ST PETERSBURG

CENTRAL MUSEUM OF RAILWAY TRANSPORT OF RUSSIA
50, Sadovaya ul. St Petersburg
Tel: 7(812)168-80-05/ 7(812)315-14-76
http://www.museum.ru/Museum/RAILWAY/museng.htm
Locomotives: *PROVORNY* (¼-scale replica) – (Chapter 10)

UTRECHT

NEDERLANDS SPOORWEGMUSEUM (Dutch Railway Museum)
Maliebaanstation, 3581 XW Utrecht
Tel: 030 2306206
http://www.spoorwegmuseum.nl/home.html
Locomotive: *DE AREND* (Operable replica) – (Chapter 10)

VIENNA

TECHNISCHESMUSEUM WIEN (Vienna Technical Museum),
Mariahilfer Strasse 212, 1140, Wien
Tel: (+43) 1 89998 0
Locomotives: *AJAX* – (Chapter 10)
           STEINBRÜCK – (Chapter 12)

North America

AUGUSTA

MAINE STATE MUSEUM
230 State Street, Augusta, Maine 04330
Tel: (+1) 207 287 2301
http://mainestatemuseum.org/
Locomotive: *LION* – (Chapter 17)

BALTIMORE

B&O RAILROAD MUSEUM
901, West Pratt Street, Baltimore, MD 21223
Tel: (+1) 410 752 2490
http://www.borail.org/
Locomotives: *Stourbridge Lion* (original components) –
           (Chapter 4)
           John Stevens' *Steam Waggon* – (original
           components) – (Chapter 8)
           TOM THUMB (replica) – (Chapter 8)
           ATLANTIC – (Chapter 9)
           JOHN HANCOCK – (Chapter 9)
           LAFAYETTE (replica) – (Chapter 12)
           MEMNON – (Chapter 17)

CHARLESTON

THE BEST FRIEND OF CHARLESTON RAILWAY MUSEUM
The Citadel Mall, 2070 Sam Rittenberg Drive, Charleston,
South Carolina
Tel: Not listed
http://www.bestfriendofcharleston.org/MUSEUM.html
Locomotive: *BEST FRIEND* (operable replica) – (Chapter 8)

CHICAGO

MUSEUM OF SCIENCE AND INDUSTRY
57th Street and Kale Shore Drive, Chicago, IL 60637
Tel: (+1) 773 684 1414
http://www.msichicago.org/
Locomotives: *ROCKET* (replica) – (Chapter 5)
JOHN STEVENS (replica) – (Chapter 8)
YORK (replica) – (Chapter 8)
Mississippi No. 1 – (Chapter 11)

CHICAGO HISTORY MUSEUM
1601 N. Clark Street, Chicago, IL 60614
Tel: (+1) 312 642 4600
http://chicagohistory.org/planavisit/exhibitions/crossroads/
index
Locomotive: *Pioneer* No. 7 – (Chapter 15)

COPIAPÓ

UNIVERSIDAD DE ATACAMA (North Campus),
485 Copayapu Copiapó, Atacama Region, Chile
Tel: (+56) 52 206 500
http://www.uda.cl/
Locomotive: *COPIAPÓ* – (Chapter 12)

DAYTON, OH

CARILLON HISTORICAL PARK
1000, Carillon Boulevard, Dayton, Ohio, 45409
Tel: (+1) 937 293 2841
http://www.daytonhistory.org/contact-us.htm
Locomotive: *JOHN QUINCY ADAMS* – (Chapter 9)

DEARBORN, MI

THE HENRY FORD MUSEUM
20900 Oakwood Blvd., Dearborn, Michigan, 48124-5029
Tel: (+1) 313 982 6001
Locomotives: *ROCKET* (replica) – (Chapter 5)
DE WITT CLINTON (replica) – (Chapter 8)

HAVANA

MUSEO DEL FERROCARRIL CUBANO (Cuba Railway
Museum),
Cristina Arroyo (Cristina Station), Habana Vieja, Havana
Tel: (+53) 07 868 4256
Locomotive: No. 1 *LA JUNTA* – (Chapter 15)

HONESDALE, PA

WAYNE COUNTY HISTORICAL SOCIETY
810 Main Street, Honesdale, Pennsylvania, 18431
Tel: (+1) 570 253 3240
http://www.waynehistorypa.org/
Locomotive: *Stourbridge Lion* (Static replica) – (Chapter 4)

MONTREAL

EXPORAIL, CANADIAN RAILWAY MUSEUM
110, rue Saint-Pierre, Saint-Constant, Montreal, Québec,
J5A 1G7
Tel: (+1) 450 632 2410
http://www.exporail.org/en/welcome-to-exporail/
Locomotives: *JOHN MOLSON* (Operable replica) –
(Chapter 15)
DORCHESTER (nameplate) – (Chapter 18)

PHILADELPHIA

THE FRANKLIN INSTITUTE
222 North 20th Street, Philadelphia, PA 19103
Tel: (+1) 215 448 1200
http://www2.fi.edu/
Locomotives: *ROCKET* – (Chapter 11)
No. 3 (*Shamokin*) – (Chapter 16)

STRASBURG

RAILROAD MUSEUM OF PENNSYLVANIA
P. O. Box 15, Strasburg, PA 17579
Tel: (+1) 717 687 8628
http://www.rrmuseumpa.org/
Locomotive: *JOHN BULL* (Operable replica) – (Chapter 7)
JOHN STEVENS (Static replica) – (Chapter 8)

STELLARTON

MUSEUM OF INDUSTRY
147 North Foord Street, Stellarton, Nova Scotia, Canada
Tel: (+1) 902 755 5425
http://museum.gov.ns.ca/moi/en/home/default.aspx
Locomotive: *Samson* – (Chapter 17)

TALLAHASSEE

DEPARTMENT OF AGRICULTURE AND CONSUMER SERVICES
(Food Safety Division)
3125 Conner Boulevard, Tallahassee, Florida, 32399-1650
Tel: (+1) 850 245 5520
Locomotive: *Rochester* – (Chapter 16)

WASHINGTON DC

THE NATIONAL MUSEUM OF AMERICAN HISTORY
(The Smithsonian Institution), Division of Work and Industry,
Behring Center
Tel: (+1) 202 633 1000
http://www.si.edu/
Locomotives: *Pride of Newcastle* (Original components – in
store) – (Chapter 5)
John Bull – (Chapter 7)

BIBLIOGRAPHY

The following books, papers and articles provide further information about the locomotives in this volume. In addition to their printed form, a number of them have been digitally scanned and can be consulted on the internet. Only a few museums provide information about their artefacts on their websites.

General

Ahrons, E.L., *The British Steam Railway Locomotive, 1825–1925*, Locomotive Publishing Co., London, 1927, reprinted, Bracken Books, London, 1987.

Bailey, Michael R. (ed.), *Early Railways 3*, Six Martlets Publishing, Sudbury, 2006.

Boyes, Grahame (ed.), *Early Railways 4*, Six Martlets Publishing, Sudbury, 2010.

Guy, Andy and Rees, Jim (eds.), *Early Railways*, The Newcomen Society, 2001.

Kinert, Reed, *Early American Steam Locomotives: 1st Seven Decades: 1830–1890*, New York, 1962.

Lewis, M.J.T. (ed.), *Early Railways 2*, The Newcomen Society, 2003.

Marshall, C.F. Dendy, *A History of Railway Locomotives Down to the End of the Year 1831*, Locomotive Publishing Co., London, 1953.

Oliver, Smith Hempstone, *The First Quarter-Century of Steam Locomotives in North America*, United States National Museum Bulletin 210, The Smithsonian Institution, Washington DC, 1956.

Payen, Jacques, *La Machine Locomotive en France, des origines au milieu du XIXe siecle*, Lyon UP, 1986.

Von Oeynhausen, C. and Von Dechen, H., 'Railways in England 1826 and 1827', *Archiv für Bergbau und Hüttenwesen*, Vol. XIX, Berlin, 1829, republished in English, with translation by Forward, E.A., edited by Lee, Charles E., in collaboration with Gilbert, K.R., The Newcomen Society, 1971.

Warren, J.G.H., *A Century of Locomotive Building by Robert Stephenson & Co. 1823/1923*, Andrew Reid & Co., Newcastle-Upon-Tyne, 1923, reprinted David & Charles, Newton Abbott, 1970.

White, John. H. Jr, *American Locomotives: An Engineering History*, 1830–1880, John Hopkins Press, Baltimore, 1968, republished as *A History of the American Locomotive, Its Development: 1830–1880*, Dover Publications, New York, 1979, further republished John Hopkins UP, 1997.

White, John H., *A Short History of American Locomotive Builders*, Bass Inc., Washington DC, 1982.

White, John H., 'Railway Replicas Past and Future', *Locomotive and Railway Preservation*, Issue 37, Sept–Oct 1992, pp.50–51.

Wishaw, Francis, *The Railways of Great Britain and Ireland*, Simpkin, Marshall & Co., London, 1840.

Wood, Nicholas, *A Practical Treatise on Rail-Roads etc.*, first edition, Knight & Lacy, London, 1825, second edition, Hurst, Chance & Co., London, 1831, and third edition, Longman, Orme, Brown, Green & Longmans, London, 1838.

Chapter 1

Dickinson H.W. and Titley Arthur, *Richard Trevithick: The Engineer and the Man*, Cambridge UP, 1934, republished, 2010.

Eyles, Joan M., 'William Smith, Richard Trevithick and Samuel Homfray: Their Correspondence on Steam Engines, 1804–1806', in *Transactions of the Newcomen Society*, Vol. XLIII (1970–71), pp.137–161.

Forward E.A., 'Links in the History of the Locomotive', *The Engineer*, 22 Feb, 1952, pp.266–268.

Lewis, M.J.T., 'Penydarren Company Locomotives', in Rattenbury, Gordon and Lewis, M.J.T. (eds), *Merthyr Tydfil Tramroads and their Locomotives*, Railway & Canal Historical Society, 2004, pp.51–55.

Liffen, John, 'Searching for Trevithick's London Railway of 1808', in Boyes, Grahame (ed.), 2010, pp.1–29.

Magner, Christopher, *Catch Me Who Can: Bridgnorth and the Steam Locomotives of Richard Trevithick*, privately published, Bridgnorth, 2004.

Mason, W.W., 'Trevithick's First Rail Locomotive', in *Transactions of the Newcomen Society*, Vol. XII (1931–32), pp.85–103.

Owen-Jones, Stuart, *The Penydarren Locomotive*, Welsh Industrial and Maritime Museum, Cardiff, 1981.

Randall, John, *History of Madeley*, Wrekin Echo Office, Madeley, 1880.

Rees, Jim and Guy, Andy, 'Richard Trevithick & Pioneer Locomotives', in Bailey, Michael R. (ed.), 2006, pp.191–220.

Trevithick, Francis, *Life of Richard Trevithick*, E. & F.S. Spon, London, 1872, 2 vols, republished Cambridge UP 2011.

Trinder, Barrie, 'Recent Research on Early Shropshire Railways', in Lewis, M.J.T. (ed.), 2003, pp.10–25.

Trinder, Barry, 'Trevithick Locomotive Arrives', *Ironbridge Quarterly*, Friends of the Ironbridge Gorge Museums, 1990, Issue 3, pp.4–5.

Chapter 2

Archer, Mark, *William Hedley, The Inventor of Railway Locomotion on the Present Principle*, J.M.Carr, Newcastle, 1882.

Binnie, Colin, 'The Archaeology of the Locomotive Puffing Billy', in *Model Railways*, January 1979, pp.28–34.

Bye, Sheila, 'John Blenkinsop and the Patent Steam Carriages', in Lewis (ed.), (2003), pp.134–148.

Crompton, John, 'The Hedley Mysteries', in Lewis (ed.), 2003, pp.149–164.

Davidson, Peter, correspondence with the author, 2012.

Guy, Andy, 'North Eastern Locomotive Pioneers 1805–1827: A Reassessment', in Guy and Rees (eds.), 2001, pp.117–144.

Guy, Andy, 'Early Railways: Some Curiosities and Conundrums', in Lewis, M.J.T. (ed.), 2003, pp.64–78.

Liffen, John, 'The Patent Office Museum and the Beginnings of Railway Locomotive Preservation', in Lewis, M.J.T. (ed.), 2003, pp.206–7.

Liffen, John, 'The Iconography of the Wylan Waggonway', in Bailey, Michael R. (ed.), 2006, pp.51–75.

Loher, Eugen, *Meine Erinnerungen an die Aufnahme der Lokomotive 'Puffing Billy' in London 24 März–20 April 1906*, unpublished report, October 1933, retained in the library of the Deutsches Museum, München.

Rees, Jim, 'The Strange Story of the Steam Elephant', in Guy and Rees (eds.), 2001, pp.145–170.

Chapter 3

Barker, W.J., Letter to *The Locomotive* magazine, published 15 December 1925, with accompanying editorial notes, Vol. 31, pp.403–4.

Dunlop, James, 'The Development of Locomotive Valve Gear', No.III, *The Engineer*, 16 July 1920, p.49.

Forward, E.A., 'Links in the History of the Locomotive', *The Engineer*, 10 October 1941, pp.230–33, and 17 October 1941, pp.248–51.

Forward, E.A., 'The Stephenson Locomotives at Springwell Colliery 1826', *Transactions of theNewcomen Society*, Vol. XXIII (1941–42), pp.117–127.

Guy, Andy, 'North Eastern Locomotive Pioneers 1805–1827: A Re-assessment', in Guy, Andy and Rees, Jim (eds.), 2001, pp.117–144.

Mountford, Colin E., *The Bowes Railway*, Industrial Railway Society/Tyne & Wear Industrial Monuments Trust, 1966, second edition 1976.

Mountford, Colin E., *The Private Railways of County Durham*, Industrial Railway Society, 2004.

News article, 'An 80-year Old Locomotive Still at Work', *The Railway Magazine*, Vol. X, May 1902, pp.385–87.

Reed, Brian, *Locomotion*, Loco Profile 25, Windsor, 1972.

Rees, Jim, 'The Stephenson Standard Locomotive (1814–1825): A Fresh Appraisal', in Lewis, M.J.T. (ed.), 2003, pp.177–201.

Satow, M.G., 'Repeat Order', *The Railway Magazine*, Vol.121, Aug 1975, pp.378–381.

Satow, F., Satow, M.G., and Wilson, L.S., *Locomotion Concept to Creation … the Story of the Reproduction 1973–1975*, Beamish, 1976.

Chapter 4

Crompton, John, 'Rewriting the Record – John Rastrick's Locomotives', in *Perceptions of Great Engineers II*, National Museums & Galleries on Merseyside, 1998, pp.51–58.

FitzSimons, Neal, (ed.), *The Reminiscences of John B. Jervis*, Syracuse UP, NY, 1971, pp.85–91.

Gale, W.K.V., *A History of the Pensnett Railway*, Goose & Son, Cambridge, 1975.

Hale, Michael, 'Agenoria and Her Railway', in *The Blackcountryman*, Vol. II, No. 4, pp.8–14, later reprinted in Pardoe, Bill, and Hale, Michael, *Two Stourbridge Locomotives*, Black Country Society Studies in Industrial Archaeology, No. 3, n.d. but 1970s.

Leslie, Vernon, *Honesdale and the Stourbridge Lions*, Wayne County Historical Society, Honesdale, Pennsylvania, Enlarged Edition, 1994.

Loree, L.F., 'The Four Locomotives Imported Into America in 1829 by the Delaware & Hudson Company', *Transactions of the Newcomen Society*, Vol. IV, 1925, pp.64–72.

Renwick, James, *Treatise on the Steam Engine*, Carvill & Co., New York, 1830.

Chapter 5

Bailey, Michael R. and Glithero, John P., *The Engineering and History of Rocket*, National Railway Museum, York, 2000.

Burton, Anthony, *The Rainhill Story*, BBC, London, 1980, Chapter Eight, 'The Replicas', pp.103–113.

Coste, L. and Perdonnet, A.A., 'Machine Locomotives', *Annale Des Mines*, VI, 1829, pp.199–202 and 288–289.

Davidson, Peter and Glithero, John, 'Analysis of Locomotive Performance', in Bailey, Michael R. (ed.), 2006, pp.284–299.

Demos, John and Thayer, Robert, 'The Case of the Vanishing Locomotive', *American Heritage*, Oct 1998, pp.91–95.

Fellows, Rev. Reginald B., *History of the Canterbury and Whitstable Railway*, J.A. Jennings, Canterbury, 1930.

Kessler, William Conrad, 'The Private Library of John Bloomfield Jervis', *Bulletin of the Railway and Locomotive Historical Society*, Vol. 52, May 1940.

Kessler, William Conrad, 'Letters of John B. Jervis', *Bulletin of the Railway and Locomotive Historical Society*, Vol. 53, October 1940.

Loree, L.F., 'The Four Locomotives Imported Into America in 1829 By the Delaware & Hudson Co.', *Transactions of the Newcomen Society*, Volume IV, 1925, pp.64–72.

Marshall, C.F. Dendy, 'The Rainhill Locomotive Trials of 1829', *Transactions of the Newcomen Society*, Volume IX, 1928–1929, pp.78–93.

News Article, 'Invicta 150', *The Railway Magazine*, Vol. 126, April 1980, pp.170–171.

Reed, Brian, *The ROCKET*, Loco Profile 7, Windsor, England, 1971.

Satow, M.G., '*ROCKET* Reborn', *The Railway Magazine*, Vol.125, October 1979, pp.472–474.

State, Ray, 'The Truth Behind the *Pride of Newcastle*', *Railroad History*, 201, Fall–Winter 2009, Railway and Locomotive Historical Society, pp.71–79.

Chapter 6

Burton, Anthony, *The Rainhill Story*, BBC, London, 1980, Chapter Eight, 'The Replicas', pp.103–113.

Cowburn, Ian, 'The Origins of the St-Etienne Rail Roads, 1816–38: French Industrial Espionage and British Technology Transfer', Guy and Rees (eds.), 2001, pp.233–250.

Davidson, Peter and Glithero, John, 'Analysis of Locomotive Performance', in Bailey, Michael R. (ed.), 2006, pp.284–299.

Forward, E.A., 'Links in the History of the Locomotive: Marc Seguin and the Multitubular Boiler', *The Engineer*, December 1923, pp.638–639, 661–663.

Gibbon, Richard, 'Rings, Springs and Things: The National Collection Pre-1840', in Guy, Andy and Rees, Jim (eds.), 2001, pp.208–216.

Hills, Richard, 'Novelty in Sweden', *The Railway Magazine*, October 1981, pp.476–477.

Lamb, Richard, 'Something of a *Novelty*', in Bailey, Michael R. (ed.), 2006, pp.272–283.

Liffen, John, 'The Patent Office Museum and the Beginnings of Railway Locomotive Preservation', in Lewis, M.J.T. (ed.), 2003, pp.202–220.

Marshall, C.F. Dendy, 'The Rainhill Locomotive Trials of 1829', *Transactions of the Newcomen Society*, Vol. IX, 1928–1929, pp.78–93.

News article, 'Without Equal', *The Railway Magazine*, Vol. 126, June 1980, pp.270–271.

Paques, Joseph-Jean, 'A Reproduction is Born', *The Railway Magazine*, Vol.133, July 1987, pp.454–455.

Payen, Jacques, *La Machine Locomotive en France*, Lyon UP, 1986.

Satow, M.G., 'The "Novelty" Enigma', *The Railway Magazine*, Vol. 126, November 1980, pp.514–517.

Young, Robert, *Timothy Hackworth and the Locomotive*, Locomotive Publishing Co., London, 1923, republished 2000, The Book Guild, Brighton.

Chapter 7

Bailey, Michael R., 'The Stephenson '*Planets*' – Their History and Rebirth', *Railway World*, Vol. 50, May 1989, pp.306–310, and June 1989, pp.350–354.

Bailey, Michael R., 'Learning through Replication: The *Planet* Locomotive Project', *Transactions of the Newcomen Society*, Vol. 68 (1996–97), pp.109–136.

Bailey, Ronald T., 'John Bull; A Replica of the Past', The Railroad Museum (of Pennsylvania) Collection No. 19, *Milepost, Journal of the Friends of the Museum*, Vol. 11, No. 5, November 1993.

Boyd, Jim, 'John Bull: 150 Years – The Beginning', and 'The Celebration', *Railfan and Railroad*, January 1982, pp.34–37 and 45–48.

Klensch, Carl, 'Die Lokomotive "Adler" der Ersten Deutschen Eisenbahn und Ihre Nachbildung im Reichsbahn-ausbesserungswerk Kaiserslautern', *Organ f.d. Fortschritte des Eisenbahnwesens*, Vol. 24, 15 December 1935, pp.486–491.

de Pater, A.D. and Page, F.M., *Russian Locomotives, Volume 1 1836–1904*, Retrieval Press, Sutton Coldfield, 1987.

Schwarzenstein, Franz F., 'Centenary and Development of the German Railways', *The Railway Magazine*, Vol. LXXIV, May 1934, pp.313–316.

Thomas, R.H.G., *The Liverpool & Manchester Railway*, Batsford, London, 1980, pp.154–161.

Westwood, J.N., *A History of Russian Railways*, George Allen and Unwin, London, 1964.

White, John H. Jr, 'Resurrection: The John Bull Steams Again at 150 Years of Age', *Railroad History*, Railway & Locomotive Historical Society, Bulletin 144, Spring 1981.

White, John H. Jr, *The John Bull: 150 Years a Locomotive*, Smithsonian Institution Press, Washington DC, 1981.

White, John H. Jr, 'Old Debts and New Visions: The Interchange of Ideas in Railway Engineering', *Common Roots – Separate Branches*, transactions of international symposium, York, 1993, London, 1994, pp.74–78.

Chapter 8

Alexander, James, *John Stevens; A Replica of the 'First'*, The Railroad Museum Collection, Friends of the Railroad Museum of Pennsylvania, n.d. but 1994.

Alexander, James Jr: 'John Stevens: The Man and the Machine', in *Milepost*, Vol. 12, No. 1, Friends of the Railroad Museum of Pennsylvania, February 1994, pp.5–10.

Article, 'Famous Locomotives Now on Exhibition', *Railway & Locomotive Historical Society Bulletin*, No. 9, 1925, pp.4–6.

Article, 'History of the Best Friend of Charleston', *Railway & Locomotive Historical Society Bulletin*, No. 18, 1929, pp.60–61.

Article, 'Replica of the Col Stevens Locomotive', *Railway & Locomotive Historical Society Bulletin* No. 18, 1929, pp.68–69.

Bell, J. Snowden, *The Early Motive Power of the Baltimore & Ohio Railroad*, Angus Sinclair, New York, 1912, reprinted Glenwood, Felton, Ca.1975.

Brown, William H., *The History of the First Locomotives in America*, Appleton & Co., New York, 1871.

FitzSimons, Neal, *The Reminiscences of John B. Jervis*, Syracuse UP, NY, 1971.

Hungerford, Edward, *The Story of the Baltimore & Ohio Railroad 1827–1927*, 2 vols, G.P. Putnam, New York, 1928.

Mack, Edward C., *Peter Cooper – Citizen of New York*, Duell Sloan & Pierce, New York, 1949, pp.99–121.

Mooneyhan, Gordon and Schafer, W., 'Cradle of Southern Railroading', *Ties, The Southern Railway Historical Association Magazine*, May–June 1993, p.4.

Pennoyer, A. Sheldon, *Locomotives in Our Lives*, Hastings House, New York, 1954, pp.215–220.

Sagle, Lawrence W., 'The Tom Thumb', *Bulletin of the Railway & Locomotive Historical Society*, No. 73, 1948, pp.46–53.

Siegling, H. Carter, 'The Best Friend of Charleston', *South Carolina, History Illustrated*, Vol. I, No. 1, February 1970, p.19.

White, John H. Jr, 'Railway Reproductions Past and Future', *Locomotive and Railway Preservation*, Issue 37, September–October 1992.

Chapter 9

Hungerford, Edward, *The Story of the Baltimore & Ohio Railroad 1827–1927*, 2 vols, G.P. Putnam, New York, 1928.

Bell, J. Snowden, *The Early Motive Power of the Baltimore & Ohio Railroad*, Angus Sinclair, New York, 1912, reprinted Glenwood, Felton, Ca.1975.

Chapter 10

Book series, *The Locomotives of the Great Western Railway*, Part Two, Broad Gauge, The Railway Correspondence and Travel Society, 1952.

Bryan, Tim, *North Star, A Tale of Two Locomotives*, Thamesdown Borough Council, 1989.

Clark, E.F., 'Notes on early locomotive practice, with reference to *Lion* (1838)', *Transactions of the Newcomen Society*, Vol. 62, 1990–91, pp.111–112.

Holcroft, H., *An Outline of Great Western Locomotive Practice, 1837–1947*, Locomotive Publishing Co., London, 1957, pp.2–3.

Horn, A., *Die Kaiser Ferdinands-Nordbahn*, Harenburg, Wien, 1980.

Illustrierter Fuhrer durch die Sammlungen, Österreichisches Eisenbahn Museum, Wien, 1975.

Jarvis, A.E., 'Untwisting the Lion's Tale', *Railway World*, Vol. 41, January 1980, pp.21–24.

Jarvis, Adrian and Morris, Len, *Lion*, Booklet, Liverpool Museum, 1987.

Jarvis, Adrian, 'Lion 150', *Railway World*, Vol. 49, April 1988, pp.218–221, and May 1988, pp.277–280.

Kölsdorf, Karl, (Slezak, J.O., ed.), *Lokomotivbau in Alt-Österreich, 1837–1918*, Slezak, Wien, 1978.

Lionsheart, Occasional Newsletter of the Old Locomotive Committee 1984 – present day.

MacDermot, E.T., *History of the Great Western Railway*, Volume 1 1833–1863, Part II, Great Western Railway, London, 1927.

Martin, Evan, *Bedlington Iron & Engine Works 1736–1867*, Frank Graham, Newcastle-Upon-Tyne, 1974.

Morris, L.E., 'The Restoration of "Lion"', *Railway World*, Vol. 41, May 1980, pp.245–251.

Mosse, John, 'The Firefly Locomotive of 1839', *Transactions of the Newcomen Society*, Vol. 62, 1990–91, pp.97–112.

News article, 'Past and Present Locomotives, Austrian State Rys', *The Locomotive Magazine*, Vol. XV, 15 June 1909, p.117.

Stockklausner, Johann, *Dampfbetrieb in Alt-Österreich, 1837–1918*, J.O.Slezak, Wien, 1979.

Van Reeuwijk, G.F., *De Breedspoorlocomotieven van de H. IJ.S.M. (The Broad gauge Locomotives of the Dutch Railway Company)*, De Alk, Alkmaar, 1985.

Chapter 11

Ahrons, E.L., 'Short Histories of Famous Firms No. XVI, Messrs. Edward Bury & Co.', *The Engineer*, 2 February 1923, pp.111–114.

Corliss, C.J., *Main Line of Mid America, The Story of the Illinois Central*, New York, 1950, pp.246–248.

Fancey, W.F., 'An Old Locomotive', *The Railway Magazine*, March 1899, Vol. IV, pp.217–8.

Feature article, 'Illustrated Interviews No. 30, Mr Robert George Colhoun, Traffic Manager, Great Southern and Western Railway', *The Railway Magazine*, Vol. V, December 1899, pp.481–2.

Murray, K.A. and McNeill, D.B., *Great Southern & Western Railway*, Irish Railway Record Society, 1976.

Näbrich, F., Meyer, G. and Preuss, R., *Locomotiv-Archiv* Sachsen 1, Berlin, 1984, pp.12–17 and pp.66–67.

News article, 'Bury Locomotive at Inchicore', *The Railway Magazine*, Vol. 88, March 1942, p.92.

News article, 'An Irish Centenarian', *The Journal of the Stephenson Locomotive Society*, No. 277, Vol. XXIV, May 1948, p.109.

Pettigrew, W.F., 'History of the Furness Railway Locomotives', *Proceedings of the Institution of Mechanical Engineers*, July 1901, pp.728–730.

Schnabel, Heinz, SAXONIA Beschreibung und Rekonstruktion einer historischen Lokomotive, VEB Verlag, Berlin, 1989.

Taylor, G., '0-4-0 Locomotives of the Furness Railway', *Locomotive Review*, April 1950.

Weisbrod, M., '*SAXONIA* und der Sachsenstolz', *Eisenbahn-Journal* 6/1989, pp.30–35.

White, John H. Jr, 'The *Mississippi*, A Southern Foundling', *Railroad History*, Railway & Locomotive Historical Society Bulletin 140, 1979, pp.114–118.

Chapter 12

Austlicher Bericht über die Allgemeine Deutsche Gewerbe-Austellung Zu Berlin in Jahre 1844, Vol .II, p.542.

Bell, J. Snowden, *The Early Motive Power of the Baltimore & Ohio Railroad*, Angus Sinclair, New York, 1912, reprinted Glenwood, Felton, Ca. 1975.

Echubarth, Prof. Dr, *Verhandlungen des Vereins Zur Beförderung des Gewerbefleisses*, Association for the Promotion of Trade Diligence, Berlin, Vol. 25, 1846, pp.75–82.

Fontanellaz, Ing. Eugène, *Das Rollende Material der Schweizerischen Nordbahn (Zürich–Baden) 1847 und deren Rekonstruktion 1947*, unpublished paper, 1947, retained in Verkehrshaus der Schweiz, Luzern.

Illustrierter Fuhrer durch die Sammlungen, Osterreichisches Eisenbahn Museum, Section 8, Fahrbetriebsmittel.

Mayer, Dr-Ing. Max, *Lokomotiven, Wagen und Bergbahnen. Geschichtliche Entwicklung in der Maschinenfabrik Esslingen Seit dem Jahre 1846*, VDI-Verlag, Berlin, 1924.

Moser, Alfred, *Der Dampfbetrieb der Schweizerischen Eisenbahnen, 1847–1922*, Birkhäuser, Basel, 1923, pp.62–65.

100 Jahre Borsig Lokomotiven 1837–1937, Borsig Lokomotiv-Werken GMBH, Berlin, 1937.

Peck, Stephen R., *The Copiapó locomotive: Historical and Technical Assessment*, unpublished thesis, Colorado State University, 2002.

Pierson, Kurt, *Die Beuth – Lokomotive Von Borsig*, Information Pamphlet No. 14 of the Museum Für Verkehr und Technik, Berlin.

Pierson, Kurt, *Borsig Ein Name Geht Um Die Welt*, Rembrandt Verlag, Berlin 1973.

Reed, Brian, *The Norris Locomotives*, Loco. Profile 11, Windsor, 1971.

Scholz, F.W., 'Ein Hundertjahriger Lokomotiv-veteran', *Die Modelleisenbahn*, 1948, pp.107–110.

Stockklausner, Johann, *Dampfbetrieb in Alt-Osterreich, 1837–1918*, Slezak, Wien, 1979.

Stones, H.R., 'William Wheelwright: Nineteenth Century Railway and Shipping Entrepreneur in Latin America', *The British Overseas Railways Journal*, No. 3, Autumn 1987, pp.45–46.

Witzig, Konrad, *Die Rekonstruktion des Ersten Schweizerischen Eisenbahnzuges*, Schweiz. Bauzeitung, 65. Jahrgang, No. 25, 21 June 1947, pp.2–8.

Chapter 13

Ahrons, E.L., 1927, pp.53–58.

Bulletin de la Société Industrielle de Mulhouse, No. 744, 1971, pp.79–80.

Warren, J.G.H., 1923, pp.94 and 346–357.

Chapter 14

Bulletin de la Société Industrielle de Mulhouse, No. 744, 1971.

Chaloner, W.H., 'Alexander Allan's Own Claim', *The Railway Magazine*, Vol. 97, 1951, pp.416–418.

Clark, D.K., *Railway Machinery: A Treatment on the Mechanical Engineering of Railways*, 2 Vols, Blackie, London, 1855.

Doerr, Michel, 'Notice Historique Sur Le Matériel Rassemblé En Vue De La Création D'un Musée Des Chemins De Fer, Au Dépôt De Chalon-Sur-Saône', *La Vie du Rail*, 1965.

Feature article 'An Historic Locomotive, The "Cornwall"', *The Railway Magazine*, Vol. XLIII, September 1918, pp.143–150.

La Maquinista Terrestre y Maritima 1855–1955 (Company History), Barcelona, 1955.

Lee, Charles E., 'Genesis of the 'Crewe' Type Locomotive', *The Railway Magazine*, May 1951, pp.303–305.

Maristany, Manuel, *Un Siglo De Ferrocarril En Cataluña*, Buró Gràfic, Barcelona, 1992.

Maskelyne, J.N., *Locomotives I Have Known*, Percival Marshall, London, 1959, second edition, Model & Allied Publications, Hemel Hempstead, 1980.

Payen, Jacques and Combe, Jean-Marc, 'Crewe Engine et Machine Buddicom', *Revue d'Histoire des Chemins de Fer*, Hors Série No. 1, Association pour l'Histoire des Chemins de Fer en France, Paris, 1988, pp.119–132.

Reed, Brian, *Crewe Locomotive Works and its Men*, David & Charles, Newton Abbot, 1982.

Stuart, D.H. and Reed, Brian, *The Crewe Type*, Loco Profile 15, Windsor, 1971.

Talbot, E., *An Illustrated History of LNWR Engines*, Oxford Publishing Co., 1985.

Wais, Francisco, *Historia de lo Ferrocarriles Españoles*, Madrid, 1968, republished 1974 and 1987.

Chapter 15

Bailey, Michael R. and Glithero, John P., *The Odin Project: Design and Construction of Denmark's First Locomotive*, The Danish Railway Museum, Odense, 2004.

Brown, John K., *The Baldwin Locomotive Works 1831–1915*, John Hopkins UP, Baltimore, 1995.

Brown, Robert R., 'British and Foreign Locomotives in Canada and Newfoundland', *Railway and Locomotive Historical Society Bulletin* No. 43, April 1937, p.8.

Dambly, Phil., *Vapeur en Belgique*, Blanchart, Brussels, 1989, Vol. 1, 'Origines a 1914'.

De Laveleye, A., *Histoire des 25 Premiers des Chemins de Fer Belges*, Brussels, 1860

Feature article, 'The Railways of Cuba', *The Railway Magazine*, Vol. X, 1902, pp.129–133.

Feature article 'John Molson 1848', in connection with 'The Champlain & St Lawrence Railroad', *Railway and Locomotive Historical Society Bulletin* No. 39, March 1936, p.54.

Fisher, Charles E., 'Galena & Chicago Union Railroad Company', *Railway and Locomotive Historical Society Bulletin* No. 27, March 1932, pp.5–30.

Hall-Patch, Tony, '"Iron Duke" Reborn', *Railway Magazine*, Vol. 131, May 1985, pp.216–218.

Lamalle, Ulysse, *Histoire des Chemins de fer Belges*, Office de Publicité, Brussels, 1943, third edition, 1953.

Lavallée, Omer, 'Will the <u>Real</u> "John Molson" Please Steam Forward?', *Clearboard*, Bytown Railway Society, September 1969, pp.3–7.

News article 'Austerity Tank Locomotive Ministry of Supply', *The Locomotive*, Vol. XLIX, No. 607, 15 March 1943, pp.34–35.

Nicholls, R.V.V., 'The Impossible Dream: The Construction of the John Molson of 1971', *Canadian Rail*, October 1971, pp.270–291.

Small, W. Gordan, 'Designing the 'John Molson' of 1971, *Canadian Rail*, October 1971, pp.292–300.

Thestrup, Poul, *På Sporet 1847–1997*, 3 Vols, Jernbanemuseet, Odense, 1997, Vol. I, *Dampen Binder Danmark Sammen*.

Twining, E.W., 'Great Western Railway Broad Gauge 8ft Singles', *The Locomotive*, Vol. LVI, No. 700, 15 December 1950, pp.195–199.

White, John H. Jr, *The Pioneer, Chicago's First Locomotive*, The Chicago Historical Society, 1976.

White, John H. Jr, 'Yankee, please come home!', *Trains Magazine*, September 1984, pp.21–28.

Chapter 16

Conrad, J. David, *The Steam Locomotive Directory of North America*, 2 vols, Transportation Trails, Polo, Ill., 1988.

Smith, E.A. Frog, 'Steam Engineer at Eight', *Rail Classics*, 1984, pp.8–10.

Warner, Paul T., 'The Development of the Anthracite-Burning Locomotive', *Railroad & Locomotive Historical Society Bulletin*, Vol. 52, pp.11–28.

Warner, Paul T., *Locomotives of the Pennsylvania Railroad 1834–1924*, Owen Davies, Chicago, Ill., 1956.

Chapter 17

Ahrons, E.L., 1927, pp.33–48.

Bailey, Michael R. and Glithero, John P., *The Braddyll Locomotive and Collier Class Tender: An Assessment of Current Condition and Recommendations for Restoration*, unpublished report for the Timothy Hackworth Victorian and Railway Museum, August 1994. Now in Locomotion Museum, Shildon.

Bailey, Michael R. and Glithero, John P., 'Learning through Restoration: The Samson Locomotive Project', in Guy, Andy and Rees, Jim (eds.), 2001, pp.278–293.

Bailey, Michael R. and Glithero, John P., 'Turning a Blind Eye to Braddyll', in Boyes, Grahame (ed.), 2010, pp.259–279.

Bell, J. Snowden, *The Early Motive Power of the Baltimore & Ohio Railroad*, Angus Sinclair, New York, 1912, reprinted Glenwood Publishing, 1975.

Bell, J. Snowden, 'The New Castle Manufacturing Company', *Railway & Locomotive Engineering*, January 1922.

Bell, J. Snowden, 'The Baltimore & Ohio Baldwin Engine "Dragon"', *Railway & Locomotive Engineering*, October 1922.

Boyd, J.I.C., *Narrow Gauge Railways in North Caernarvonshire*, 3 vols, Oakwood Press, Oxford, 1986.

Brown, Robert R., 'General Mining Association', *Bulletin of the Railway and Locomotive Historical Society*, No. 41, November 1936, p.41.

Charlton, L.G., 'Early British Locomotives for Nova Scotia', *Industrial Railway Record*, No. 83, December 1979, p.79.

Clinker, C.R., 'Early Days on the Bodmin and Wadebridge Railway', *The Journal of the Stephenson Locomotive Society*, Vol. 28, 1952, pp.44–46.

Feature article, *The Locomotive Magazine*, Vol. 31, 15 June 1925, pp.183–185.

Gibbon, Richard, 'Rings, Swings and Things: The National Collection Pre-1840', in Guy, Andy and Rees, Jim (eds.), 2001, pp.215–216.

Given, Charles S., 'First Locomotives in the State of Maine', *Railway & Locomotive Historical Society Bulletin*, No. 15, November 1927, pp.34–36.

Lander, Eric, Notes on the Horlock Locomotive '*FIRE QUEEN*', Penrhyn Castle Industrial Railway Museum, 2000.

Lee, Charles E., 'The Bodmin and Wadebridge Railway', *The Railway Magazine*, Vol. 75, 1934, pp.39–42, 115–119 and 257–262.

Lee, Charles E., 'The Padarn Railway and Dinorwic Slate Quarry', *The Railway Magazine*, Vol. 80, 1937, pp.423–428.

MacDonald, Herb, 'The Albion Mines Railway of 1839–40: Some British Roots of Canada's First Industrial Railway', in Guy, Andy and Rees, Jim (eds.), 2001, pp.266–277.

News article, *The Locomotive Magazine*, 15 December 1919, p.209.

News articles, *Journal of the Stephenson Locomotive Society*, Vol. 24, July 1948, p.180, and Vol. 25, February 1949, pp.28–29.

Pearce, T.R., *The Locomotives of the Stockton and Darlington Railway*, The Historical Model Railway Society, 1996.

Rivard, Paul E., *Lion, The History of an 1846 Locomotive Engine in Maine*, Maine State Museum, in conjunction with the Machiasport Historical Society, 1987.

Ryan, Judith, *The History of Railway Developments in Nova Scotia until 1920*, unpublished report for the Nova Scotia Museum of Industry, 1991.

Sweetser, James, *The Lion Locomotive*, Paper to the Newcomen Society of North America, Chicago, 1938.

Tomlinson, William W., *The North Eastern Railway Its Rise and Development*, Andrew Reid, Newcastle, 1914, p.536.

Turner, S., *The Padarn and Penrhyn Railways*, David & Charles, Newton Abbot, 1975.

Walker, Harold S., 'The Whitneyville and Machiasport Railroad', *Railway & Locomotive Historical Society Bulletin*, No. 98, April 1958, pp.76–78.

Weaver, C.R., '"Fire Queen", A Technical Appreciation', *Penrhyn Castle Industrial Railway Museum*, guide, The National Trust, first published 1991.

Young, Robert, *Timothy Hackworth and the Locomotive*, Locomotive Publishing Co., London, 1923, republished 2000, The Book Guild, Brighton.

Chapter 18

The Locomotives of the Great Western Railway, Part Two, 'Broad Gauge', Railway Correspondence and Travel Society, 1952.

MacLean, John S., *The Newcastle & Carlisle Railway*, Newcastle-upon-Tyne, 1948.

Spark, Stephen, 'Tornado and Warlock: A Society Mystery', *Stephenson Locomotive Society Journal*, Vol. 87, No. 871, September–October 2011, pp.208–212.

Walker, Harold S., 'Bangor, Oldtown and Milford Railroad 1836–1869', *Bulletin Railway & Locomotive Historical Society*, No. 106, April 1962, pp.40–48.